MW01089599

Developing Human Service Leaders

To David, Kate, Sarah, and Kate

SAGE was founded in 1965 by Sara Miller McCune to support the dissemination of usable knowledge by publishing innovative and high-quality research and teaching content. Today, we publish more than 850 journals, including those of more than 300 learned societies, more than 800 new books per year, and a growing range of library products including archives, data, case studies, reports, and video. SAGE remains majority-owned by our founder, and after Sara's lifetime will become owned by a charitable trust that secures our continued independence.

Los Angeles | London | New Delhi | Singapore | Washington DC

Developing Human Service Leaders

Deborah Harley-McClaskey

East Tennessee State University

Los Angeles | London | New Delhi
Singapore | Washington DC

Los Angeles | London | New Delhi
Singapore | Washington DC

FOR INFORMATION

SAGE Publications, Inc.
2455 Teller Road
Thousand Oaks, California 91320
E-mail: order@sagepub.com

SAGE Publications Ltd.
1 Oliver's Yard
55 City Road
London, EC1Y 1SP
United Kingdom

SAGE Publications India Pvt. Ltd.
B 1/I 1 Mohan Cooperative Industrial Area
Mathura Road, New Delhi 110 044
India

SAGE Publications Asia-Pacific Pte. Ltd.
3 Church Street
#10–04 Samsung Hub
Singapore 049483

Acquisitions Editor: Kassie Graves
Editorial Assistant: Carrie Montoya
Production Editor: Bennie Clark Allen
Copy Editor: Renee Willers
Typesetter: Hurix Systems Pvt. Ltd.
Proofreader: Rae-Ann Goodwin
Indexer: Terri Morrissey
Cover Designer: Anupama Krishnan
Marketing Manager: Shari Countryman
eLearning Editor: Lucy Berbeo

Copyright © 2017 by SAGE Publications, Inc.

All rights reserved. No part of this book may be reproduced or utilized in any form or by any means, electronic or mechanical, including photocopying, recording, or by any information storage and retrieval system, without permission in writing from the publisher.

Printed in the United States of America

Library of Congress Cataloging-in-Publication Data

Names: Harley-McClaskey, Deborah, author.

Title: Developing human service leaders / Deborah Harley-McClaskey.

Description: Los Angeles : SAGE, [2017] | Includes bibliographical references and index.

Identifiers: LCCN 2015038936 | ISBN 9781483393100 (pbk. : alk. paper)

Subjects: LCSH: Human services—Management. | Social work administration. | Leadership.

Classification: LCC HV41 .H375 2017 | DDC 361.0068/4—dc23
LC record available at http://lccn.loc.gov/2015038936

This book is printed on acid-free paper.

16 17 18 19 20 10 9 8 7 6 5 4 3 2 1

Brief Contents

Detailed Contents

The companion website at http://study.sagepub.com/harleymcclaskey provides password-protected instructor resources created by the author to accompany this book, including a test bank, PowerPoint® slides, and video resources.

Note: PowerPoint is a registered trademark of Microsoft Corporation in the United States and/or other countries.

Preface

Developing Human Service Leaders is the culmination of a teaching career spent coaching students to become leaders. I have always bristled at the notion that leadership is an aspiration for someone else, a select few, the chosen. It is time to be proactive about how this society chooses its leaders. Society will make choices from inclusive pools of candidates if education becomes serious about teaching the skills, theories, attitudes, and behaviors of leadership with the same intentionality as math, science, and English.

Education has compartmentalized leadership into the world of politicians, business, military, and school principals. Yet leadership is needed in every facet of society, from the playground to families to that broad spectrum of careers known as the human services sector.

Leadership is not a tool we pick up when it is necessary. Leadership is both a personal and organizational operating system of quality and excellence. When our neighbors, colleagues, and global citizens can interact in a system that fosters personal development, setting common missions with measureable goals, support, respect, and collaboration, imagine the difference in our lives!

The voice in this book is that of a coach, first defining the general topic, and then cultivating the readiness and need for the lessons in the chapter. This book does more than teach about leadership, it can help students start the process of adopting leadership behaviors. It provides initial feedback to start a personal change process. It begins by asking the students to reflect. How does this topic touch their daily lives? The next step is to diagnose. Like the doctor asks, "Where does it hurt," the learning process is designed to ask the students to assess their level of skills and ability for each topic. It is the dissonance of what students have experienced and what they see is possible that motivates them toward change. The last step in each section provides a prescription of ideas for the students to adopt increasing their strength in the topic area.

I invited my students to read several initial chapters of the book to assess this learning format. They gave a resounding "thumbs up!" The reflect, diagnose, prescription format makes this book unique and allows my teaching voice to shine through. (My students also noted that they could hear me on every page.) I am excited by the choice of topics in the book and believe that they will prepare a student in the human services sector for the necessary skills and abilities needed for a leader in the 21st century.

Acknowledgments

Thank you, SAGE Publications, for providing this first-time author with a talented team to produce this book. I appreciate Kassie Graves and Carrie Montoya for their support and assistance with the manuscript and permissions. I give additional thanks to production editor Bennie Allen Clark and copy editor Rene Willers for their production and copy editing talents. It is their magic that transformed the initial Word document into a beautiful textbook.

It is with the deepest sense of appreciation, love, and gratitude that I share the success of this book with my daughter, Katherine Craig, who served as initial editor, helped with ancillaries, and was my ongoing cheerleader throughout this process. Thank you to Benjamin Ryan Lynch, East Tennessee State University undergraduate student, who provided helpful feedback as well as research for the ancillaries. Many thanks for the love and support of my husband, David, and his perspectives on leadership, quality, and performance excellence. Thanks for the love and support of daughters, Sarah and my "other" Kate for encouragement and perspective. And I salute my leadership students, who over the years have taught me how they wish to learn as well as shown me their appetite for this subject.

Deborah Harley-McClaskey, EdD

SAGE Publications gratefully acknowledges the following reviewers:

Greg Allinson, *Beaufort County Community College*

Michael D. Forster, *The University of Southern Mississippi*

John L. Hudgins, *Coppin State University*

Heather A. McCabe, *Indiana University School of Social Work*

Desalyn De-Souza, *SUNY Empire State College*

Barry Thomas, *Stevenson University*

About the Author

Deborah Harley-McClaskey, EdD, is an associate professor in the Department of Teaching and Learning in the Clemmer College of Education at East Tennessee State University. For more than 30 years, she has led university departments and served on boards of nonprofits as well as directed service-learning coalitions and community leadership programs. For the last 15 years, she developed, coordinated, and taught in the Interdisciplinary Minor in Leadership at East Tennessee State University. She infused leadership into the undergraduate curriculum in the College of Education. She taught in the human services program and developed courses for the Tennessee Regents Degree graduate program in strategic leadership. Her research interests include leadership assessments and the development and outcomes of youth leadership programs. She provides leadership training for many nonprofits in the surrounding community. She is a leadership consultant for Pal's Business Excellence Institute, designing leadership learning experiences for local, national, and international organizations, training leadership teams as well as employee groups. She holds a doctorate in educational leadership and policy analysis from East Tennessee State University and master's and bachelor's degrees from the University of South Florida.

Introduction

Why Are You Taking This Course and Reading This Book?

Imagine today is your first day on the job at a human services organization. You survived the application and interview process and accepted the job offer. All of those skills you learned in college about managing your assigned case load of clients, teaching, coaching, counseling, making referrals, and delivering programs and services must have prepared you for what you are about to face. But is that enough? The stakes surrounding this first professional job are higher than any of the part-time jobs you have previously held. You want and need to do well. Is success on the job as simple as following your job description and showing up on time every day?

You may suspect there are some "other duties as assigned," which is a common workplace phenomenon. Could there be other responsibilities and expectations not assigned, but assumed? Yes, in fact, the other duties are not only expected by your employer but also sought after by your supervisor and all your new colleagues. Did your professors teach you how to work collaboratively with your new colleagues, facilitate a professional meeting, or build and mentor a team? Can you give feedback to a colleague with candor and be regarded as helpful not hurtful? Will you be able to establish new and important team goals and receive acceptance, support, and commitment from the group? Will you be seen as not only able to carry out a "stretch" assignment and show your supervisor that you're not only competent but also able to grow in the position? Employer requests are overwhelming for new employees to have professional attitudes, work habits, leadership, and people skills in employer satisfaction interviews conducted by universities. In a recent interview with the program director of a local, faith-based nonprofit, Amanda Beattie, a 16-year veteran in the human services field, described the qualities she looked for in human services applicants:

- Someone who loves his or her work as well as the clients served
- Someone who is teachable
- Someone whose values mirror the organization's values
- Someone who exhibits skills in leadership: self-management, teamwork, communication, planning, mission and vision, multicultural competencies, training and feedback, resource management and development

(Interview with Amanda Beattie, 2010)

Direct service to clients is the work for which the typical bachelor's or associate degree in human services professions prepares. Courses teach skills such as client intake; counseling/advising; understanding client response; case management; lifespan development theory, marriage and family dynamics, community program resources, psychology, and sociology; service as a volunteer or intern; family structure and culture; and crisis response protocol. These skills are important, and yet the jobs in human services require so much more. Beattie went on to describe the skill sets she found to be invaluable when she first entered the human services field:

- Collaboration
- Planning
- Training and mentoring
- Policy development
- Outcome measures
- Teamwork
- Team leadership
- Supervision and feedback
- Networking
- Child development theory
- Aural, oral, and written communication

PREPARE YOURSELF

Now consider how your job could evolve over the next year by opportunities to partner with other organizations, grant programs, or new ideas learned at a professional meeting. This could be attributed to the influence you've had as well as the changing needs of the organization, community, and clients. This is a more typical timeline of the transition into your new position:

- Year 1: You are getting to know your supervisor and your colleagues. You attended a staff retreat, met many new people, and are sorting out your manager's expectations of you and the files of the previous person in the job. You may be tested with a "light duty" leadership responsibility. You are hoping to find some order to the new employee chaos.

- Year 2: Maybe your supervisor adds responsibilities or even rewrites your job description, while you have struggled to meet your current deadlines and responsibilities. You have a better idea of the organization mission and goals. You are asked to chair an important program committee. How do you manage your responsibilities and others expectations to maximize your productivity? How do you as a committee chairperson set expectations for your team? How do you make sense of what you do in the framework of the organization's goals?

- Year 3: You might discover that your organization's services are missing the mark and not meeting your clients' needs. You may also discover that government regulations are tying your hands, restricting your ability to serve your clients. How do you find your voice, influence others, and initiate changes within your organization to better serve your clients and community?

- Year 4: How deep are your skill sets for leadership, management, and community outreach? How will you develop partnerships with other organizations to better serve your clients and the community?

- Year 5: What additional skills will you need after 5 years on the job? What would you say if the manager of the department asked you to step into his or her role because he or she is leaving the organization? Are you prepared to lead?

During your career, you will be asked to lead work teams, chair committees, develop community partnerships, supervise your colleagues or even direct your entire organization. What skills have you learned that will enable you to lead and manage effectively? You have seen leaders in movies, read about them in magazines and blogs, heard about them on the nightly news, and certainly complained about them with your friends. But now YOU get to become one.

DEVELOPING AS A LEADER AND MANAGER: WHAT ARE THE CHALLENGES?

Through this book you will start your journey to bring your dreams to reality as a practitioner, leader, and manager of a human services organization. Opportunities for leadership abound in this job sector. Human services nonprofits alone account for one third of all public charities – the largest subsector of nonprofits as measured by the number of organizations (Wing, Pollack, & Blackwood, 2008). These are typically smaller organizations (by measures of staff and other resources) and are reliant on government funds, which account for 23% of their revenue (Wing et al., 2008). Given the challenges created by dependence on outside resources, the smaller size of the organization's human resources, the relative low pay of staff (high turnover), the inconsistencies of volunteer support, and the vital mission of these organizations for a community's most vulnerable populations, leaders of human service organizations must be prepared with the strongest leadership skill sets.

Leaders are people who we trust for guidance, direction, feedback, coaching, strategy, and encouragement. Frequently leaders have a position of authority (like your supervisor), but sometimes leaders are respected colleagues with no formal position of authority. Leadership is the sum of the actions, skills, knowledge, and behaviors leaders use to motivate and inspire people to follow them. Consider the equation:

$$\text{Leadership} = [\text{Development of Self and Team}] + [\text{Development of the Organization}] + \text{Influence}$$

Although these components can be viewed from several lenses, we will look at them through the lens of a new leader: you. Review the questions clustered below based on their respective leadership development components from the equation. Consider how they apply to you and your current or future job. As a current or future employee engaged in the human services sector of the workplace, answer the questions posed.

- **Development of Self** – How do I fit in my organization, my community? What are my talents? Am I continuing to learn, stretching my skills and talents? How can my talents be utilized in the workplace? Have I paused to reflect on my patterns of behavior to know how I respond to others as well as how they respond to me? Do I manage my time and emotions well? Am I open to feedback and change? Am I a good steward of resources?
- **Development of Team** – Am I helping others learn and stretch their skills and talents? Do I contribute positively to the goals of the team? Do I enable others to positively contribute to the team? Do I practice good relationship-building skills within the team? Do I share feedback on the team's progress? Do I help build a trusting work environment? Am I fully committed to the organization and the profession?
- **Development of the Organization** – What is the primary purpose of the organization? Are my goals in line with the goals of the organization?

How does my job move the mission and goals of the organization forward? Am I focused each day on the accomplishment of these key tasks? Do I have a clear picture of the organization's mission? Can I see and describe the organization's goals? Can I measure my results against those goals?

- **Influence** – How do others see me? How do I see myself? Do I "walk my talk" based on my values? How do my actions align with the values of my organization? How wide and deep are my connections? Will others trust me? Is my feedback valued? Do I value others' feedback? Can I put the goals of the group above my own? Do the members of the organization value my contributions?

You may not know how to answer some of these questions now, but that's okay. You will be exploring the questions in this leadership equation as you study this text. Through the following chapters, the leadership skills of personal growth, leading teams, organizational development and influence will be detailed for your study and application. Each chapter follows a pattern:

- Reflection on your current practice of the specific skills
- Diagnosis of your leadership learning needs
- Prescribing new knowledge, new skills, and new approaches to grow your leadership abilities.

Consider this text your leadership coach. Your entry into the world of leadership development begins here. Answer the questions posed within the chapters and spend time on the exercises. The questions in the chapter exercises are important. Leadership skills are not learned by simply reading about them, you must open yourself to the ideas, work through the discussion in the chapters, and determine how they fit into your experience.

Good leadership development is synergistic. Synergy is the sense that by everyone pulling together, one can achieve more. As a member of a team, you may have felt that leadership synergistic chemistry with a special boss, work team, teacher, or community group. The synergy in leadership development is through the integration of all the skill sets and behaviors described in the leadership equation. Together they are stronger than each behavior and skill set weighed individually. There is a special synergistic chemistry felt when it all comes together. As an individual developing leader you will be more confident in your choices and strategy. As you apply these in your workplace, the synergistic chemistry of the organization/workplace is successful, employees are happy, feel valued, and stay longer. Likewise, the organization's clients are more satisfied, needs are being met, the community points to the organization with pride, and other organizations seek ways to collaborate.

The need for quality leadership in human services professions is important. It is a field that unites a diversity of people and organizations to improve the human condition. Professionals in this field are at the forefront of change for individuals and for communities. Human services leaders have great opportunities to work with other leaders to bring about real change. The common denominator among these leaders is their ability to synergistically employ the skill sets in the components of the leadership equation.

YOUR LEGACY

It is exciting to think about your human services career committed to the improvement and sustainability of a quality life for all. There are many amazing leaders in the human services field who have established important institutions on which we have come to rely and build today's programs. Consider these:

William Booth founded the Salvation Army in the mid 1800s, an organization that still thrives today.

Jane Addams founded Hull House in Chicago and won the 1931 Nobel Peace Prize.

C. Henry Kempe led his peer physicians in the research on Battered Child Syndrome in the 1970s.

Cesar Chavez founded the National Farm Workers Association and advocated for the rights of farm workers from the 1970s through the 1980s. He was the recipient of the Presidential Medal of Freedom.

Ryan Hreljac founded Ryan's Well Foundation in 1999 at age 7 with his family to build wells and bring clean water to communities internationally.

Malala Yousafzai and Kailash Satyarthi struggled against the suppression of children and advocated for the right of children to an education; they shared the 2014 Nobel Peace Prize.

Now, it's your turn to step up to the plate. What legacy will you leave?

My goal is to prepare you for a successful human services career as a practitioner and leader by giving you the tools required to serve your organization's mission and community needs. It will be an exciting journey!

REFERENCES

Addams, Jane: http://www.nobelprize.org/nobel_prizes/peace/laureates/1931/addams -bio.html

Booth, William: http://www.salvationarmy.org

Chavez, Cesar: http://www.clnet.ucla.edu.edu/research/chavez/

The Kempe Foundation: http://www.kempe.org

Interview with Amanda Beattie. (2010). *YouTube ETSU*. Retrieved from http://www.youtube.com

Satyarthi, Kailash: http://www.npr.org/blogs/goatsandsoda/2014/10/11/355141727/nobel-laureate-kailash-satyarthi-aims-to-eliminate-child-labor

Ryan's Well Foundation: http://www.ryanswell.ca/about-usaspxbio

Wing, K. T., Pollack, T. H., & Blackwood, A. (2008). *The nonprofit almanac 2008*. Washington DC: Urban Institute.

Yousfzai, Malala: http://www.malala.org

Leadership Development and Organizational Management at Work in the Human Services Professions

Chapter 1

Leadership in Human Services and Workplace Vocabulary of Leaders and Managers

LEARNING OBJECTIVES

The student will

- describe the human services work sector and the leadership skill sets needed;
- explain the benefits to human services organizations if employees develop improved leadership skill sets;
- identify and explain leadership and management vocabulary as described giving a workplace example; and
- engage with the flow of the learning process used through out the textbook: reflection, diagnosis, and prescription.

The scope of this text will focus on the full range of key organizational processes and personal skills of leaders and managers within a human services organization.

LEADERSHIP IN HUMAN SERVICES

Effective leadership starts on the inside. This text will provide growth and development for both personal and organizational leadership as well as management. The impact of learning from this text will equip you to establish strong foundations and key skill sets within your organization to become a manager and leader in the field.

Your action will be to read, reflect, diagnose, and apply the various skills to personal and organizational situations (prescription). Don't think of it as a medication for an illness but instead as a treatment of multivitamins for your leadership growth and development. You will be learning not just theory but application of the theories. This challenge requires more than memorization on your part. In each chapter, the concept is introduced, followed by an opportunity to reflect on how the concept is currently active in your life. After reflecting, you will have the opportunity to take a short assessment to see how effective you are in utilizing that leadership concept. This step is called diagnosis. Your need for the third step, prescription, is determined here. Once you know what you want to do differently to become more effective as a leader, you can apply the prescription appropriately. Following the study of each chapter's concepts, utilize the textbook's extra resources and seek feedback from peers, faculty members, and human services professionals on the progress of your ability to apply your new learning in leadership. And of course, practice, practice, practice! Learning new skills and behaviors requires practice.

WHAT IS THE HUMAN SERVICES SECTOR?

Agencies, community centers, some government services, educational organizations, health clinics, and many nonprofits fall under the umbrella of the human services sector. Sometimes these organizations are partnered with or are part of national, state, and local governments. Each organization's outreach varies depending on the community need, organizational mission, functional technology, human resources, and funding. The field of human services can be defined as one that helps individuals cope with problems of a social welfare, educational, psychological, behavioral, health, or legal nature (Mehr & Kanwischer, 2011, p.13).

THE HUMAN SERVICES LEADER: A SNAPSHOT

Due to the diverse services and programs human services organizations deliver, leaders within human service organizations have obtained a variety of degrees and experiences that qualify them to be direct service providers, media and marketing coordinators, educators, public health officials, social workers, grant writers, or volunteer coordinators. Leaders of human services organizations work with teams inside and outside of their organization, establishing partnerships as well as ensuring their customers', clients', or patients' needs are met. They have to balance not only the diverse set of needs and talents of their staff but also the diverse set of needs and characteristics of their clients. A typical workday in a human services leadership position will include a substantial number of meetings and communications with staff, clients, board members, and community partners. Leaders find themselves engaged in planning, supervising, handling crises, fundraising, returning phone calls and emails, building the organization's brand, leading teams, managing large numbers of documents and appointments, reviewing and monitoring budgets, and approving expenditures. Human services organizations are typically challenged with limited fiscal and human resources whether in government, for-profit, or nonprofit sectors. Most employees' roles include administrator, service provider, program planner, as well as clerk and receptionist, because support staff is a luxury for most of these organizations. Few leaders of human services organizations spend their time engaged in only leadership activities such as documenting and measuring the positive impact of their services, fundraising, providing feedback to staff and other stakeholders, leading board meetings, networking with potential community partners, and assessing community needs and resources. Many leaders of human services organizations also provide direct client services.

THE STUDY OF LEADERS IN HUMAN SERVICES ORGANIZATIONS

Since the 1990s, interest has grown in understanding civic leadership in communities and the human services field. As you will see in Chapter 2, much of the early historical focus regarding the study of leadership concentrated on military leaders, political leaders, and for-profit business leaders. As you progress in your study of leadership in the human services sector, the overall best practices, skill sets, strategies, and processes of leadership will have many commonalities among the many workplace sectors. However, because the missions-orientation, values, environmental contexts, and operating systems of human services organizations differ from other workplace sectors, this textbook will emphasize and present leadership skill sets, strategies, and processes in a human services organizational context. In other words, leaders in human services use the same tools but may use them in a different way, have a different emphasis, or spend more time with some tools than others. Included in a section of this chapter will also be key vocabulary used in the study of leadership and organizational management that might be unfamiliar or unclear to those who studied only for human services careers.

REFLECTION: LEADING A HUMAN SERVICES ORGANIZATION

Begin by comparing the characteristics of a human services and a for-profit organization. Did you realize a human services organization serves a client base and a community while a for-profit organization serves stockholders, owners, and customers? A for-profit organization produces a product that must be sold and return a cash profit. A human services organization produces a product most often in the form of a program, service, or assistance that is not always expected to return a cash profit with returns to stockholders. These products are delivered to clients to alleviate a difficult situation, enabling them to return to a state of well-being. They may compete with programs and services of another agency, but such a marketplace is usually limited by location or rules of eligibility. A for-profit organization competes in a global marketplace of many similar products and services. Leaders in human services organizations always seek to make an impact at the micro level, which can be described as running an effective organization that provides quality, direct services to individual clients. A for-profit organization works to impact at both the micro and macro levels, seeking to gain the loyalty of the customer as well as a larger market share. Now that you can recognize the different characteristics of for-profit and human services organizations, are the characteristics of leadership requirements different in the two sectors? The Table 1.1 defines the needed skill sets for each of the different leadership levels within an organization.

Although this list of skill sets is common to leaders in both sectors, leaders in human services organizations require additional skills. Over time, leaders in human services organizations will observe patterns of client risk factors and bureaucratic rules, resulting in a possible need to problem solve at a macro level (to investigate through a larger unit of analysis such as a multiple community study or a national study). By collaborating with other community leaders, human services organizations become part of a collaboration that champions, makes recommendations, and establishes policies on a variety of issues regarding social, educational, health care, and socioeconomic issues. Human services leaders play a vital role in advocating for and building the public policy agendas that shape programs and policies government undertakes (Denhardt, Denhardt, & Aristigueta, 2002). Leadership in this field is more than influencing followers toward a common goal. Human services leaders must consider roles and responsibilities of all, the comprehensive network of community issues and problems, as well as seek to understand the value systems of different populations. Heifetz (1994, p. 22) refers to this as "adaptive work." Human services leaders are tasked with a difficult job of helping communities learn to adapt to new ways of thinking, living, and accepting people of all backgrounds as valued and deserving of services designed to improve their quality of life. Human services leaders, such as government policy makers, working at the macro level to impact large-scale issues will partner with many organizations, agencies, and community leaders to achieve

Table 1.1   Leadership Skill Sets

Level of Leader or Manager	Key Requirements of the Job
Top Level Leader Director/ CEO/President	• Sets the organization's strategic direction (vision and mission) • Approves and provides resources for processes, services, and programs • Approves operational processes, program designs, strategies, and goals • Ensures adequate standards are enacted for services to meet the organization's mission and vision • Reaches out to shareholders, constituents, stakeholders, peers, and communities
Middle Manager	• Designs (redesigns) and implements key processes, services, and strategic projects • Sets standards for each process, service, and program • Recommends and monitors resources for processes, services, and programs • Approves hiring decisions
First-Level Manager	• Communicates standards to employees • Trains and coaches employees to implement processes, services, and programs at the expected standards • Executes the processes, services, and programs • Builds relationships with clients, customers, and patients • Assesses employee performance and recommends consequences • Recommends improvements to processes, services, and programs • Requests and utilizes allocated resources • Recommends which employees to hire

Source: Adapted from Bossidy, L., & Charan, R. (2002). *Execution: The discipline of getting things done.* New York, NY: Crown Business.

their goals. The traditional skills of organizational management skills useful in micro-level work are not adequate at the macro level. These leaders need skill sets to become conveners, facilitators, advocates, and conflict negotiators. They must think strategically and motivate others to do the same. They must keep a positive, proactive attitude; possess high personal integrity; and maintain focus on the mission and results (Denhardt et al., 2002). Human services leaders working at the micro level help community members address individual and family needs; later they shift to the macro level to provide advocacy that may diminish the gap between a community's values, legislative policies, programs, and services and between the disparities community members face. As a future leader in this sector, imagine the breadth of the roles you will play, the skills you will employ, as well as the impact you will have.

DIAGNOSIS: LEADERSHIP SKILL SETS NEEDED IN THE HUMAN SERVICES PROFESSION

How is your academic program and future profession preparing you to succeed as a leader in the human services sector? In 2005, Scotland's government convened a group of leaders in the social work profession to review current practice of leadership preparation, project the leadership and management needs within the profession, and make recommendations on how to improve and strengthen their services (Leadership and Management Sub Group, 2006). The group determined that a future of increasing demands, greater complexity, and rising expectations of social work services required an upgrade from their current ability levels. Their research concluded needs for a changing service delivery model with engaging clients as active participants, consistently improved outcomes, new collaborative service delivery, and a shift from a welfare-based approach to a delivery of well-being for individuals and communities. Their report highlighted recommendations for improvement in strategic leadership, succession planning, outcomes measures for programs and services, greater accountability, management and leadership training at all levels of the organization, standards of professional practice, and integrated service delivery. In short, the skill set needs were identified, and a call to action was declared. In 2012, the Center for Creative Leadership in the United States facilitated an online discussion of nonprofit professionals to discuss leadership challenges driving today's nonprofit landscape (Clark, 2012). The first challenge noted was the struggling economy, which created an environment of fierce competition for funding from foundations, donors, and grants. All funders have raised the bar to require demonstrations of impact and statistical measures of change for the dollars received. The second challenge discussed focused on the leadership capacity of nonprofits. It is critical that nonprofit organizations intentionally develop a pipeline of leaders within the organization both to carry out the mission and strategic plan of the organization and to be trained and ready to fill a vacancy or void. Succession planning builds an organizational pipeline, ensuring one person does not have all of the expertise and experience regarding a particular niche. The third challenge of human services organizations is to evolve with the changing needs of the employees, clients, and board members by adding new leadership development programs and updating leadership tools. Leaders must develop skills that facilitate new ways to operate that favor team approaches and interagency collaboration, new methods to engage board members, creative use of resources, retaining and utilizing volunteers, as well as hiring and retaining highly trained staff. As you can see from these two different studies, it is imperative for successful human services leaders to adapt to changing demands, changing needs of their communities, diverse employees, and environments that evolve due to ongoing social and economic change. Earlier academic programs did not prepare human services professionals for the skill sets required to face today's leadership challenges. These studies specifically make recommendations to train and develop leaders in the human services sector, to establish bench strength and succession planning, to train leaders for both the micro and macro roles of the organization, to establish a network of shared leadership at all levels of the organization, and to establish a discipline of resource accountability by demonstrating consistent, measured results. Complete this survey as you consider the strength of your skill sets in these diverse leadership success factors.

Survey of Human Services Leadership Skill Sets

Use the scale of 1 = no knowledge, no practice; 2 = small knowledge, no practice; 3 = some knowledge, little practice; 4 = knowledgeable, some practice; 5 = knowledgeable, successful practice.

1. Able to sustain a community partnership: I am knowledgeable of and can apply the key behaviors and requirements that make a community partnership successful.

    1   2   3   4   5

2. Teamwork: I can work with a team to make decisions and implement policies and programs.

    1   2   3   4   5

3. Influence: I can lead others to see and adopt new ways of thinking and living in a diverse community.

    1   2   3   4   5

4. Lead change: I can work at the micro level to influence others to make positive changes for themselves and their families.

    1   2   3   4   5

5. Political influence: I can work at the macro level to influence policy makers and leaders in peer organizations to initiate change.

    1   2   3   4   5

6. Mission driven: I can coach my work team to stay focused on the mission and results.

> 1   2   3   4   5

7. Demonstrate measurable results: I am able to frame results in a quantifiable way so that progress can be measured and compared.

> 1   2   3   4   5

Where are your leadership skill sets strong? How many 4s and 5s did you score and in what areas?

Where do your skill sets need strength? What areas did you score 1s, 2s, and 3s?

PRESCRIPTION: GUIDING YOUR LEADERSHIP JOURNEY

The scope of this text will focus on the full range of key organizational processes and personal skills of leaders and managers within a human services organization. You will see measurable improvement in the seven identified leadership skill sets and more. Ken Blanchard (2007) wrote in *Forbes* that one of the many mistakes E-MBA programs (i.e., online MBA programs) make is spending too much time on teaching strategy and other organizational management concepts before ensuring students have adequately addressed their own credibility as a leader. Kouzes and Posner (2007) and Covey (1989) further emphasize that leadership development begins with an assessment of personal management, values, and credibility. By spending time in each chapter with an honest assessment and real application of new behaviors, you will become that credible leader.

Teaching leadership and management in one textbook for what will likely be a one-semester course might seem like entering an eating contest to see how many sandwiches you can eat in 15 sittings. The intention is not to give you indigestion or information overload but to teach you the critical skill sets of successful leaders and managers in human services organizations. In *How Great Leaders Grow*, Ken Blanchard (2012, p. 1) calls this learning process "walking toward wisdom." In his book, Blanchard states leaders grow when they are willing to receive feedback, open to learning, willing to seek counsel, able to reach out to others, and willing to stretch outside their comfort zones. Be open to reflecting on yours and your classmates' experiences. Consider adopting new ideas into your repertoire of leadership skills. Picture yourself in a first-level leadership role, in a middle-level leadership role, and as the executive director. The goal is to help you gain confidence as you make the skills within this text your skills. The leadership skills you develop rely solely on how far you are willing to study; use the questions, exercises, feedback, and practice. Welcome to the journey.

THE WORKPLACE VOCABULARY OF LEADERS AND MANAGERS

Every workplace has a culture and a language peppered with a vocabulary designed to communicate unique concepts and ideas in a profession. Human services, leadership, and management are no different than other professions in their use of specialized terms. In your study of human services, you have gained a rich understanding of that special vocabulary. Now it is time to avail yourself of the important terms in leadership and management.

REFLECTION: SPEAKING A NEW LANGUAGE

Becoming a confident and respected leader requires the ability to use the language employed by leaders in the workplace. In fact, let's start with those two words. Are they interchangeable? Is a leader the same as a manager? Actually, they are not the same. To simplify the concepts, think about a pair of work colleagues in terms of roles they each play on the job. Reference Table 1.2 below to note the role differences between leaders and managers.

As you can see, leaders and managers play different yet vital roles ensuring an organization's success. The manager provides steady and consistent processes and procedures. The leader is looking to the future to keep the organization and staff strategically positioned for the inevitable changes, which will maintain an organization's future readiness for growth and success. Organizations need the stability and steady progress managers provide. Some organizations have a large enough staff to hire two executives who have complementing skills in leadership and management. Some organizations have a very small staff and must seek an executive director who has

Table 1.2   Roles of Managers and Leaders

Role of a Manager	Role of a Leader
• Focus on policy and procedure	• Focus on improvement and change
• Plans for the stability of the organization	• Looks ahead and envisions the future
• Maintains quality operations and procedures	• Seeks new ideas and best practices
• Supervises and appreciates employee contribution	• Engages others in the process of future planning
• Provides training for employees	• Mentors others in the leadership pipeline

both skill sets. Because many human services organizations are resource-challenged, resulting in fewer staff, the ability to play both roles is beneficial and necessary for a human services leader.

How strong is your vocabulary in the world of organizations, business, management, and leadership?

DIAGNOSIS: BORROWING WORDS FROM OTHER PROFESSIONS

In addition to words such as manager and leader, there are other words and ideas that are common in the business world and useful in the world of human services. Can you give a working definition of these words?

___Asset	___Competitor
___Process	___Client/Customer
___Mission	___Stakeholder
___Brand	___Accounts Receivable/Payable
___Profit Margin	___Measure
___Sustainability	___Strategy

It is possible you may have worked in the for-profit sector, and this language is familiar to you. You may also believe that words such as these are necessary in only the for-profit world. Be assured that this vocabulary will be important to you as well as to other human services leaders and partnering community leaders. Can you use these words correctly as a leader in a human services context? Do you currently use these words regularly in the workplace?

You will find that management and leadership language translates as easily to small business entrepreneurs as it does to human services organizations and Fortune 500 companies. Rather than give you the *Webster's Dictionary* definition of each term, I've created a story to help you understand vocabulary concepts through a human services lens.

PRESCRIPTION: BUSINESS VOCABULARY TRANSLATED INTO HUMAN SERVICES SPEAK

Business vocabulary is spoken by leaders in all sectors of the workplace, and many business leaders will be represented on your board of directors, advisory board, community stakeholders, and community partners (depending on your organization's for-profit/nonprofit status). Your ability to use and understand these terms builds your leadership credibility. The vocabulary was selected from *What the CEO Wants You to Know: Using Business Acumen to Understand How Your Company Really Works* by Ram Charan (2001), and from the 2015 Criteria for the Tennessee Center for Performance Excellence (http://www.tncpe.org/framework) The order is based on the sequence of the fictional case study that uses these terms in a human services context.

The case: As agency director, you are considering establishing a new service for your health education agency to better serve its clients. This new service will provide to-go healthy meals for families dealing with Type 2 diabetes using after-work (5–7 p.m.) support group services at your agency. A survey of evening support group participants uncovered that fast food consumption (a problem area for those with Type 2 diabetes) had increased among participants of after-work programs. This was an unintended consequence of hosting otherwise convenient after-work programs for working adult participants. If the agency could send the 5 to 7 p.m. participant out the door with healthy to-go meals for the participant and the family, fast food consumption would decrease and participants would have healthier diets, a goal for those with Type 2 diabetes.

Mission – This mission is the engine driving your organization in the human services sector. The mission should be able to answer why your organization exists and what it hopes to accomplish? What unique, high quality purpose does it deliver to your community? The mission is the compass by which your leadership steers the agency. *Mission: The XYZ Health Education Agency seeks to educate and support citizens in making life-changing decisions for a healthier XYZ community.* What programs and services should your organization agree to deliver, and what should other organizations deliver are two of the most important questions a human services organization must determine. In the context of this case study, you must answer the question, Will healthy to-go meals for the 5 to 7 p.m. participants enhance the delivery of your organization's mission?

Anticipate Demand – If you decide the program of healthy to-go meals aligns with your organization's mission, the next step is to discover if your clients want and need such a service. If they do, are they willing or able to pay a nominal fee for the meals? A willingness to pay a small fee is an indicator of the client value placed on the service. Through this process, you will learn if clients desire and value the meal service and if there is a portion of the cost you can recoup by charging a fee.

Market Survey – One way to determine if a healthy to-go meal service will be successful is to interview and survey the clients your organization serves. Here you can ask more detail questions regarding the nominal fee and the client need to determine the extent of the demand. It will also be helpful to research your competitors to determine if similar meal services exist and would therefore compete for funding and clients. A competitor's program model can help you establish certain baselines such as operations, staffing, costs, facility impacts, and client responses.

Competitor – Competition exists in all sectors of the marketplace, even nonprofits. Name the organization(s) that offer similar services as your organization. Then go one step further and ask who offers similar meal services in your market area? The organizations you name are your competitors. It is always beneficial to know who is in your marketplace offering similar services and the details regarding what they offer.

Core Competency – A core competency is your organization's area of greatest expertise. Your organization may be excellent at health education but not excellent in meal preparation. Although a good idea, this new healthy to-go meal service may be better executed by a partnering agency whose expertise is quality meal preparation.

Products – In the human services sector, these are deliverables to the clients. The deliverables are programs and services that benefit the clients of your organization. The proposed healthy to-go meal plan would be classified as a service provided by your organization.

Sales Forecast – This is an attempt to predict the number of meals you anticipate delivering each day you are in operation. You can compare this number to your actual served meal count each day to see if you are meeting your goals and reflect on opportunities for change.

Merchandising – Any service (food especially) must look appealing and fresh. Even if the clients want the service, if it does not look or smell appealing, they will not participate. How will you package and make the healthy to-go meals attractive to current and future clients?

Advertise – Once your agency adopts the healthy to-go meal service as one of its programs, how will you communicate this service to your clients? How will you secure their loyalty to the program? How will you reach out to potential clients and ensure their future loyalty?

Product Mix – When you offer the healthy to-go meals, you will likely have choices for what makes up the meal. Some of these decisions can be fleshed out during the market research phase. However, there will inevitably be some clients who are unsatisfied due to the lack of variety, gluten-free, or vegetarian options. Therefore, it is important to determine if your organization will meet these needs or evolve to discontinue some of the unpopular choices after the service is in place.

Cash – This term has a different meaning in many organizations within the human service sector. Yes, all organizations operate with cash. The sources of that cash are as varied as the types of organizations. Cash can come from sales of products, fees for services, insurance reimbursements, donors, and grants. If your organization is a government or nonprofit agency, you will need to know that the expenses for the service do not exceed what you budgeted for the cost and that the service provided value to the client. Measuring this value is in effect a demonstration of your profit. If your organization is a for-profit agency, you will need to know the cost of delivering the program; not only should the program not exceed the total expenses incurred, but also there must be a profit (cash for the agency to keep) to show for the work.

Profit Margin – This term means the same as net margin. It is a calculation to help an organization know how closely priced the item is to its cost. For example, jewelry is sold at a higher margin than groceries. Margin is not the same as the markup on an item. The profit margin formula looks like this:

$$\text{Net Profit Margin} = [\text{Revenue} - \text{Cost}]/\text{Revenue} \times 100$$

Let's say you spent $400 on 4,000 pounds of ingredients for the healthy to-go meals. If all to-go meals are sold at a 2% profit margin, assuming the staff salaries are covered and there is no food waste, the agency has a profit of $80. Therefore, your organization will make a 20% return on assets (80/400 = .20 or 20%), which can either be reinvested to grow the program, grow other programs, or support other new programs.

Client/Customer/Patient Focus – Agencies strive to know whether their services and programs create value and return clients to a sense of well-being. One way they do this is to put themselves in their clients' shoes to determine if the services alleviate the problem and are delivered in a way that pleases the client. Clients have choices today in selecting their service providers. In the health care arena, patient focus is a key determinant in the accreditation ratings of clinics and hospitals. Foundations and government-funded grants are also interested in value to client and client satisfaction. Clients have the ability to choose most service providers. A healthy to-go meal will have to be convenient, high quality, high choice, and a good economic deal to interest the client.

Brand – Funding streams tend to follow organizations that create client demand and show results. That reputation is known as the agency brand. As a leader, the organization's focus is not only to deliver on the agency mission but also to deliver in such a way that clients are well served. This translates into an enhanced brand. Any new service or program added to the agency must deliver in a way that continues to enhance the brand. Delivering a quality, healthy to-go meal causes clients to want to return to your service/organization as well as rave about their experience to other current or potential clients. Today that conversation method includes texts, emails, twitter, blogs, and so on. Your agency's reputation can be elevated or reduced by a few keystrokes. Many human service organizations rely on their brand reputation to secure donors, grant funds, and ensure ongoing government funding. Although your agency's goal is not to become a long-term competitor to McDonalds, you want your funders and board members to understand the agency has a new quality, healthy to-go meal service that adds to the reputation of your organization's brand.

Stakeholders Versus Shareholders – The for-profit term is shareholders and refers to those who have made a monetary investment in the business, and will expect a return of cash on that investment. A stakeholder in a nonprofit expects a return on the investment in the form of an enhanced community. The term stakeholder applies to all types of organizations and is someone who is impacted by the organization: a key stakeholder is impacted directly. Using this definition, the list of stakeholders for an organization is large. Adding a new service to your organization certainly impacts its internal stakeholders such as employees and board members as well as external stakeholders such as clients, competitors, and community partners. When you pitch the idea for the healthy to-go meals to internal stakeholders, you must be able to articulate the organizational impact on staff, resources, future clients, board members, major donors, and so on.

Accounts Receivable/Accounts Payable – Accounts receivable are funds clients owe the organization. These can be agency fees or even the discounted cost of the new healthy to-go meal service. Accounts payable are funds the agency owes to suppliers. These can be utility bills or the cost of the food items for the to-go meals. Organizations must have appropriate cash on hand to pay for those items in the accounts payable column. Therefore, leaders must know what it will cost to incorporate the new meal service and if the money is not in the current budget, how you will intend to raise the funds.

Asset – These are things (not people) you have invested in for your organization. Ownership of the facility, equipment, technology, and vehicles are considered assets. Supplies such as paper or packaging for the healthy to-go meals are not assets since those are items that are consumed. It might be that the new food service will require purchase of assets such as new kitchen equipment: ovens, microwaves, stoves, and refrigerators.

Return on Assets – Leaders must understand the value of an investment of funds for an asset. They will refer to it as an ROA (return on assets) or ROI (return on investment). The terms are interchangeable. How might you describe the ROI of cash and staff-time to add the new meal service? Is the return an increase in participation? A return could mean healthier eating patterns for participants and their families, resulting in a reduction of their out-of-pocket medical expenses? Most organization boards of directors will ask such questions before approving expenditures for new equipment to support new programs like the healthy to-go meal service.

Effective – This term describes whether a service achieves its intended purpose. What are the intended purposes of the healthy to-go meal? (1) Meal convenience maintains client participation. (2) Healthy meal choices support the organization's clients overall well-being as well as the after-work programs that educate families impacted by Type 2 diabetes. (3) The healthy to-go meal service provides families an economic option to eat healthy. Using these purposes, you can measure effectiveness of the new service.

Goals – A goal is a performance level an organization intends to attain. In launching the new healthy to-go meal service, your goal might be to reduce after-work program participation decline by 50% in 6 months. Participants reported it was too difficult to manage a healthy evening family meal and attend 5 to 7 p.m. programs. If the new meal service caused 25 of those participants to return to after-work programs over 6 months and the organization had previously seen a decline of 50 participants, we would say the goal had been met.

Measure – This is numerical information that quantifies input, output, and overall outcomes of a program or service. In an organization that provides services designed to provide clients with a sense of well-being, measuring the impact of services is challenging. Programs and services in human services organizations are usually directed to produce behavior changes, which can be attributed to multiple influences. A sustained behavior change presents even more challenges to measure since the organization will need to monitor the change for months or even years. If your after-work program is one that provides education and support on weight loss, the program is an input to the participant's goal to lose weight. Another input is participating in the healthy to-go meals. An output in the process is the number of times the participant attended the 5 to 7 p.m. program. The overall outcome is the number of pounds the participant lost or gained. Each of these items can be measured. Each plays an important part in measuring the behavior change.

Process – A set of linked activities with the purpose of producing a program or service for clients is a process. Many times the sequence of activities is important to a process. The case study program describes linked activities that make up the programs and services for families with Type 2 diabetes. Teaching families to prioritize healthy eating is part of the process of successfully living with Type 2 diabetes. The healthy to-go meal is an optional part of the services that support learning about healthy eating processes. Other parts of a healthy eating education change process could be teaching how the body uses different nutrients in foods, how exercise changes metabolism and burns calories, how to read product labels, how to change recipes to use healthier ingredients, and how to plan your week to include shopping, cooking, and exercise instead of relying on typical fast food.

Strategy – Engaging in a strategy session requires analyzing all internal and external impacts of an organization to determine a plan of action that allows the organization to achieve intended objectives and positive growth. Such a strategy session may have produced the idea for the healthy to-go meal service, or a decision within the strategy session may have been made to eliminate other programs so that limited resources could be focused on this initiative's specific long-term goals. Strategy can expand or focus an organization's work.

Sustainability – The organization's ability to address needs, to evolve, and to strategically plan to successfully prepare for the future needs of the community in their market area is work to sustain the long-term success of the organization. To have long-term viability, organizations must look at both internal and external factors. Factors may include workforce capability, technology, resources, facilities, and so on. It is the social responsibility of the organization to act in a manner that benefits all stakeholders. As an organization, taking on many small new services can reduce its capability to respond to major community needs as they arise. To preserve your organization's agility and future resources, leaders may choose not to offer the innovative, healthy to-go meal service, so that resources are not spread too thin. Leaders of human services organizations must focus on both the sustainability of the organization as well as the sustainability of its programs and services upon which your clients and community depend.

Values – Guiding principles that embody how the organization and its people are expected to operate are its values. Examples of organizational values usually include demonstrating integrity and fairness, valuing diversity, and striving for excellence in the organizations programs and services. Your organization may value nutrition and want to help clients make healthy eating choices. Therefore, the healthy to-go meal service is aligned with your organization's values.

Vision – This is a statement that describes in a sentence or two a picture of what the organization is striving to be in the future. The organization focusing on services for families with Type 2 diabetes may seek to create an all-encompassing set of programs and services to facilitate a health and wellness focus on Type 2 diabetes with support to empower clients toward healthy weight loss. The organization's vision might be "All families deserve the knowledge to make healthy choices." With such a vision, this organization may see the healthy to-go meals as a new service in alignment with their vision statement.

SUMMARY

Diving into new material can feel like learning to swim all over again. Don't worry; this content will help you learn how to swim in these new waters. The material in this text will prepare you to step into your first leadership position as well as to move into progressively increasing responsibility-laden leadership positions in the human services sector. You were able to appreciate a snapshot of the skill sets required of human services leaders, admire the depth and variety of leaders' varied organizational duties, as well as gain an understanding of the likelihood of needing to wear both the leader and manager hat in the organization. Human services leaders play both a micro role in the organization and a macro-leadership role in the larger community. You studied the current needs of human services organizations and the profession shared through research studies regarding leaders and leadership development within this sector. And through the use of a human services case study, you have been able to translate key business, management, and leadership terms into situations you might encounter. In the next chapter, the history and development of leadership and management theory will guide you to understand this new applied science and the art of its practice.

REFERENCES

Application Criterial. (2015). Tennessee Center for Performance Excellence. Retrieved from http://www.tncpe.org/framework

Blanchard, K. (2007). Why we can—And should—Teach leadership. *Forbes.* Retrieved from http://www.forbes.com/2007/10/05/executive-mba-teaching -lead-cx_kb_1005blanchard.html

Blanchard, K. (2012). *How great leaders grow: Becoming a leader for life.* Oakland, CA: Berrett-Koelher.

Bossidy, L., & Charan, R. (2002). *Execution: The discipline of getting things done.* New York, NY: Crown Business.

Charan, R. (2001). *What the CEO wants you to know: Using business acumen to understand how your company really works.* New York, NY: Crown Business.

Clark, S. (2012, Oct. 23). Top three issues facing nonprofit organizations in 2012. *Leading Effectively* [Center for Creative Leadership blog]. Retrieved from http://www .leadingeffectively.com/top-three-issues-facing-nonprofit-organizations -in-2012-2

Covey, S. R. (1989). *The seven habits of highly effective people: Powerful lessons in personal change.* New York, NY: Simon and Schuster.

Denhardt, R. B., Denhardt, J. V., & Aristigueta, M. P. (2002). *Managing human behavior in public and nonprofit organizations.* Thousand Oaks, CA: Sage.

Heifetz, R. A. (1994). *Leadership without easy answers.* Cambridge, MA: Belknap Press.

Kouzes, J. M., & Posner, B. Z. (2007). *The leadership challenge* (4th ed.). San Francisco, CA: John Wiley and Sons.

Leadership and Management Subgroup (2006). *Strengthening leadership and management capacity across social work services: The leadership and management subgroup report.* 21st Century Social Work. Retrieved from http://www.knowledge.scot.nhs.uk/changinglives/resources-library/resource-detail.aspx?id=9247

Mehr, J. J., & Kanwischer, R. (2011). *Human services: Concepts and intervention strategies.* Boston, MA: Pearson.

Schawbel, D. (2012). *Ken Blanchard on How Great Leaders Grow.* Retrieved from www.Forbes.com

Chapter 2

Theories of Leadership and Management—Building a Philosophy of Leadership

LEARNING OBJECTIVES

The student is expected to

- trace the history of the development of leadership and management theories,
- identify and paraphrase the important outcomes of each theory of leadership and management, and
- draw conclusions from each theory to inform his or her own philosophy of leadership.

Theories of leadership and management have their roots in the theories of psychology and sociology. When analyzing leadership as a study of the actions of a group of people who intend to work together to achieve a set of goals, it becomes apparent that the same influences on individual human behavior come to bear on group behavior.

REFLECTION: THE COMPLEX DYNAMICS OF LEADING

Consider the human interactions you experience as a participant and observer at home, work, and school. What influences people to communicate, think, interpret, and behave in certain ways? And why do we respond in particular ways to others' words and actions? If more than two people are involved in an interaction, do the dynamics change? Now let's insert some complexity to the interaction by adding a few deadlines, differing cultural perspectives, or uneven power dynamics. The mixture becomes even more intense when a healthy dose of environmental influence and differing levels of motivation are added. With all these ingredients, we have created a "leadership stew" for researchers in the fields of psychology, sociology, education, military science, political science, and management sciences to "taste." Research in leadership seeks to observe, interview, measure, and analyze seeking patterns, responses, and outcomes that result in consistent explanations, predictable behaviors, and common interpretations to test in a variety of situations. What follows is a historical summary of leadership theory development, derived from decades of scientific research, which serves to inform the recommended practices of developing leaders today.

As each leadership theory unfolds, watch how the focus on the leader as a perfect hero with a defined set of attributes, transitions to an imperfect hero who must make choices to evaluate and use several leadership skill set options. Also, become familiar with the discovery of how different situations and teammates affect the choices of skills leaders use. Eventually the "hero leader" realizes that he or she must rely on others to solve complex problems. The focus of the theory broadens from individuals as leaders, leaders and situations, leaders and team relationships, empowerment, collaboration, and a diverse perspective of solutions to problems.

"Leadership is one of social science's most examined phenomena," according to Antonakis, Cianciolo, and Sternberg (2004, p. 4). The amount of research on leadership and management increased after World War II as countries acquired new borders, names, and powers; selected new political leaders; and internally rebuilt industries. Given the crisis all had survived as well as the global complexity of the leadership situation, the desire for quality leaders was a high priority and is reflected by the increase in research in universities, industry, and the military. This research continues throughout the decades fueled by the leadership needs of communities, diverse populations and organizations, as well as the interdisciplinary nature of the contributing theories. Scientists expect the magnitude of leadership information and findings to increase exponentially as increasingly more research studies are conducted during the coming years. Many authors of leadership books have classified leadership research into different categories or schools of thought. Antonakis et al. (2004) identifies six schools of thought that will be used to describe each theory indicating key researchers and authors for each theory, the impact of the theory on the field of leadership, and the important takeaways you will apply to your own philosophy of leadership. Studying the history of leadership theory and research should be done with a purpose. One of the reasons you choose to study leadership is to increase your chances of finding a job in human services and to improve career performance. Having a philosophy of leadership will do both. Your growing philosophy of leadership will become your guide as you navigate the succeeding lessons in this chapter's sections, understand the impact and implications of each theory, and apply your acquired knowledge in real-world leadership situations.

DIAGNOSIS: THE PROCESS OF BUILDING A PHILOSOPHY OF LEADERSHIP

What is your philosophy of leadership? This is not an uncommon question in a job interview or essay for graduate school admission. Building a philosophy of leadership begins by understanding your personal values and asking yourself key questions regarding how those values influence your choices about how you interact with others in work groups. Review the 10 questions listed below (adapted from Chalker, 2015), and keep them in mind as you read this chapter. You will use them at the conclusion of this chapter to draft your philosophy of leadership.

1. List the top three values you embody that speak to your role as a future leader.

2. Do you believe that others on your team are capable of working toward a common goal or are only motivated by what is in it for them?

3. What is the contribution you want to make by serving as a leader?

4. How do you want to treat others and how do you want others to treat you?

5. Describe the leadership style you think others see in you.

6. In a group, do you think first about group tasks or relationships with the group members?

7. How do others describe their working relationship with you?

8. How do others describe the way you accomplish tasks?

9. How do you work to build your influence with others?

10. Do you believe your leadership skills are already set and are waiting to be uncovered, or do you believe you must actively grow and cultivate these skills?

Making theories come alive for readers is challenging. Compiling ideas from various theories into a philosophy can feel overwhelming. This chapter will guide you through the process of connecting with each theory and evaluating its place in your philosophy of leadership. During your tenure as a student of leadership, you will engage in reflective thinking and picture the theory's impact on you, the team, and shared goals. You will resonate with certain ideas and values, and through this process, you will develop your leadership philosophy. For those readers engaged currently in a workplace full or part time, you might conduct what Ferrance (2000) describes as action research, a process in which participants reflectively examine their own practices systematically. It is carried out in the context of the observations you make in your working environment posing questions about the leadership theories you see demonstrated around you. If you are a team leader, the research questions you pose relate to your actions. If you are a team member, the research questions you pose relate to your perceptions of the supervisor or team leader. In your workplace, internship, classroom, or community organizations,

- observe and reflect on the leadership you see practiced around you,
- gather data about the leader's effectiveness,
- interpret the data and reflect on its relationship to the leadership's practices,
- connect the related theory as presented in this chapter,
- determine the actions to change and related skills to learn, and
- measure the resulting change, if possible.

To examine the effectiveness of the leadership results (data), a context is needed. As a human services professional, you are actively engaged in the study of theory and action research every day, helping clients achieve an improved state of well-being. In human services, the context comes from the study of psychology, sociology, human development theory, and so on. In leadership, the context comes from the scientific research and resulting theories examined in the rest of this chapter. You must know the whole story in order to interpret your data and recommend a better course of action as a leader. Understanding the story and the theory will allow a diagnosis of the leadership problem and a supported recommendation for change in thinking and action. At the close of each leadership school discussion, you will be asked four questions:

1. How would you describe the theories in action in your workplace, school, or home?

2. What evidence do you see regarding the theory's effectiveness?

3. How does this evidence support your conclusions about the theory's effectiveness?

4. How will you include the theories of this school into your leadership philosophy?

Schools of Leadership

Trait School

Before the 19th century, leadership was a social and biological concept that revolved around the great man theories, which are rooted in the belief that the heredity and intermarriage of the elite would produce exceptional, individual leaders (Komives, Lucas, & McMahon, 1998). Bass (1990) explains that all societies created myths that gave exaggerated explanations for the strength of their leaders and the powerless submission of their subordinates. The greater the economic injustice in the world, the more distorted the realities of the leaders' powers, morality, and effectiveness. Historically, leaders were selected from the upper classes, disconnected from the realities of everyday life, and educated in the world of crisis management, fear, and privilege. Leadership was exhibited through power in military, government, religious organizations, and families. In the pre-19th-century era, leaders were male and in most cases, leadership positions were handed down from one male family member to another. Legal and social standing in these times did not allow women to participate fully in government, religious, social, and work-related organizations; therefore, it was rare for a woman to hold a leadership position.

Goffee and Jones (2011) explain that the modern study of leadership began in the early 1900s, about the time of World Wars I and II, with the primary purpose to improve the process of identification and selection of military leaders. Because of the long-held belief that leadership was a set of inherited traits, trait patterns were explored to determine whether such characteristics were inherited (Bass, 1990). As the study of traits became more popular, defining the list of traits considered imperative to leadership became increasingly more complex. Characteristics such as self-confidence, intelligence, agreeableness, persistence, command of voice, extraversion, and many more comprised the profile of a perfect leader. Research regarding traits continues; yet, one trait, intelligence, consistently correlates positively with leadership effectiveness (Bass, 1990).

Eventually, trait theories broadened to include not just the traits of the leader, but also the traits of the situation or crisis. Researchers studied patterns of matching the needs of the situation with the traits of the leader. Leaders were identified and selected for skills that matched the situation to solve the problems at hand (Bass, 1990). Eventually research determined that there was not one definitive set of perfect leadership traits. Keep in mind the era in which this research was conducted and its original purpose. The participants in leadership research until the late 1900s came from large employers, usually the military and manufacturing, and therefore were predominantly Caucasian males. Until the last quarter of the 20th century, the participants of leadership research were not representative of the population by gender, race, or ethnicity.

Overall, the impact of organizations choosing leaders based only on traits is usually negative. First, there is a level of bias toward certain traits that results from the person or group making the decisions. People tend to select team members who look and sound like themselves. Members of minority groups usually are not considered for leadership positions, as their physical and cultural traits are different from the preconceived familiarity of the majority group. Given that preferred leadership traits are thought to be inherited, the idea of developing leaders and valuing alternative leadership perspectives becomes a moot point. Choosing leaders based only on traits assumes that quality leaders are born, and therefore, leadership is not a learned skill. People are described as "born leaders" every day based on their appearances and perceptions of abilities to influence. Subscribing to that perspective has in turn created many ill-prepared leaders that have made unfortunate decisions across the world throughout history. The trait school of thought is a leader-centered perspective, one that is focused on finding that perfect person to heroically fix the problem. It was and still is not uncommon to see organizations conduct a search for the ideal leader. Unfortunately, citizen voters, based on their historical voting patterns, subscribe to the trait theory as well when casting a ballot at the voting booth. (Lipman-Blumen, 2005)

Traits, and the assumptions that accompany those traits, establish your initial expectations about others as you make a quick and sometimes superficial assessment of someone else's abilities. In other words, traits become the palette by which you create a first impression of another person, and likewise, how others make initial impressions regarding you. First impressions are the baseline from which you build leadership influence with others. Those first impressions cause people to make choices about the level of influence someone initially has. People become gatekeepers, allowing some to have influence and others not. Closing the gate based only on the assumptions and perceptions of a leader's traits too often limits opportunities for important voices to have access to both formal and informal positions of leadership.

Today, we acknowledge flaws with the trait theory in which someone's leadership ability isn't strictly attributed to genealogy, personality, or physical characteristics. We know now that leadership is a learned set of skills that involve our ability to work with people and manage the operational side of the organization. Leadership philosophies based only on trait theories are not congruent in an organizational structure that includes shared leadership responsibilities that are more typical of today's diverse organizations with team-oriented expectations. Today's workplace requires shared responsibilities and support for the learning and growth of the whole team as opposed to the cookie cutter notion of a definitive list of leadership traits.

Tapping your understanding of trait theory, respond to these questions:

1. How would you describe the trait theories in action in your workplace, school, or home?

2. What evidence do you see regarding the theory's effectiveness?

3. How does this evidence support your conclusions about the theory's effectiveness?

4. How will you include the theories of this school into your leadership philosophy?

Behavioral School

In the 1930s, behavioral researchers began to identify what leaders do as a learned set of behaviors and skills instead of genetically inherited innate characteristics. In 1939, psychologist Kurt Lewin's research team identified three types of leaders based on the leader's interactions with a group: authoritarian, participative, and delegative (Lewin, LIippert, & White, 1939). Later, the three styles were referred to as autocratic, democratic, and laissez-faire. Lewin's study, which used school children as the subjects, found that participative/democratic leadership was both productive and allowed for high quality, creative contributions from the followers. The children in Lewin's study also demonstrated that authoritarian/ autocratic type leaders were productive in results while delegative/laissez-faire leaders were neither highly productive nor creative. In 1955, Katz published one of the first articles regarding effective administrative skills in the *Harvard Business Review*. Katz described three essential areas of skills as technical, human, and conceptual, defining skill "as ability which can be developed, not necessarily inborn, and which is manifested in performance, not merely potential" (pp. 33–34). Stogdill and Coons (1957) described two major clusters of leadership behaviors: (1) "consideration" behaviors that centered on concern for followers, and (2) "initiation of structure" behaviors that centered on goal attainment. This breakthrough was important since most current theories focus on these two constructs to describe and categorize leader behaviors. Today these clusters are referred to as relationship versus task behaviors. Blake and Mouton (1964) first depicted a model of managerial behavior in a diagram that also conceptualized Stogdill and Coon's two manager behavior constructs: leaders' concern for people and the need to complete the task (results or production). This well-known leadership grid maps five different leadership styles on a graph with two axes: The vertical axis represents concern for people, and the horizontal axis represents concern for tasks. Each square is numbered one through nine to represent the strength of the concern. Five leadership styles emerge from the grid: (9,1) authority-compliance, (1,9) country-club, (1,1) impoverished management, (5,5) middle of the road, and the most desirable style (9,9) team management.

The leaders whose behaviors are illustrated by (1,9) on the upper left side of the grid are more concerned with the people on the team and least concerned with the tasks and results. Leaders who are most focused on the tasks and results

Figure 2.1   The Leadership Grid

9	1,9										9,9
8											
7											
6											
5							5,5				
4											
3											
2											
1	1,1										9,1
	1	2	3	4	5	6	7	8	9		

Concern for Relationships (vertical axis)

Low Concern for Results High (horizontal axis)

Source: Blake, R. R., & Mouton, J. C. (1964). *The managerial grid.* Houston, TX: Gulf Publishing.

and least concerned with the people on the team are deadline driven and usually seek compliance for the one way to accomplish the task (9,1). The leader whose behaviors are described in the (1,1) impoverished frame are generally not engaged with the team and are perceived as disconnected with the goals of the organization. The (5,5) leader is somewhat unsure of the commitment from the team and seeks to compromise for fear of conflict among the team members. There is progress toward the tasks assigned, but a lack of confidence in leadership ability keeps this team from their full potential. A (9,9) leader exhibits confidence in himself or herself and the team. They share ownership of the tasks and results, frequently celebrating and empowering others to higher levels of performance.

Behavior theories opened doors to the idea that certain behaviors and skills leaders used can be identified, observed, and learned. This meant people weren't just born with an ability to lead, but instead that these skills could be learned through modeling, teaching, and feedback. Acceptance of this theory exponentially increased the pool of potential leaders for organizations. In addition to the wider pool of potential leaders, new understanding regarding the framework of the two clusters of leader behaviors—(1) consideration (people focused) and (2) structure (task focused)—are foundational to understanding yours and others' actions in the workplace.

Tendencies to be relationship or task focused are each observable in interactions with coworkers, classmates, and even interpersonal relationships. Due to these tendencies, some people relate better to task-focused leaders while others relate well with relationship-focused leaders. Even without reading a leadership theory textbook or having a formal leadership style assessment in hand, you can determine the relationship and task-focused preferences of those you interact with on a regular basis. Think about your own tendencies. Some may resonate well with others who are task-oriented and be motivated to complete the task at hand. Others might think that was rude and would rather spend time engaged in icebreakers to get to know the entire team before getting to work, the tendency of a relationship-oriented person.

Behaviorists using Blake and Mouton's (1964) managerial grid believed that a perfect leader was both high task and high relationship focused. In reality, most people have style tendencies in one direction or the other on the continuum. But the continued search for the perfect leader actually raises this question: Is there a perfect leader? Some researchers (trait theorists and behavioral theorists) are still focused on describing the ideal leader. Then a different group of researchers made a breakthrough with connections to the Lewin et al. 1939 study with the school children, integrating his findings with the newly developed contingency leadership school.

Tapping your understanding of behavior theory, respond to these questions:

1. How would you describe the behavior theory in action in your workplace, school, or home?

2. What evidence do you see regarding the theory's effectiveness?

3. How does this evidence support your conclusions about the theory's effectiveness?

4. How will you include the theories of this school into your leadership philosophy?

Contingency School

Research from the behavioral school was focused on leadership styles: task centered versus relationship centered, as well as other characteristics involving a leader's tendencies and preferences when interacting with teams. Questions by contingency school researchers asked if different behavior styles worked effectively in all situations. Fiedler (1967) studied contingency theories seeking to demonstrate that different situations called for different leader behaviors. He later determined that leadership style alone was not sufficient to determine leadership effectiveness (Fiedler & Chemers, 1974). In general, contingency theories work to match situational characteristics to the appropriate leadership style. The contingency school extends our view beyond the individual leader and broadens our attention to include additional variables: the characteristics of those being led and the details of the situation. Hersey and Blanchard introduced situational theory, also in the contingency theory family, in the 1960s. Their research found that the leader's choice of leadership style is best determined by the followers' task-related maturity (Hersey & Blanchard, 1993). Task-related maturity is the level of experience one has in the ability to complete a task similar to the one previously performed. If you have successfully completed task A and your supervisor assigns a similar task B, you would feel confident (mature) in your ability to be successful at task B. In situational theory, leaders were expected to be cognizant of the followers' abilities and have the flexibility to choose from several types of leadership behaviors as the ability, confidence, and maturity of the followers in the situation required. Hersey and Blanchard (1993) determined that a leader's ability to self-assess, as well as observe and assess the followers and then choose the appropriate approach, was an integral part of a leader's success. The leaders choice to respond in a more directive manner (task orientation) or supportive manner (relationship) is based upon the group members' competence (knowledge and experience doing the specific task) as well as commitment (motivation to want to accomplish the task; see Figure 2.2). Blanchard, Zigarmi, and Nelson's (1993, p. 26) model divides followers abilities into four developmental levels:

- Development Level 1 – Group members new to the organization are typically enthusiastic but not knowledgeable. They are excited to start something new but untrained in the expectations of the organization.
- Development Level 2 – Generally group members have some experience at this level but now understand how far they have to go to become a master at the task. It can seem overwhelming and motivation can wane.
- Development Level 3 – By this time, group members have learned and practiced the skills required for the job and are considered highly competent. Motivation levels can vary greatly from team member to team member, requiring leaders to listen to individuals, to support and grow the confidence of others, and to troubleshoot individual problems.
- Development Level 4 – The highest level of development demonstrates the impact of motivated and competent team members. Through careful and deliberate coaching, as well as a razor sharp focus on results, leaders can build and sustain high performing teams.

The third situational variable studied in the contingency school during the1960s was the workplace environment and its prominent role in creating situational influences on team members. Three important elements of the workplace situation include leader–member relations (group atmosphere), task structure (clarity, simplicity, and urgency), and the level of the position with the corresponding power of the leader (authority to reward and punish).

Figure 2.2   The Situational Leadership Model II

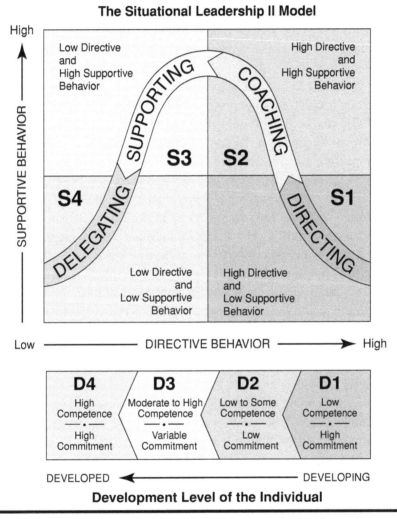

Source: Blanchard, K. H., Zigmmi, D., Nelson, R. B. (1993). Situational leadership after 25 years: A retrospective. *Journal of Leadership and Organizational Studies, 1*(21), 22–36. doi: 10.1177/107179199300100104.

An individual's motivation is a strong influence on performance and increases as an individual meets physical, emotional, and intellectual needs. Herzberg's (1966) research on motivation theory found that meeting workers' lower level (hygiene) needs prevented dissatisfaction in the workplace. If workers higher level needs (motivators) were met, it would drive workers to a higher level of performance. Hygiene factors met physical needs such as sufficient weekly pay (food and shelter), tools to accomplish the job, and a consistent work schedule. Motivators (intellectual and emotional needs) included the ability to make suggestions in the workplace, feel appreciation, and know your work is important to the success of the organization

(Bass, 1990). McGregor's Theory X and Theory Y (1966) contrasted a supervising leader's perspectives about the nature of employees as driven by needs of power and rewards as opposed to their need for responsibility and internal satisfaction. Theory X represents a negative view of human nature, assuming workers are naturally lazy and resulting in a belief that workers need close management supervision. Theory Y represents a positive view of human nature, assuming workers naturally want to work and resulting in a belief that workers want to believe they are trusted and to participate in decision making; therefore, they do not need close supervision. House (1971, 1996) studied the influence of a leader's task and relationship orientation on follower motivation and satisfaction, which is referred to as path-goal theory. This research question asked which focus (task or relationship) motivates employees and how leaders can modify their own behaviors and choices to influence followers desire to achieve. The study of path-goal theory added task characteristics as well as the needs of motivated followers to the previous situational research results of leader style and follower characteristics. House learned the more challenging the path toward goal attainment, the more appreciation followers have for a manager with a structured leadership style. Followers seek more autonomy in less difficult tasks choosing to engage in some leadership roles in the group. The importance of relationship in the workplace is important to most followers at a basic level (respect and appreciation) and increases with the preferences and needs of the worker (House, 1971). The importance of task orientation is high when the followers are navigating unknown waters.

Contingency theories do not subscribe to the belief that there is a perfect leader, perfect team, or perfect situation. Instead, the impact of the leader's style choices, the details surrounding the task, and the characteristics of the team create multiple sets of complex and fluid variables in organizational leadership.

As demonstrated by Figure 2.3, team members are influenced by the leader and the situation, while the leader is influenced by the team and the situation, and the situation is influenced by the team and the leader. The important takeaway is that successful leaders must be observant, thoughtful, and conscious of their own patterns and tendencies as well as others behaviors, while analyzing

Figure 2.3   Key Relationships in Contingency Theories

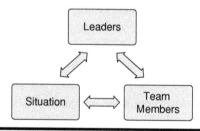

the situational variables. The take-charge leader, responding without thoughtful attention to the task, employees' competence and commitment, and environmental influences, might feel good emotionally but likely is not making the best choices that consider all the important variables. Creating a short checklist of questions that considers the variables of a leader's style, situational characteristics, as well as the team's knowledge and commitment can help you learn and practice the process of a thoughtful analysis of variables in situational leadership decisions. Practicing this mental analysis in calmer moments will provide you with a go-to tool when the situation is tense and time sensitive. This a sample go-to tool, a checklist of questions, that will help you evaluate the major components of situational leadership:

1. Describe the team. Rate them on a scale of 1 to 10 on factors of experience in similar problems, emotional maturity, motivation, demonstration of good teamwork, loyalty, and trustworthiness.

2. Describe and rate the leader on a scale of 1 to 10 on factors of experience with similar problems, emotional maturity, motivation, demonstration of good skill sets in leading teams, loyalty, and trustworthiness. Is the leader more task or relationship focused? Is the leader in a formal or informal position of power?

3. Describe the situation. Is it under control or out of control? Does it have the potential to explode in conflict? Is it time sensitive? Is the leader clear about the task? Are there clear processes in place? Will new skills be needed?

As you can see from the set of questions, the choice of leadership approach flows from the leader's assessment of the variables. Generally a more task-focused approach is best for teams who either know what they are doing and work well together or for groups who are new and not yet acclimated to operating as a team. A leader's choice of a stronger relationship focus shows more success when work groups faced with uncertain decisions or environments test their expertise first, gain new skills, and build confidence. This theory is not trying to promote leadership by formula, but researchers noted patterns that lend themselves to one approach more than another. Historically, the industrial age, command and control environments that existed until well into the 1970s, believed followers worked best in a consistent high power, high structure, and high achievement work environment. Contingency theories not only demonstrate the success of multiple leadership approaches but also demand the need and skill of leaders to operate with flexibility to be successful. Leaders now know to analyze followers and situations and then choose from multiple leadership methods. If a leader is only successful at applying one method to every situation, success in the endeavor and in the leadership relationship is unlikely, and as the saying goes, "if the only tool in the leader's toolbox is a hammer, then every situation looks like a nail."

Tapping your understanding of contingency theory, respond to these questions:

1. How would you describe the contingency theory in action in your workplace, school, or home?

2. What evidence do you see regarding the theory's effectiveness?

3. How does this evidence support your conclusions about the theory's effectiveness?

4. How will you include the theories of this school into your leadership philosophy?

Relational School

The interactions of leaders and followers are the focus of study in this school of thought. Leadership is not a solo practice; you are in a leadership role because you are working with followers. Relationships are built around the reciprocal desire of Person A to meet the needs of Person B, and for Person B to meet the needs of Person A. Leader–member exchange theory (Graen & Scandura, 1987) emphasizes the one-on-one relationship between a leader and a follower. Each leader–follower relationship may be slightly different because each person is unique. Some relationships are easier to establish and maintain because of common experiences and values. A high quality relationship between the leader and follower is labeled an in-group relationship and results in positive outcomes for both parties. Leader–follower relationships characterized by a lack of understanding between the leader and follower or between some followers and less engaged followers are referred to as out-group relationships. The relationships among the followers can sometimes influence the leader to be less welcoming to those excluded. These types of relationships usually result in unsatisfactory outcomes for the follower, leader, and the organization.

This in-group/out-group phenomenon happens on playgrounds, in classrooms, in offices, and even in families. Those who share more common experiences tend to become increasingly friendly with each other and are chosen more often by leaders of the same group for new opportunities. In-groups are also referred to as "cliques" and exist in the workplace as well. Leader–member exchange theory illuminates the responsibility of the leader to build relationships that move as many followers from the out-group into the in-group status and to foster relationship building between in- and out-group members, thus facilitating acceptance of new in-group members. Too often leaders have had an ambivalent attitude or worse, have sought opportunities to transfer or dismiss out-group followers. Later we will see how this theory is connected to the multicultural school and to our own familiarity with such terms as "glass ceilings" and "cement walls."

Organizations have become more heavily dependent on the success of work teams. Team leadership theory is part of the relational school and involves a complex array of leadership functions, which can be classified as maintenance (relationship) functions and task functions. Maintenance functions include establishing a culture of trust, meeting team member/follower needs, creating a culture that respects team members and encourages their development, and providing resources for team members to achieve their goals. There are several excellent books about teams and trust (*The Five Dysfunctions of a Team* by Patrick Lencioni, 2002; *The Speed of Trust* by Stephen M. R. Covey, 2006) that articulate the importance of a work environment built on high trust. Trust is the foundation of all relationships and therefore foundational to teamwork. Team members must be able to "be vulnerable with each other about their needs, talents, weaknesses, fears, and commitment," states Lencioni (2002, p. 7). Once trust is established, the team's effectiveness is increased due to the additional four steps of Lencioni's teamwork model: (1) sharing differences of opinion, (2) willingly listening to all voices around the table, (3) building confidence so each team member will come through on promises, and (4) establishing alignment so all are working for the benefit of the team. Without trust, the team cannot open the door to the four steps of Lencioni's teamwork model in order to succeed.

Larson and LaFasto (1989) found eight consistent characteristics of highly successful teams:

1. Quality leadership

2. Clear, elevating goal

3. Results-driven structure

4. Competent team members

5. Unified commitment

6. Collaborative climate

7. Standards of excellence

8. External support and recognition

Assessing the level of these eight characteristics within a team is useful for troubleshooting problems or training team leaders. Summarizing Larson and DeFasto (1989), the two key components of leading teams are (1) the foundational work of establishing team trust and (2) attending to the eight characteristics of successful teams. Leading a team is a complex job, but it does not require a hierarchy (formal organizational power structure). With a flatter structure (fewer positions of power), more team members are sharing in the leadership functions of the team. Sharing leadership with the team positively impacts trust, commitment, interpersonal relationships, and motivation to succeed. Strategies for building trust will be shared in Chapter 4 in this text.

These theories connect to the relationship school because of the leader's desire to create a positive work environment and meet the needs of followers/team members. A leader's ability to be inclusive is invaluable to the trust and work ethic of all team members. Workplace cliques are not conducive to successful teamwork or the health and empowering culture of the organization. If moral reasons are not convincing enough, there are legal protections in place against unfair employment practices and the segregation of employees. Therefore, leaders must be committed and skilled in listening, negotiation, and embracing a diverse work team. Historically, certain members of organizations have been relegated to out-group status because of their gender, race, ethnicity, ability, sexual orientation, and gender identity to name a few. The US Equal Employment Opportunity Commission (EEOC) was created to protect minority groups from unfair firing, hiring, and other illegal workplace practices. (Note that EEOC currently does not protect all the classes named here although many organizations and some states have taken that extra step.) It is the responsibility of the leader to develop trust and respectfully lead every member of the team.

Tapping your understanding of relational theory, respond to these questions:

1. How would you describe the relational theory in action in your workplace, school, or home?

2. What evidence do you see regarding the theory's effectiveness?

3. How does this evidence support your conclusions about the theory's effectiveness?

4. How will you include the theories of this school into your leadership philosophy?

Multicultural School

In the 1980s and 1990s, skeptics began to question the validity of leadership research as well as the impact of leadership on organizational performance (Meindl & Ehrlich, 1987; Bass, 1990; Antonakis, Cianciolo, & Sternberg, 2004). The study of leadership "benefitted from such questioning by A) using more rigorous methodologies, B) differentiating top-level leadership from supervisory leadership, and C) focusing on followers and how they perceive reality" (Antonakis et al., 2004, p. 262). Even the data collected for the previous 50 years was questioned due to the minuscule numbers of nonwhite male participants. Prior to this, most participants in leadership research were white males, since the majority of mid- and high-level leaders in for-profit, nonprofit, and government work sectors hired very few women, Latinos, African Americans, or other races and ethnicities. Political leadership suffered the same homogenous membership. The Center for American Women and Politics (2011) at Rutgers University and the Congressional Research Service maintain statistics documenting examples of gender and race disparities of elected officials in the US Congress; the 95th US Senate (1977–1978) had only one more woman member than the 87th US Senate (1961–1962) for a total of two. In the 113th US Congress, there are 20 women serving in the Senate. Six African American males have served in the US Senate while only one is currently serving, elected in 2013: two during reconstruction (1870–1881) and seven between 1967 and 2013 (Manning & Shogan, 2012). These are just a few examples of disparities that caused leaders to question the validity of leadership research because it excluded significant portions of the population and rendered findings to be not generalizable across all populations.

These assertions caused greater scrutiny of leadership research normative data sets for participation to be inclusive of gender, race, and ethnicity. From *Brown v. Board of Education of Topeka* in 1954, to the passage of Title IX of the Education Amendments in 1972, as well as the Americans with Disabilities Act passed in 1990 (and amended in 2009), our paradigms are beginning to shift regarding how we see others, leading to more inclusive perceptions about who is qualified to be a leader. Students of leadership research results must question the normative data, and ask to see participant demographics. Practitioners of inclusive leadership will seek to facilitate acceptance for the whole team to ensure an "us" versus "them" culture does not exist. As an employee, evaluate leadership teams in your organization or department. Are all stakeholders represented? Are all employee demographics represented? Are meeting outcomes communicated quickly to all who need to know? As a leader, are the members of your team clear about your expectations on acceptance, value, and respect? Question the representativeness of community collaborations in which your organization participates. Advocate for inclusiveness in nominated and elected bodies such as the city council, community advisory boards, nonprofit boards, and school boards. Are there policies and procedures within your control that prevent out-group members from full participation? Multicultural leaders seek to advocate, coach, mentor, and serve as role models for acceptance, understanding, and a willingness to work together effectively. Seek to become a multiculturally competent leader.

Tapping your understanding of multicultural leadership theory, respond to these questions:

1. How would you describe the multicultural leadership theory in action in your workplace, school, or home?

2. What evidence do you see regarding the theory's effectiveness?

3. How does this evidence support your conclusions about the theory's effectiveness?

4. How will you include the theories of this school into your leadership philosophy?

The New Leadership School

The late 1970s began an era of reciprocal leadership theories (Komives et al., 1998). Transformational leadership (Burns, 1978), servant leadership (Greenleaf, 1977) and followership (Kelley, 1992; Kellerman, 2008), and authentic leadership (George, 2007) are the major theories in this category. Transformational leaders change the behaviors of followers as well as themselves because of the compelling vision and action that inspires and engages both leaders and followers. It is reciprocal because of the change that transforms all involved. To understand transformational leadership, it must be distinguished from transactional leadership. Transactional leaders engage in a formal or informal contract with their followers promising something in exchange for a desired outcome or level of effort. Examples of such transactions manifest as pay bonuses for meeting a work quota, high grades for a quality level of work in a class, or a treat for earning a good grade on a major exam. Transformational leaders work with followers, inspiring the team to fulfill a high level common goal, while raising the morality of all in the process. These leaders have inspired people to believe the impossible is possible. They have encouraged players in athletic competition, students in lecture halls, congregations in houses of worship, families in homes, and clients of human services professions. They have inspired citizens to volunteer, collect signatures for petitions, adopt a healthier lifestyles, or given people confidence to make important career choices.

The impact of transformational leaders resonates with followers' emotions. Their message feels good, captures imaginations, and inspires commitment. Transformational leaders are passionate about an issue, cause, or celebration; members of their team call them influential and inspirational. They are focused on the needs around them—the beneficiaries of the cause as well as the team with whom they work. Authenticity enables these leaders to have earned the trust of their followers and therefore, be influential and inspirational. Authentic leaders have strong internal values and ideals and they make choices in alignment with their core values. Charisma is not a requirement, but they do engage well with others. They are well versed in the situation, the organization, and the leadership process. It is a level of leadership to which many aspire. It is within your capability to achieve the skills of a transformational leader. Transformational leaders must attend to these questions:

- What social issues are you determined to change?
- How dedicated are you to this mission; what sacrifices will you make?
- Does this cause align with your core values?
- Are you authentic in your words and actions?
- Are you well read on all sides of the issue?
- Do you engage well with others?
- Can you communicate your ideas clearly with your determination visible?

If your responses connect to your deepest passion about the issue or idea, you will be able to transform your team to carry this effort forward with you.

Servant leaders serve those around them first and emerge as leaders from the trust and competence demonstrated to the group. Servant leadership is reciprocal from the trust relationship that is built between the one serving and the followers. Trust is what empowers the followers to seek the servant as their leader. The leader builds trust with the followers because followers can see and feel the leader's commitment and passion for the cause. A communication manager at AT&T, Robert Greenleaf, first described this theory in the leadership world. He wrote extensively on servant leadership and its use in the workplace, in boardrooms, and in education. Greenleaf (1970) described servant leaders as those who are "servants first. Then conscious choice brings one to aspire to lead" (p. 15). He goes on to describe a kind of "litmus test" for servant leadership. Greenleaf (1970, p.15) writes,

> It begins with the natural feeling that one wants to serve, to serve first. Then conscious choice brings one to aspire to lead.... The best test...is do those served grow as persons? Do they, while being served, become healthier, wiser, freer, more autonomous, more likely themselves to become servants? And what is the effect on the least privileged in society? Will they benefit or at least not be further deprived?

In order to illustrate the development of servant leadership in a group, let's examine a group of college students at East Tennessee State University, in Johnson City, Tennessee, and how they interacted in a servant leadership living-learning environment. This group of students chose to have no formal constitution or bylaws with established officer positions. Their purpose was to enhance their leadership abilities by meeting weekly, reading and discussing selected books on leadership, and serving the community. In addition to their leadership education, they also lived in groups of four students per apartment in one campus apartment building adjacent to the university. They learned to live and work together, to establish their own expectations, and to serve each other as well as the campus and community. Each year through an informal process of serving each other day-to-day, the group came to identify and respect one or two members who had earned everyone's trust. Those students were the servant leader of the community for that academic year, guiding the members in their leadership and academic journeys. There was no vote or discussion, simply a transformation though service and trust. Since most students did not remain in the living-learning program for more than 2 years, the servant leader role quietly transitioned each year, always through the same process.

It is common to think of servant leadership in service-oriented professions such as leaders of faith organizations, teachers, counselors, or other human services careers. It is also common to think this leadership philosophy is only practical in less formal and lower level positions. The strength of Greenleaf's philosophy is that no matter the type of organization or the level of position in the organization, one must serve others. Have you participated in a group with members who stepped into a similar service role? In this leadership culture, the servant leader chooses to serve as a way of leading the team. The leadership culture is built first with trust. It takes time to become a servant leader. Trust isn't built in a day … week … or month. It is a series of big and little things done from your heart that signals to others your courage, compassion, and commitment.

The recent emphasis on followership is a paradigm shift that lifts the term follower from the Industrial Age perspective of one who needs to be led, Theory X (McGregor, 1966), to one of an equal who chooses to be led, educated, and respected as a future leader, Theory Y. Followers, according to Kelley (1992), can be anywhere on a continuum from active and loyal to passive or even alienated. Kellerman (2008) placed followers on a continuum of engagement:

- Isolated – totally detached
- Bystander – observes but does not participate
- Participant – invests himself or herself to try to have an impact
- Activist – works hard on behalf of leaders or against them
- Diehard – devoted, all-consuming

Deeper yet in this study of the relationships between leaders and followers is the understanding of why followers seek out leaders. Jean Lipman-Blumen's (2005) research explores the phenomenon of toxic leaders. Toxic leaders practice negative leadership through charm and manipulation, which leads to the mistreatment and devastation of their followers. Humans have a subconscious need to feel secure and chosen, to belong, and to be identified as competent. Toxic leaders can manipulate followers based on their needs and create a psychological dance between the leaders and followers, trapping either in a bad leadership relationship. For example, executive leaders in and around the Nixon presidency manipulated the citizens to trust them because of the citizens' trust and need to feel secure with the institution of the federal government. Watergate (1974) ushered in a heightened societal awareness of ethics and integrity in all leadership positions and a growing distrust for institutions of authority. The trust was shattered between American citizens and their political leaders (Kellerman, 2004).

The impact of the loss of trust in government and social institutions is pervasive. Dealing with the fears associated with this loss is the only path to an intercultural leadership community of nontoxic leadership (Lipman-Blumen, 2005). The illusion of the "white knight leader," a leader who swoops in to save followers, offering to deliver on impossible promises, is a toxic expectation. Followers must work beyond their fears to find the leader inside themselves. Empowering each other to become leaders brings communities/groups together, enabling them to work toward a shared authentic dream. Organizations are strengthened by the human potential of its members. When that potential is engaged, all share in the responsibilities and rewards. Goals become selected by most, not a handful. Trust levels are high, and members bring their authentic selves to the organization. When followers share responsibilities with the leader, the need to be rescued is eliminated and a "white knight leader" becomes unnecessary. Leaders and followers together devote the time necessary to engage all members of the group/organization. Engagement is the key for this effort to be sustained. Members become engaged both logically and emotionally. Stephen Covey (2004) calls this whole person leadership. Leaders and followers must be willing to engage both head and heart to have an organization engaged at its full potential.

Tapping your understanding of the new leadership school, respond to these questions:

1. How would you describe the new leadership perspectives in action in your workplace, school, or home?

2. What evidence do you see regarding the theory's effectiveness?

3. How does this evidence support your conclusions about the theory's effectiveness?

4. How will you include the theories of this school into your leadership philosophy?

Emerging Issues in Leadership

New perspectives on leadership theories revolve around the view of leaders and followers as human, imperfect, teammates, and diverse. Leaders are leading in increasingly more complex situations:

- In organizations with multiple locations both locally, cross country, and internationally.
- In person and virtually through many kinds of electronic communication tools.
- In extreme situations of conflict across languages and cultures that do not understand each other.

Therefore, no one leadership theory is a fit for all leaders in all situations. The construction of hybrid theories will be the next frontier for leadership researchers. (Antonakis et al., 2004) These research studies include the unique perspectives of cultures (House, Hanges, Javidan, Dorfman, & Gupta, 2004), the GLOBE Studies; the impact of technological tools, envisioning the future (Friedman, 2005); and a return to the foundations of character, communication, trust, and ethics (George, 2007; Covey, 2004, 2006). Ethics and moral development have become essential elements of leadership research (Antonakis et al., 2004) as government, institutions, and organizations from many sectors of the workplace and communities appear to have lost their moral compass. Concerns of accountability and transparency continue to make headlines from proficiency testing in education to the quality of consumer goods, as well as the investments of the financial industry. The actions and results of leadership decisions are reviewed and monitored by the public and media. Followers also have found new power in social media for organizing, communicating, and influencing organizations. The speed of communication and accessibility of the Internet empowers and enables citizens to quickly know how decisions are made, who is responsible, and what action is required. Presidential elections, government shutdowns, Middle Eastern revolutions, as well as decisions of nonprofit boards, and for-profit CEO's have all triggered national and international waves of citizen action and resistance.

Tapping your understanding of management theory, respond to these questions:

1. How would you describe the management theories in action in your workplace, school, or home?

2. What evidence do you see regarding the theory's effectiveness?

3. How does this evidence support your conclusions about the theory's effectiveness?

4. How will you include the theories of this school into your leadership philosophy?

Management Theories and Their Application

The history of management is a study of facilitating the many processes that bring products, programs, and services to market. As far back as you may have studied in history, there are stories and examples of crafts artisans who individually created products to sell or trade. Such products were crafted to the individual specifications of the artisan. It was not until the time of the US Civil War that the idea of replaceable parts and common equipment standards was widely entertained. The magnitude of equipment needs for wagons and battle implements during this war was huge. To have craftspersons using common specifications meant equipment didn't have to be continuously replaced but could be repaired economically by someone other than the original craftsperson. A few decades later, the industrial revolution caused everyone to evolve and accept new ideas regarding mass production, products and services, standards, and manufacturers needing to meet customer expectations. Leaders of manufacturing companies determined that production of products could be improved by separating two management processes: production of the product and inspection of the product quality. It was during this era that Frederick Taylor, the father of scientific management, studied time and motion of workers on assembly lines and made recommendations for proper tools, training, incentives, and methods so workers could better accomplish their tasks. In 1914, Henry Ford sponsored the development of a moving assembly line, which created yet another separation in the product development process. Planning, production, and inspection became separate processes and required management to oversee each function. World War II intensified the need for mass production and quality assurance. Lives as well as an international victory depended on quality ships, planes, ammunition, radios, boots, uniforms, and other equipment. Taxpayers and political leaders were unwilling to support the war if the soldier's equipment wasn't deadlier than the enemy. Wartime innovations led to Walter Shewhart's development of the statistical quality control chart. In 1951, J. Edwards Deming, Shewhart's student, was a member of a group of engineers General McArthur assembled to aid the Japanese in rebuilding their industry after World War II. Another member of this prestigious group of engineers was Joseph Juran, editor of the now classic *Quality Handbook*. Together their work in quality management, along with Peter Drucker, creator of the six stages of management by objectives (MBO) and considered the father of modern corporate management, made the 1950s a renaissance era in management theory. The goal of managers in the manufacturing sector was to bring standardized products to the marketplace while simultaneously meeting consumer expectations. To maintain consistent quality required management to monitor the steps of each process and create production lines with the most efficient systems. The six stages of MBO are as follows:

1. Define corporate objectives.

2. Analyze management tasks and devise formal job specifications for frontline managers.

3. Establish performance standards.

4. Achieve agreement for specific objectives.

5. Align goals with organizational objectives.

6. Establish a management information system to monitor achievements against objectives.

Between the 1960s and 1980s, leaders and managers of manufacturing companies in Japan took to heart Juran, Deming, and Drucker's lessons. By the 1970s, "Made in Japan" took on new meaning for high quality electronics, automobiles, and other consumer products. To compete with Japan and encourage American efforts in quality management principles, the federal government established the Malcolm Baldrige Award in 1988 to provide an assessment tool and presidential recognition for manufacturing organizations that achieved quality in performance excellence. After a few years, the award was expanded to include all sectors of the workplace: manufacturing, service, nonprofit, education, health care, and government. There are seven key areas of the organization that are assessed for this award:

1. Leadership

2. Strategic planning

3. Customer focus

4. Measurement, analysis, and knowledge management

5. Workforce focus

6. Operations focus

7. Results

A human services example of the principles of good management processes is in the development of Case Management procedures. Case management is a profession with standards and is practiced in law, social work, health care, and mental health care. Its purpose is to provide the best treatment plan and coordination of care for clients using systematic processes. Principles of quality management and assessment of workplace processes are becoming standard practice in health care, education, and government agencies.

Tapping your understanding of management theory, respond to these questions:

1. How would you describe the management theories in action in your workplace, school, or home?

2. What evidence do you see regarding the theory's effectiveness?

3. How does this evidence support your conclusions about the theory's effectiveness?

4. How will you include the theories of this school into your leadership philosophy?

PRESCRIPTION: YOUR LEADERSHIP PHILOSOPHY

As stated earlier, building a philosophy of leadership begins by understanding your personal values and asking yourself key questions about how those values influence your choices in decision making and how you interact with others in work groups. Reflect on the various theories you studied in this chapter. Consider how leadership has been viewed and evolved over the last century. Review the 10 questions below (adapted from Chalker, 2015), and answer each one.

1. What are the top three values you embody that speak to your role as a future leader?

2. Do you believe that others on your team are capable of working toward a common good or are only motivated by what is in it for them?

3. What is the contribution you want to make by serving as a leader?

4. How do you want to treat others, and how do you want others to treat you?

5. What is the leadership style you think others see in you? Describe.

6. In a group, do you think first about group tasks or relationships with the group members?

7. How do others describe their working relationship with you?

8. How do others describe the way you accomplish tasks?

9. How do you work to build your influence with others?

10. Do you believe your leadership skills are already set and are waiting to be uncovered, or do you believe you must actively grow and cultivate these skills?

Return to the end of each section in this chapter and review your comments. Note especially your answer to number four in each group. Record your notes on the appropriate lines for each group of theories.

Leadership Theories

- Trait Theories
- Behavior Theories
- Contingency Theories
- Relational Theories
- Multicultural Theories
- The New School Theories
- Management Theories

Connecting your values and the key areas of importance from the theories, write five or six statements that capture your comprehensive view of leadership, how you want to see others, and how you want the team to see you. Your leadership philosophy is personal. There is no right or wrong, just the clarification of your fundamental truths. Your philosophy captures who you are, the values you live by, and the expectations you have of yourself and others.

SUMMARY

From early historical views of leadership to the now widely accepted complex views of today, our world seeks to find and develop leaders who are able to guide us to a better tomorrow. Theories are still evolving in this relatively young body of research on leadership. Now that you understand the context of the theories and how they evolved, you can better interpret the experiences surrounding your leadership development journey up to this time and identify your intentions as a new leader in human services.

The study of leadership began with a need to identify military and business leaders for a world and economy in crisis. Given the thinking of the times in the early 1900s, trait theory seemed a natural place to start investigating leadership as a theory. There are still expectations of certain traits in leaders today such as intelligence, confidence, and integrity. The behaviorists continued on the path of seeking the perfect leader by investigating patterns of behaviors through the lenses of task oriented and relational leaders. Contingency theories opened the door to the notion of leaders having the ability to flex and choose from a repertoire of behavior style options after analyzing the ability of the followers and the nature of the situation. This is a big step in the study of leadership, shifting the focus from the leader to the three major players in the leadership equation. Relational leadership theories analyzed the dynamics between leaders and followers, while multicultural theories brought self-examination of the current processes of leadership research to correct research participant selection methods, welcomed new voices to the field, and provided feedback to establish new paths to leadership in multiple sectors. New school theories provide a personal development orientation to leadership development. Management theories create the interface between human actions and the operations of the organization.

* * *

The remainder of this text will use a combination of reflection, diagnosis, and prescription processes for improving your leadership skills. As we prepare for this leadership journey through the next chapters, let me recommend how we will travel and what you need to pack. Fill your travel bag with the ability to be open to new ideas, honesty in your self-assessments, and willingness to try a new and better way to lead.

Although I will refer back to related leadership theories found in this chapter, the focus will be on their application to specific skills and techniques in the remaining chapters. The teaching approach is similar to a coaching experience. You will be coached through new and improved skills for your future career as part of a team of leaders and managers in the human services sector. In the table of contents, you will notice two types of chapter content areas: Self-Management and Organizational Management. Self-management chapters will focus on areas of personal change and learning new behaviors. Organizational management chapters will focus on skill sets that help leaders improve the processes and systems of the organization. Both are important to becoming a good leader. Chapter content is organized in a sequence such that related topics flow from one to the next. The organization of the chapter itself involves a consistent pattern of learning about the skill and situations for its use. Application is all about real skills in real situations with real people. Chapters are ordered as a leadership coach might introduce each skill. Change is never easy, but when you understand how the leadership concepts relate to you, the outcomes (i.e., prognosis) will become very clear.

REFERENCES

Antonakis, J., Cianciolo, A. T., & Sternberg, R. J. (2004). *The nature of leadership.* Thousand Oaks, CA: Sage.

Bass, B. M. (1990). *Bass and Stogdill's handbook of leadership.* New York, NY: Free Press.

Blake, R. R., & Mouton, J. S. (1964). *The managerial grid.* Houston, TX: Gulf Publishing.

Blanchard, K. H., Zigarmi, D., & Nelson, R. B. (1993). Situational leadership after 25 years: A retrospective. *Journal of Leadership and Organizational Studies, 1*(21), 24–36. doi: 10.1177/107179199300100104

Burns, J. M. (1978). *Leadership.* New York, NY: Harper and Row.

Center for American Women and Politics. (2011). *Facts on women in Congress.* Rutgers University Eagleton Institute on Politics. Retrieved from http://www.cawp.rutgers.edu

Chalker, A. (2015). Ten questions to identify your leadership philosophy. *Suntiva.* Retrieved from http://www.suntiva.com/blog/185

Covey, S. R. (2004). *The 8th habit: From effectiveness to greatness.* New York, NY: Free Press.

Covey, S. M. (2006). *The speed of trust: The one thing that changes everything.* New York, NY: Free Press.

Ferrance, E. (2000). *Action research.* Providence, RI: LAB at Brown University. Retrieved from http://www.brown.edu/academics/education-alliance/sites/brown.edu.academics.education-alliance/files/publications/act_research.pdf

Fiedler, F. E. (1967). *A theory of leadership effectiveness.* New York, NY: McGraw-Hill.

Fiedler, F. E., & Chemers, M. M. (1974). *Leadership and effective management.* New York, NY: Scott, Foresman.

Friedman, T. L. (2005). *The world is flat: A brief history of the twenty-first century.* New York, NY: Farrar, Straus and Giroux.

George, B. (2007). *True north: Discover your authentic leadership.* San Francisco, CA: Jossey-Bass.

Goffee, R., & Jones, G. (2011). Why should anyone be led by you? In *HBR, On Leadership* (pp. 79–95). Boston, MA: Harvard Business School Review Press.

Graen, G. B., & Scandura, T. A. (1987). Toward a psychology of dyadic organizing. In B. Staw & L. L. Cumming (Eds.), *Research in organizational behavior* (pp. 175–208). Greenwich, CT: JAI.

Greenleaf, R. (1970). *The servant as leader.* Westfield, IN: The Greenleaf Center for Servant Leadership.

Greenleaf, R. (1977). *Servant leadership: A journey in the nature of legitimate power and greatness.* New York, NY: Paulist.

Hersey, P., & Blanchard, K. H. (1993). *Management of organizational behavior: Utilizing human resources* (6th ed.). Englewood Cliffs, NJ: Prentice Hall.

Herzberg, F. (1966). *Work and the nature of man.* Cleveland, Ohio: World Publishing.

House, R. J. (1971). A path-goal theory of leadership. *Administrative Science Quarterly, 16,* 321–338.

House, R. J. (1996). Path-goal theory of leadership: Lessons, legacy, and a reformulated theory. *Leadership Quarterly, 7*(3), 323–352.

House, R. J., Hanges, P. J., Javidan, M., Dorfman, P. W., & Gupta, V. (Eds.). (2004). *Culture, leadership, and organizations: The globe study of 62 societies.* Thousand Oaks, CA: Sage.

Katz, R. L. (1955). Skills of an effective administrator. *Harvard Business Review, 33*(1), 33–42.

Kellerman, B. (2004). *Bad leadership.* Boston, MA: Harvard Business School Publishing.

Kellerman, B. (2008). *Followership: How followers are creating change and changing leaders.* Boston, MA: Harvard Business Press.

Kelley, R. (1992). *The power of followership.* New York, NY: Doubleday.

Komives, S. R., Lucas, N., & McMahon, T. R. (1998). *Exploring leadership for college students who want to make a difference.* San Francisco, CA: Jossey-Bass.

Larson, C. E., & LaFasto, F. M. J. (1989). *Teamwork: What must go right/what can go wrong.* Newbury Park, CA: Sage Publications.

Lencioni, P. (2002). *The five dysfunctions of a team: A leadership fable.* San Francisco, CA: Jossey-Bass.

Lewin, K., LIippert, R., & White, R. K. (1939). Patterns of aggressive behavior in experimentally created social climates. *Journal of Social Psychology, 10,* 271–301.

Lipman-Blumen, J. (2005). *The allure of toxic leaders: Why we follow destructive bosses and corrupt politicians—and how we can survive them.* New York, NY: Oxford University Press.

Manning, J. E., & Shogan, C. J. (2012). *African American members of the United States Congress: 1870–2012* (CRS Report No. RL30378). Retrieved from Congressional Research Service website: http://www.crs.gov

McGregor, D. (1966). *Leadership and motivation essays.* Boston, MA: MIT Press.

Meindl, J., & Ehrlich, S. B. (1987). The romance of leadership and the evaluation of organizational performance. *Academy of Management Journal, 30,* 91–109.

Stogdill, R. M., & Coons, A. E. (1957). *Leader Behavior: Its description and measurement.* Columbus: Ohio State University, Bureau of Business Research.

Part II

Development of Self and Team

Chapter 3

Self-Management— Understanding Self and Managing Conflict

LEARNING OBJECTIVES

The student will

- describe the four behavior styles,
- demonstrate how knowledge of the styles improves a leader's ability to lead teams,
- explain the advantages of a normed assessment,
- diagnose team conflict through knowledge of behavior styles, and
- manage conflict.

UNDERSTANDING SELF

It is said that the journey of leadership development begins with knowing yourself. This chapter begins the process of finding who you are and how you respond to others in work or school situations. Once you have developed an understanding about yourself, you can choose to manage your behaviors in ways to increase your effectiveness. This chapter begins your process of self-management.

Outside the classroom, what tests have you taken that assess your experiences or personality traits? Do you and your friends take quizzes in magazines or other forms that make the rounds via email or social media? It is fun to check results and laugh at yourself and your friends for your "animal likeness" or "movie character trivia" the assessments reveal. However, true self-assessment is derived from the instruments of social science research. Questions for this type of research are first tested with hundreds of volunteers exhibiting broad yet representative demographics of the population before they are utilized in official studies of larger populations. This process enables researchers to determine if their study is reliable. They also need to ensure the research questions measure the subsets of the construct they seek to identify. The researcher's diligence ensures that as you take a reputable assessment regarding your personality, behavior, or tendencies and answer honestly, you will be rewarded with better insight about yourself.

REFLECTION: WHO AM I?

As unique as we are as human beings, we have over time established a set of typical responses to certain kinds of stimuli. Understanding these nature/nurture reactions is a growing social science. We respond in a consistent pattern to the cues, tones, and body language expressed by different people as they share their feelings, thoughts, and ideas. Undoubtedly, there are people with whom you interact in your life who put you on edge, and others who set you at ease. You also respond in different ways when asked to consider information to make a decision. Some of you can jump right into a discussion while others prefer time to consider the details. Similarly, there are some meetings you attend where you thrive and are highly engaged in the discussion. Then there are others whose pace or choice of agenda make you wish you were having a root canal. Should these signals mean anything to you? These feelings are clues about how you prefer to communicate, interact, and make choices. The bottom line is that success in the workplace revolves around what type of team player you are and the professional relationships you build. As you recall from Chapter 2, according to Robert Greenleaf's (1977) discussion on servant leadership, group members will not want to follow someone they do not trust or respect. Trust and respect are partially built out of our comfort with and perceptions of someone's style. Many leadership careers are derailed because the person in charge did not develop trustworthy and respectful relationships. Valuing a diverse array of personality, behavior, and decision-making styles will directly correlate to your future success as a leader. The first place to start is to better understand your style.

DIAGNOSIS: UNDERSTANDING STYLES

It is important to know what an assessment measures and what it does not. This section will lead you through the basics of a behavior style analysis as a place to start learning about yourself. You may have taken other types of assessments that provided measures of career interests or personality during the undergraduate years.

These types of assessments are different from a measure of your behavior style. Let's begin with an explanation of how a behavior style develops. During childhood, you developed learned preferences that influenced your behavior style. The learned preferences came from a range of experiences occurring over time, which triggered similar responses resulting in a pattern of synapses growth in the brain. The responses and preferences became learned habits and at the same time were interwoven into your thinking patterns. Your experiences, habits, and preferences influenced how your brain synapses connected and developed (Buckingham & Clifton, 2001; Pink, 2009). That is how you developed preferences for your behavior styles, which will soon be described in this chapter.

Your style preferences are learned, and the strength of each preference is a function of both your age and your life experiences, causing the learning and synapse growth through childhood, adolescence, and young adulthood. Through the development and maturation process of the brain, preferences and habits are typically set in a person of 20 years of age. Therefore, administering behavior style or other similar assessments to high school age and younger students will likely yield inconsistent results. Although learned, such patterns are usually consistent over time for most people. A significant life event may reshape or change a behavior style preference later in life.

In Chapter 2, the discussion of leadership theory, you learned about research questions that built on leader behavior tendencies toward relationships and tasks. It was particularly prevalent in the sections on style and situational theories. People and task tendencies are significant in both leadership theory and practice. These tendencies are important to recognize in your own style preferences. Which way do you lean toward, people or task? Devising a way to measure tendencies on the people-task themes provides leaders an understanding of their choices in how emails are written, what behaviors start the workday, and even the tone of chit-chat in the office. Chapters 5 and 9 provide a strong focus on results as leaders maintain focus on managing time, people, and other resources to deliver excellent programs and services. You may find that these chapters resonate with you as you see yourself accomplishing projects in great quantity and with high quality. In Chapters 6 and 11, the sections on teambuilding, motivation, and communication skills may be more to your interest. You might feel that there can be nothing greater than mentoring a colleague to develop new skills or coaching others to achieve a stretch goal. The two dimensions, people and tasks, reveal themselves in your choice of words, need for working with others, importance of task completion, dislike for conflict, speed of thought, body language, and depth of detail necessary for completing a task or making a decision.

It is important to understand that anyone can operate with either task or people as a primary focus, but you do have a preference. The preference is not something most people actively think about or choose; it happens automatically, especially when you are stressed, tired, in a time crunch, or unaware of your behavior preferences. Through this study of behavior styles, you will better understand your preferences and recognize the preferences of others. The ability to do this is dependent on aware-ness. The ability to recognize the behaviors that make up your preferences helps you to recognize the style preferences of others. Taking the time to observe and listen to yourself and others enhances your awareness level. One of the benefits of growing your personal awareness is becoming tuned in to your preferences and the knowledge of the strengths each preference style brings to a group. If your team is style-heavy in one direction, the ability to shift your style can be helpful in leading teams when members' styles tend to cluster in one area. As you will soon see, these preferences and tendencies of style have their own strengths and blind spots. A shift in your response style provides a change in your communication style or project manage-ment choices depending on the situation. Flexibility of style enables the leader and team to take advantage of style strengths and to work around style preference blind spots and tendencies. *No one style is best or more important than another.* Every organization benefits from the combination and presence of all styles in work teams.

Scales About People and Task Behaviors

To generate accurate results using the questions and scales in Figure 3.1 and Figure 3.2, you must answer all questions in the table openly and honestly, based

Figure 3.1 People and Emotions Scale

9	8	7	6	5	4	3	2	1	0	1	2	3	4	5	6	7	8	9
"A" Behaviors										"B" Behaviors								

"A" Behaviors	"B" Behaviors
• Guarded facial expressions and limited use of gestures • In person — communicates with few words • Waits to be approached in social settings • Gives stronger weight to facts in decision making • Difficult to get to know, rarely talks about self • More focused on task accomplishment • Tends to mask feelings • Prefers working alone, feels stressed work-ing with others • Does not always think to give praise and appreciation to others • Keeps conversation on point • Prefers private appreciation	• Easy to read emotions from facial expressions and body language • Talkative, very expressive • Outgoing in social settings • Gives stronger weight to feelings in decision making • Easy to get to know, openly shares about self • Prioritizes maintaining relationships • Easily expresses feelings • Prefers working with others, feels stressed working alone • Regularly gives praise and appreciation to others • Speaks enthusiastically about big idea • Prefers public praise

Figure 3.2   Task and Results Scale

9	8	7	6	5	4	3	2	1	0	1	2	3	4	5	6	7	8	9
"C" Behaviors										"D" Behaviors								
<ul><li>Needs thinking time (pause), then speaks slowly</li><li>Prefers the agenda at least the day before</li><li>Asks rather than tells</li><li>Sits or stands back from others</li><li>Stays out of others personal space</li><li>Softer tone of voice</li><li>More relaxed handshake</li><li>Tends to look away while speaking</li><li>Makes less direct requests (hints)</li><li>Change brings stress</li><li>Seeks quality through monitoring details</li></ul>										<ul><li>Voice engages while thoughts are forming</li><li>Brings something else to the meeting in case of boredom.</li><li>Tells rather than asks</li><li>Sits or stands directly across from others</li><li>Leans into others' personal space</li><li>More emphatic tone of voice</li><li>Firm handshake</li><li>Makes direct eye contact while speaking</li><li>Direct, up-front requests</li><li>More comfortable with change</li><li>Seeks the best through newer and faster ideas</li></ul>								

on what you currently think and do. Do not answer the questions based on how you wish you were. There is not one scale or description to aspire to be. No one is going to judge you on your preferences. Instructions for completing the questions are below:

- Read the word or phrase in each column.
- Circle each phrase that describes you most of the time in a work or school situation.
- Count the total circled for each column of the scale, and shade in the number line (1–9) for the total number of each side you scored.
- The longer the line (higher number) is considered your preference.

Of these behaviors, which did you find to be greater?   A or B

Of these behaviors, which did you find to be greater?   C or D

Now let's apply four labels from the Effectiveness Institute's work in behavior style studies and measures to your scale feedback (http://www.effectiveness institute.com):

- If you have a high (A) and a high (D), you are a controller.
- If you have a high (B) and a high (D), you are a persuader.
- If you have a high (A) and a high (C), you are an analyzer.
- If you have a high (B) and a high (C), you are a stabilizer.

Figure 3.3   Behavioral Styles

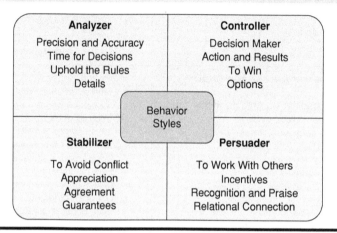

Source: Adapted and used with permission by the Effectiveness Institute.

Behavior Styles Characteristics

The tendencies, needs, strengths, and weaknesses of the styles are noted in the Table 3.1:

A good method for understanding behavior style tendencies is to note the differences of how each style might purchase a car. These scenarios are not absolutes but on the whole are typical behaviors of individuals with these style tendencies. Note also, that everyone wants a reliable, quality, and reasonably priced car. The differences appear in the order of the questions asked, time on topic, data needed to make a decision, the people chosen to participate in the decision, the willingness to pay for extra features, and so on.

- Analyzers – Individuals with this style have been reading the reliability and fuel economy reports from experts for many months. They have analyzed the cost benefit of fixing the old car versus purchasing a new one. When they go to the dealership, they will have those reports in hand including information about their current (possible trade-in) vehicle from Carfax or Kelley's Blue Book. They will have researched the best price for the new car from multiple dealerships as well as online services that send a printout of the best-negotiated price for the car. The sales person will need to be almost as knowledgeable about this data as the analyzer for the transaction to be successful. The analyzers will likely make several visits to dealers over several months, most likely alone. Time spent in the business office will be longer than most as they will most likely read everything in the paperwork signed. The goal is to get the best price and value for the new vehicle and the trade-in.
  - o Key learnings about analyzers: details, research, data driven, slow the process.

Table 3.1 Behavior Style Characteristics

Characteristics	Analyzer	Stabilizer	Persuader	Controller
Need	To Be Right	To Have Harmony	To Be Liked	To Be in Control
Strengths	• Plans • Conducts Research • Examines Facts • Follows Rules	• Monitors • Seeks Agreement • Loyal • Team Player	• Verbalizes • Generates Enthusiasm • Optimistic • Imaginative	• Expedites • Enjoys Competition • Separates Facts and Feelings • Quick Decision Maker
Weaknesses	• Reluctant to Express Emotions • Hesitant to Change • Holds on to Past • Appears Unemotional	• Avoids Risk • Does Not Initiate Quickly • Being in Confrontation • Overly Concerned for Others	• Impulsive • Overly Emotional • Following Systems • Figurative Sounds Factual	• Moves Too Quickly • Loses Interest • Does Not Actively Listen • Does Not Show Empathy
Tendencies	• Expects High Standards • Perfects Ideas • Works Carefully	• Slow to Change Opinions • Has a "Radar" About People • Expects Harmony	• Expects Freedom • Works Fast • Trusts Intuition	• Willing to Express Disagreement • Works Independently • Results Focused

Source: Used with permission of the Effectiveness Institute, http://www.effectivenessinstitute.com

- Stabilizers – These individuals have been reading data about the cars as well, especially the guarantees, warranties, and safety features. The process will start with the dealer and brand that they or their families have trusted over the years. They will discuss this decision among the entire family to ensure that the vehicle will meet the needs of everyone. The stabilizers will seek advice from a few trusted friends and relatives. Rules of the warranty will be followed to the letter. Because stabilizers do not like conflict, negotiating the price is one of the most difficult parts of the process. They may even pay a bit more for the vehicle rather than risk losing the relationship with the dealership. However, if they feel they were taken advantage, it will not be forgotten and their loyalty will be lost.
  - Key learnings about stabilizers: require a low risk venture with guarantees, loyal to organizations and small circle of friends, tuned to read the satisfaction/happiness of those involved, will play by the rules.
- Persuaders – They will make this car purchase decision relatively quickly. They want value and reliability, but features such as style, color, sound system, technology access, interior comfort, and what their friends will think of it are first in their mind. It is most likely they will take friends or family members to the dealership to share the experience. Thoughts and opinions will also be garnered from text messages, phone calls, as well as photos posted in social media of the cars of interest. As soon as the car is selected for purchase, photos of themselves with their chosen car will be posted on Facebook before the ink on the contract is dry. Before they leave the dealership, they will have met and made friends with the sales and business office staff.
  - Key learnings about persuaders: quick decision makers, will involve a large social circle of friends, attracted to new and better ideas
- Controllers – These customers will keep the needs and wants about this purchase to themselves, only consulting experts, friends, and family after they have thought about and researched the decision on their own. An announcement to friends and family about needing a new car will shortly precede a visit to test drive the vehicles on the short list. They are looking for the most highly rated brand and vehicle for the money. Price negotiation is the most enjoyable part of the process for controllers. They enjoy the challenge and opportunity to sharpen their negotiation skills. However, deciding the options package is the least enjoyable part of the car buying process. Directors want to pick and choose the options wanted, not buy a package with things they do not want. To score a vehicle with the most unique and sought-after feature combinations is a plus. Their end goal is to have the best car as promoted by expert ratings, looks, and value.

   o Key learnings about controllers: competitive, seek excellence, like options, like to direct, not afraid of conflict.

PRESCRIPTION: HOW LEADERS USE SELF-KNOWLEDGE

Taking professionally designed psychological assessments provide an objective look at yourself and the patterns of behavior you practice. Asking friends and co-workers can provide ongoing insight into your behavior patterns. However, unless this person is trained in this subject matter, the feedback may not be reliable when interpreting your behavior styles. Your patterns, tendencies, and styles are best discovered and interpreted through formal assessments. The most reputable assessments have been statistically normed with thousands of participants and describe that process in their materials. There are assessments for a multitude of psychological and behavioral characteristics. Students are encouraged to seek services offered by your campus counseling or career center, both of which can administer and interpret a variety of assessments. The cost to students to receive these services is either covered or partially covered by tuition and fees at most campuses. On some campuses, such services are extended to alumni.

Though online versions exist, they are possibly less complete and do not offer a professional interpretation of the findings that are so critical to the usefulness of the assessments. Similar to why physicians should not self-diagnose and prescribe prescription medicines, you will be better served to use a professional to interpret your assessments. Listed below are some additional assessments you may wish to consider.

Additional Assessments

- Myers Briggs Type Indicator – the most commonly used personality inventory
- DISC – personality styles applied in the workplace
- Learning Styles – preferred learning methods
- Strengths Finder – a positive psychology approach to learning about strengths with a focus on the top five talents
- Emotional Intelligence – the ability to be aware of and manage emotional responses
- 360 Assessment – a performance perspective assessment from colleagues, direct reports and the boss

There are many assessments designed to help you discover more about yourself. This list provides you with a starting point. If you do not have access to a college career or counseling center and you are employed full time, your employer's human resources department may have access to leadership and psychological assessments as well as professionals that are trained to interpret the results. Here are some self-help resources for access to these assessments:

- Jung's Typology (Myers Briggs), http://www.humanmetrics.com/cgi-win/JTypes2.asp. This site is free and offers a good abbreviated version of the personality assessment. It also provides good follow-up materials for you to print. Time to allocate: 25 minutes for the assessment, 45 minutes to read interpretation materials.
- DISC Personality Styles, http://www.free-disc-profile.com
  - A free 12-question assessment is available. The full profile is available at www.disc-personality-testing.com for a fee.
- Learning Styles, http://www.learning-styles-online.com
  - There are also good follow-up materials to print at this site. Time to allocate: 10 minutes for the assessment, 30 minutes to read interpretation materials.
- Strengths Finder Assessment can be accessed through the purchase of a book on leadership published by the Gallup Organization and authored by Donald Clifton, Tom Rath, or Marcus Buckingham. (Note: Although second-hand books are a better price, the access code to the Strengths Finder Assessment will most likely have been used by the first owner. Once used, it cannot be reused.) This assessment is timed. Allow 50 consecutive minutes for assessment and 60 minutes to explore the website resources and read interpretation materials. Retain your online login user name and password for future access to site and materials. A college campus can arrange through the Gallup organization to provide codes for the Strengths Finder assessment at a current cost of $15 without a book purchase.
- Emotional Intelligence and or Social Intelligence, http://www.queendom.com/queendom_tests/index.htm Results are free if you choose "View Sample Report." Allow 70 minutes for Emotional Intelligence Assessment and 40 minutes for Social Intelligence Assessment. Allow 30 minutes to read interpretation materials for each. You may receive follow-up emails for 3 to 4 weeks encouraging you to purchase the full assessment. Ignore or unsubscribe your email from their mailing list.
- 360 Assessments can be done in groups, individually, and online. If you can have input into the selection, pick an instrument that fits your organization culture, asks questions that relate to your job, and has a format that is easily understood by those outside your area. Usually you have input into who completes the survey that rates your skills. Choose those who have enough experience and time working with you. Most quality 360

assessments come with a professional to help you interpret your results and recommend resources for additional learning.

(Note: Some of these and other assessment sites may send follow-up emails to encourage your participation with additional free interpretive materials or to encourage you to take an additional fee-based assessment. These are options, not required. You may unsubscribe at any time.)

Becoming versed in recognizing your style tendencies as well as the characteristics of other styles is necessary in your journey to self-discovery. Knowledge and awareness of your behavior characteristics provides keys to the puzzle that is you. A leader is one of the most observed and scrutinized professionals on the team. You certainly want to know as much about yourself as your teammates think they know about you. The clues will reveal why you have an easier time working with some colleagues than others. It can even be applied to family and significant relationships. As you answered questions and reviewed tables to reveal your tendencies (Table 3.1 and Figures 3.1, 3.2, and 3.3), did you notice you were reading descriptions of behaviors? You reflected on your behaviors as you answered the questions in Figures 3.1 and 3.2. Now review those same questions and answer them about your best friend, your supervisor, and a parent. The more you practice observation and reflection about others behaviors, the more accurately you will be able to identify other's behavior styles. This will help you build diverse teams that enjoy all the strengths of each style represented.

Establishing a successful team is a treasure hunt that brings together a group with talents and skills that complements each other, yet does not mirror each other. There are talents, skills, and perceptions in each behavior style that are both nice and necessary to successful teams. When teams are mostly one behavior style, the group can have tendencies such as the following:

- Risk averse
- Blind to want to study the necessary details
- Overly conversant, talking over one another
- Lost in the minutia
- At odds over whose idea will win, not listening to the others

Leaders should never apply their knowledge of styles to create teams whose styles are carbon copies of the team leader. That is a recipe for failure. Leaders who value all the behavior styles seek team members who bring a variety of perceptions and talents to the group. Successful leaders seek to select teams that bring the broadest array of talents to the table.

MANAGING CONFLICT

Handling conflict is one of the least understood and least confident skill sets of most individuals, leaders included. Conflict is defined as a disagreement or collision of ideas. Being in conflict fuels a rash of emotions. Conflict can be productive or destructive depending upon the cause and how it is managed. Although this section will not make you a seasoned conflict manager, it will provide you with a basic understanding of how conflicts erupt, how our differences aggravate conflict situations, and tips on how to handle a difficult conversation during a conflict.

REFLECTION: THE ANATOMY OF STYLE CONFLICT TENDENCIES

Your supervisor asked you to take on a leadership role at work. The prospect of working with a team, achieving the assigned goal, impressing your boss, and celebrating a new accomplishment excited you. However, by week 6 of the assignment, you believe the word leader is code for "chief blamee," and the team's unwillingness to get along killed your excitement for this opportunity to lead. You are concerned your boss is going to blame you for the lack of progress toward the goal and that feedback from the team will look poorly on your next performance review.

What began as minor team irritations grew to members making accusations and complaints about other members of the team regarding the division of work, the quality of work from other members, indecision in planning, big talkers taking credit for others' work and ideas, and unequal allocation of resources. The group's cohesiveness had dissolved into chaos. Part of the group took sides and was quite vocal while others were hiding in foxholes waiting for it to blow over, leaving the assigned tasks neglected. Without proper leadership, this conflict could be potentially fatal to the team. How do you begin to analyze and seek a solution to this conflict?

DIAGNOSIS: A DIFFERENT LOOK AT CONFLICT

When working with people, conflict is inevitable. Some conflict is healthy and necessary, as you will see in the Chapter 6 on teamwork. Many times conflict is a misunderstanding related to our priorities and methods of communication. Those things are influenced by our behavior style tendencies. Unfortunately, those not in the same style preferences can interpret others' behaviors as intentional disrespect. In most cases, it is a behavior pattern as natural to one person as breathing but impacts the other person as intentionally pushing a "hot button."

Looking through the behavior style lens in Table 3.1 and Figure 3.3, we can see how certain tendencies when taken to an extreme will cause fingers to point and harsh words to be spoken.

- Analyzers can be obsessive about reviewing data and cause delays when trying to make the perfect decisions.
- Analyzers can be seen as antisocial because they prefer to work alone.
- Analyzers are buried in minutia and can't see the big picture.
- Analyzers seem to be stuck in a data review loop, never quite having enough to feel safe in moving forward.
- Stabilizers can be fearful of speaking up so as not to anger someone else who thinks differently.
- Stabilizers sit on the fence, unable to decide.
- Stabilizers remain silent, even when they are hurt.
- Stabilizers and analyzers can be bogged down in a sea of rules and policies.
- Persuaders do everything at the last minute because they waste time talking.
- Persuaders only do things in order to get credit and attention.
- Persuaders dominate airtime and have to have the last word.
- Persuaders and controllers need to see action, even if the team is not ready to decide.
- Controllers love their ideas above all others.
- Controllers enjoy defending their position and don't want to change their minds.
- Controllers tend to be competitive, bossy, and love to win.

Can you see the varying perceptions and tendencies of each style? Some individuals are almost destined to have disagreements just based on how their style preferences fall on the people/emotions and tasks/results continuums (Figures 3.1 and 3.2). Analyzers and persuaders have preferences that are opposite each other, as do stabilizers and controllers. Can you see how the behaviors of each style can irritate or cause misplaced assumptions and expectations in a team? Have you experienced tension and emotional outbursts from misunderstandings and conflict in the workplace?

When a high level of tension is present, the team becomes caught in bad behaviors on all sides of the argument, particularly fear, anger, and embarrassment (Weeks, 2010, p.113–114). Fear makes it hard to think and, therefore, is a limiting emotion. In order to manage your fear, ask to step away to collect your thoughts and form a strategy. There are no rules in conflict that says a pause in the situation is not allowed. This strategy is helpful to all parties, as long as everyone knows when to reassemble. Anger can be a powerful motivator for taking up the conflict and even maintaining the verbal volleys (Weeks, 2010). Anger fuels the adrenalin, which helps us feel stronger and more justified. Anger is hard on the people we work with and on our reputation, and it paints us as aggressive.

"Speak when you are angry and you will make the best speech you will ever regret."

– Ambrose Bierce

The third emotion, embarrassment, is more significant than many expect in a conflict confrontation. Weeks (2010) stated that self-respect is central to an individual's well-being. Losing self-respect has been compared to a loss of oxygen in a room. It is the first thing a person seeks to retrieve. In a conflict situation, all three emotions are surging and capturing our ability to think and act rationally.

As a leader, what will you choose to do?

Rank each of the responses below, 1 through 6, (1 is what you would likely choose to do first) to indicate what you will likely do when you have a conflict to resolve in the workplace.

___ End the team meeting, ask everyone to return to their offices, and chill. Tell the group you will reconvene tomorrow for a more rational discussion. You do not reconvene the meeting.

___ Raise your voice to join in the fray.

___ Meet later with my favorites on the team to get their opinions.

___ Dictate your solution to the conflict, after all they had a chance to work it out.

___ Make notes about what happened for future performance reviews and/or complaints to your supervisor.

___ Pause, step away, and think. Develop a strategy.

You likely were able to choose and rank a response that seemed appropriate in managing conflict. This is an imaginary situation; the shouting is all in the paragraph. Now picture yourself in a real conflict situation. Can you sketch an outline of how you will begin the conversation to manage such a team situation? I will assume that you are similar to 98% of the working world and have not had a good role model or training to handle a difficult conversation.

PRESCRIPTION: MANAGING YOURSELF AND DIFFUSING A CONFLICT

Imagine yourself prepared to know how to diffuse a conflict among team members. It begins with the last option of the list above. Patterson, Grenny, McMillan, and Switzler (2005) have established several steps to start you in the right direction.

Step 1: Decide what you want.

Problems are rarely singular in nature. Unbundle it and determine what is the most important to solve. Patterson et al. (2005) recommend looking past the offender to investigate the consequences of the problem, the underlying intent of the offender, and what you want and don't want for yourself, the other parties, and the relationship.

Step 2: Decide if you should speak up.

Sometimes issues are better left alone. A fear of speaking up or uncertainty of how to approach the problem is not a reason to stay silent.

Step 3: Pause! Reprogram your brain.

Stop the villain story you typically tell yourself says Patterson et al. (2005). It takes people to find a solution. You can't partner in a solution with someone you have just told yourself is ugly and abusive. Be curious instead of judgmental. Look at the whole situation.

Step 4: Describe problem as a "gap" statement.

Describe factually what was expected and what was observed. Be respectful of the other person and describe the mutual purpose of the concern. Don't play games, sandwich the bad between good statements, use sarcasm, inappropriate humor, or a surprise attack warns Patterson et al. (2005).

Step 5: Make it easy and motivating to follow through.

Patterson et al. (2005) advise leaders to remove barriers and refuse the option to force or bribe someone into compliance. Use natural consequences if necessary.

Step 6: Agree to a plan and follow up.

Patterson et al. (2005) recommends staying focused with a rhythm of regular meetings and a dose of flexibility because life happens.

Armed with a plan, new strategies and skills can help you diffuse a conflict with effective conversation. But knowing what to do is only half the skill set. Engage in some role-play and mock interviews. Use the skills in all areas of your life. By practicing these steps, you will become more confident and better able to manage conflict.

SUMMARY

When you look in the mirror of your behavior style, do you understand what you see? There are many reputable assessments that help leaders understand how and why they make choices and communicate in predictable patterns. Educate your team about behavior styles and preferences. Have a teambuilding day that includes understanding individual styles as well as appreciating and valuing the styles of others. Observe those around you. Watch for patterns. Take advantage of opportunities to learn about yourself utilizing campus and employer services.

What can you do to help yourself and others value styles that are unlike your own? Learning about preferences is not for the purpose of labeling others, but instead for the purpose of valuing others. Seek to create a diverse team. Learn how to be flexible by intentionally shifting your behavior to a non-preferred style if you can't balance the team with current personnel or peers. It is too easy to fall into the trap of only bringing those to the table who think just like you.

Diffusing conflict is more about managing yourself than others. This is not a blame game. It is about respect and mutual benefit. The six steps listed in the Prescription section focus on your choices, your self-control, and a perspective of win-win for all the stakeholders of the organization. If you detect patterns of problems, that is, a different situation, it will likely involve human resources or additional members of the leadership team.

REFERENCES

Buckingham, M., & Clifton, D. O. (2001). *Now, discover your strengths*. New York, NY: The Free Press.

DISC Personality Styles: http://www.free-disc-profile.com

DISC Personality Styles: http://www.disc-personality-testing.com

Effectiveness Institute: http://www.effectivenessinstitute.com

Emotional Intelligence: http://www.queendom.com/queendom_tests/index.htm

Greenleaf, R. (1977). *Servant leadership: A journey in the nature of legitimate power and greatness*. New York, NY: Paulist.

Jung's Typology: http://www.humanmetrics.com/cgi-win/JTypes2.asp

Learning Styles: http://www.learning-styles-online.com

Patterson, K., Grenny, J., McMillan, R., & Switzler, A. (2005). *Crucial confrontations: Tools for solving broken promises, violated expectations, and bad behavior*. New Your, NY: McGraw-Hill.

Pink, D. H. (2009). *Drive: The surprising truth about what motivates us*. New York, NY: Riverhead Books.

Weeks, H. (2010). *Failure to communicate: How conversations go wrong and what you can do to right them*. Boston, MA: Harvard Business Press.

Chapter 4

Self-Management—Attitude, Values, Ethics, and Trust

LEARNING OBJECTIVES

The student will

- contrast the outcomes of a growth mindset attitude from a closed mindset,
- identify five personal core values and describe how each value is visible in his or her life,
- explain the purpose and results of shared organizational values,
- describe an example of each of the four types of responsibilities upheld by ethical organizations, and
- identify and give examples of 13 basic trust building behaviors.

ATTITUDE

Attitude is the positive or negative perspective about the world around you. It channels the way you think and feel, affecting the behaviors you exhibit. Maintaining control of your behaviors and exhibiting a positive outlook with others is called having a positive attitude. In leadership parlance, it is called self-management. Employers seek those who

- genuinely enjoy their work and are positive about the mission of the organization;
- are trustworthy and act with integrity;
- communicate enthusiastically;

- share credit and ideas willingly;
- relate concerns, but do it proactively; and
- chose to be self-motivated and go the extra mile.

You will notice what is not on this list: being loud, bossy, negative, abrasive, arrogant, a "lone ranger," timid, a 9–5er, or a self-promoter. Others notice and remember these negative characteristics and in turn, make you the person they want to avoid on their work teams. You recognize how attitude impacts your willingness to spend time with people either by the positive or negative experiences you have had in your classes, team projects, workplaces, and even your friendships. The people who are upbeat, show up early to help, deliver what you request and more, and are enthusiastic in the process are the people you want to invest in with your time and energy.

REFLECTION: REACTION TO THE NEGATIVE

Think about how you feel on a difficult day, a day that seems to beat you up — from morning commute traffic, to family crises calls and texts, to the unexpected surprise from your boss or faculty member. How do you handle unexpected stress? Do you pause, count to 10, and calm yourself, or do you spew like a shaken carbonated drink, inundating everyone within earshot of your terrible and unfair day. Spewing is different than confiding in a close friend. Instead, it is an ongoing stream of complaints directed at anyone who crosses your path that day or even the next. Everything is unfair and certainly not your fault. And like a lingering cold that won't go away, "carbonated individuals" perceive most situations as being victimized by a world that has turned against them. Are you the bottle of carbonated soda ready to spew, or are you the bottle of cool, calm water?

DIAGNOSIS: WHAT IS YOUR MINDSET?

Environments saturated with positive people—people who are not just happy on the surface, but who talk and act as if they enjoy what they do—are inspiring workplaces. Having a manager or executive director who is proud of the people, programs, and services is a place employees want to apply their time and talents. Consider your current workgroup, study group, or even family members. Answer these questions as you assess the environment surrounding your attitude. If you answer yes, give that answer an "A" if it happens daily, a "B" if it happens weekly, and a "C" if it happens occasionally.

- Do conversations at work, school, or home revolve around stories or examples of bad group leadership or organizational gaffs?
- Do family members complain about each other to friends and colleagues? Do work or school colleagues complain to others, likewise?
- Does humor center around other's mistakes?
- Are suggestions for change met with resistance and a perspective of hopelessness?
- Are other's successes met with feelings of jealousy?
- Is wisdom owned by the most critical?
- Is feedback ignored due to fear of revealing a lack of knowledge?

While you may feel this is acceptable behavior because a better bond with your colleagues will solidify professional and personal connections, you are really demonstrating your lack of loyalty and an eagerness to play the victim. However, it is unlikely that you seek out victims and whiners or others who demonstrate disloyalty as leaders for your organization when you need assistance or are building a work team. You look to those who find positivity, praise others, and seek to problem solve and create solutions as leaders.

Behaviors described by the questions above, if demonstrated more than just occasionally, may also be symptomatic of a mindset detrimental to one's success. Carol S. Dweck (2006) shares her ideas about a growth and a fixed mindset. A fixed mindset sees success as proving superiority by an almost natural ability. If the challenge cannot be accomplished with one's natural talents, the challenge will be either avoided or determined to be unimportant. A growth mindset sees success as hard work, accepting a new challenge, experiencing failure along the way, learning new skills, and persistence to the achievement of the goal. Dweck's review of several leadership studies determined that the growth mindset is necessary to organizational success.

PRESCRIPTION: RETOOLING FOR A GROWTH MINDSET

A positive attitude is easy to identify in others yet difficult to identify in yourself. You might believe you are a positive person, but your words might be betraying you. And chances are, whatever you practice in one environment is likely practiced in all aspects of your life. As obvious as this might seem, finding such a positive work-place is as close as the end of your nose. This is one of those common knowledge behaviors not commonly practiced. The finger of blame is often pointed to others, but it is the individual who controls his or her work environment. To help you correctly identify whether others perceive you as a positive person, enlist the help of a trusted family member, friend, or colleague. Describe for them the negative type of behavior you are trying to mitigate. Ask them to pay attention to what you say, and then follow up with them at the end of the day to let you know what they heard. Here are some examples of what their responses could be:

- When you share the details of your day, you only mention your aggravations and disappointments.
- When you socialize with your colleagues, you vent to everyone your grievances with the organization. Rarely do you offer positive comments or a constructive solution to a colleague, work team, or your boss.
- You frequently complain about colleagues but rarely own up to your share of the situation.
- You frequently complain about your spouse, in-laws, or children to your social group and rarely offer anything you are proud of.

Developing a positive attitude results from the ability to reframe the events of your day or the ability to put the bad events in perspective with the good. One step to develop this skill is to look for opportunities to say positive things. Think about the many good things that happen during your day. Not everything that happened in your day was bad. Even if you have to start small, list the positive events that have happened and share them with others. Instead of pointing out problems, research related situations and make informed suggestions to decision makers. Learn to push the "pause button" when you catch yourself going down the negative rabbit hole. Over time, this will become easier and more natural. Until you get there, you could coordinate a signal with your spouse or colleague to alert you if you have turned onto the negative road. Model your behavior after the positive people in your life by observing their style and habits. Note how others respond positively to them. Celebrate small successes! Focus on what you did accomplish. Too often our minds get stuck on the negative part of our day. Teaching ourselves to flip that mindset allows us to let go of needless worry and concentrate on adding value to the positive part of our day.

Seeking to change from a fixed to a growth mindset is possible as well. Dweck (2006, pp. 53–54) makes five suggestions for growing your mindset:

1. Have you considered or even tried to learn a new skill, sport, language, or musical instrument? Then after a few short weeks, the lessons became more difficult, so you quit. This is a sign that your fixed mindset took control. Using the support tactics in Chapter 13 of this text, build yourself a bridge to success in learning something new.

2. As leaders, it is tempting to surround ourselves with those who think we are geniuses. It feels wonderful to hear from others that we are outstanding in our profession and seen as role models to others. It is difficult to trade this view

for one of constructive criticism, but we must. Be open to feedback. Find ways for others to communicate frequently and safely.

3. Is there a turning point in your life that was a difficult yet defining moment? It changed the planned trajectory of your life. We all have those moments; they can be painful to remember. Go through the work to remember, emotions and all. Examine honestly your part in the situation as well as others. What aha thoughts come from this process? Using this growth mindset, separate your self-worth from the incident. It does not define your whole person.

4. On days when you are feeling low, how do you respond to life? Do you easily turn away from potential opportunities? Is making an effort just too difficult? A growth mindset is one that views challenges as a source of potential energy. There can be excitement and motivation derived from new initiatives. Working with others to help you tap into the positive energy is a needed step in this journey. Again, Chapter 13 is a great resource.

5. Is there a bucket list wish item in which fear is holding you back? A behavior change plan as outlined in Chapter 13 can help you achieve this dream.

SUMMARY

Attitudes are contagious. As a leader you must be able to be positive in the face of adversity. A temperament of calm, a demeanor of strength, a focus on problem solving instead of blame, and the ability to manage your emotions will serve you well as you build trusting relationships with followers, peers, and supervisors. No one wants to be led by a whiner and complainer.

Personal growth from a fixed to a growth mindset is a development process that takes time and new behaviors. (Additional suggestions to accomplish behavior change are in Chapter 13.) You will find a growth mindset to be beneficial not only in leading organizations but also in your personal relationships as well. A growth mindset is one that welcomes challenges, sees success as conquering the journey and achieving the goal, and believes in lifelong learning.

VALUES

Personal values are the internal rudder by which you steer your life. They are the personal truths you use to make daily choices. Values are learned through your experiences, observations, and understandings with family, faith organizations, schools, and society. "The quest for leadership, therefore, is first an inner quest to discover who you are and what you care about, and it's through this process of self-examination that you find the awareness needed to lead" (Kouzes & Posner, 2010).

REFLECTION: THE SELF-AWARE LEADER

The key to becoming a leader is self-awareness (Bennis, 1989; Kouzes & Posner 1993). As a leader, you will face many decision opportunities to direct, support, create, teach, buy, hire, serve, partner, or sell. As you tackle the onslaught of competing priorities each day, the more you know yourself, the more confident you will be with your decisions and the more consistent your decisions will be. Knowing the core values by which you steer your life is key to consistency and confidence. It is the alignment between what you believe and how you act that compels followers to listen and learn from you. Kouzes and Posner (2007) studied characteristics of admired leaders in the United States as well as those of nine other countries in Europe, Asia, and South America. Their research revealed that regardless of country, participants desired the same four characteristics in a leader: honesty, forward-looking, inspiring, and competent—the components of credibility. Leaders who are credible must be believable, trustworthy, conceptual thinkers, and have positive outlooks.

Finding your inner voice is a solitary journey. "Clarity of values," said Kouzes and Posner (2007, p. 50), "is essential in knowing which way, for each of us is north, south, east, and west." Discovering your values is a process of reflection and projection. As you work through the following scenarios, reflect back on the steps that brought you to the present choice. Then project forward what future results might be if you continued making choices using similar guidelines. The "remember whens" and "what ifs" will help you process through decisions you have previously made as well as the ones sitting on the horizon. Look for patterns as you uncover your core values, finding alignment within your decisions.

Think about the first time you visited a different state or country. Remember the comparisons you made between your community and the one you saw. Did you notice differences in the types of buildings, businesses, parks, schools, families and how they engage with others? Imagine what their daily life might be like and what your life might be like if this was your community. How might your priorities be different, your choices, your experiences, your basic truths? Or consider the casual conversation you had with a supervisor during lunch or coffee break and the personal insight you gained through a story and photos she shared. After, did your perspective of the supervisor change? Did you feel closer after stories were shared and family photographs presented? Or did you feel more distant due to the values differences that were revealed?

When you experience other communities and connect with the people who live there, you are able to see their values on display. Communities may invest in schools, economic development, safety, beautification, the arts, and bring attention to other items of importance. Have you looked at your community through the eyes of your guests and visitors? What guiding values do they see? Families display values by how they travel together on a sidewalk, where they choose to shop, or what they purchase. Businesses may show their values through advertisements that display desired products or social roles. Conversations with others demonstrate what they value or conversely what they may not value depending on the tone and context. What stories do you choose to share and with what tone and context? Have you ever considered what choices in your family traditions might convey? Take a moment to analyze your media. What was the last book you read, song you chose to download, or movie you watched? What was the most recent news item that invoked emotion or passion? What cause do you wish you could dedicate more time to as a volunteer? Your values are showing.

Tell Your Story

In this exercise, values are visible in our stories. Tell a story, your story. Craft a short story below by filling in the blanks to make the story your own:

Once upon a time I was reading a leadership textbook that asked me to write my story. I grew up in a family of _____ (brothers, sisters, parents, other relatives, and pets) in _____ (city), _____ (state), and _____ (country). My favorite ways to spend my out-of-school/work time are _____, _____, _____ _____, _____, and _____.

When facing this _____ (amazing, humorous, life-changing, other?) situation is when I chose to act _____, _____and experienced_____resulting in my learning _____
_____
_____.

A few (months, years) later when facing _____ (amazing, humorous, life-changing, other?) situation is when I chose to act

_____, _____

_____ and experienced _____

_____ resulting in my learning _____

_____.

Of the lessons learned from my family, I know I will share these with my children:
_____
_____
_____.

Of the lessons learned in my community, I know I will share these with my children:

_____

_____

_____.

If I had to leave for an extended period of time to travel to Jupiter as part of a collaborative mission from Earth, what would I want these new beings to know about me and my interests to serve my world? _____

_____

_____

_____

_____.

As I think about my future, I know I can pull from experiences like these: _____, _____, and _____ to demonstrate my commitment to _____.
If I do nothing else in my life, I want to make _____
_____better.

What values are prominent throughout your story? Circle the key words in your story and compile them in a list. If there is a personal core value that is missing from your story, add it to your list as well. What does this story reveal to you regarding what is important about your values?

DIAGNOSIS: ACTING IN ALIGNMENT WITH VALUES

Not only must you know what your values are, but you must also be able to act on them in a way others recognize. You must be able to answer the question "Do you walk your talk?" Through the reflection questions and the story you completed, you likely uncovered several important personal values. Review the list of your values.

Personal Values List

In this next exercise, you will work to achieve some clarity regarding your values. If you wish to fine-tune some of the descriptions and words you have written so far, the list below may provide some assistance in building a comprehensive list of important personal values.

Adventure	Freedom	Loyalty	Balance	Generosity
Patience	Beauty	Gratitude	Compassion	Professionalism
Humility	Health	Quality	Excellence	Responsibility

Courage	Creativity	Honesty	Respect	Teamwork
Faith	Integrity	Wisdom	Fitness	Leadership
Family	Citizenship	Service	Truth	Stewardship
Love	Fairness	Unity	Diversity	Peace
Growth	Learning	Justice	Happiness	

Start by building on the list of your values from the story you just wrote. Review the list above and other sources of your choosing to complete your comprehensive list of personal values. Now narrow your comprehensive list to only five personal core values. Narrowing the list can be difficult; therefore, here are six questions (Kouzes & Posner, 2007, p. 83) to aid in this process:

1. Did I freely choose this value?

2. Have I considered alternatives to this value and explored their meanings?

3. Have I considered the alternative consequences of this value?

4. Do I cherish this value? Am I passionate about it?

5. Am I willing to affirm publicly that I hold this value?

6. Will I act on this value repeatedly, over time, and in a consistent manner?

Other ways to narrow the list are to put the values into three categories (top, middle, and lessor). Ranking your values can help eliminate several if your list is long.

Once you have arrived at your core five values, it is time to determine how visible they are in your life. The purpose of this exercise is to help you clearly identify the actions and behaviors you exhibit daily that relate to your values. For each of the five core values, you will write four or five clarifying statements depicting how you visibly live that value today on a daily basis. As an example, one of this author's core values is learning. The five clarifying statements that demonstrate how I live this value are as follows:

- I spend time weekly learning about myself, my profession, and my world.
- I seek daily to learn about others, my family, my colleagues, and my students.
- I apply my learning at every opportunity to effect positive change.
- I actively seek new information to share with others.
- I seek new information to make monthly improvements in my personal and professional life.

With the five clarifying statements, you can see how my values are visible in daily learning. Select one of your five core values and write five clarifying statements that show how you regularly live, see, and act on your value. Repeat this process for your other four core values. After you have clarifying statements for each value, analyze them and ask yourself if you are living your values. Are these values visible to yourself and others through your actions?

Values are formed from experiences that shape you from the years of your youth through young adulthood. Although your values are not set in the same way your personality is, it does require a significant event to influence or alter the perspective and foundation used in your personal guidance system. Society's values have evolved as social change occurs. The civil rights and the women's movements are examples of social change that have altered the values of many on a global level.

PRESCRIPTION: LEADERSHIP AND ORGANIZATIONAL VALUES

A leader's purpose is to rally the organization's members in a common direction to achieve a universally recognized important goal. To do this once might require less technique and intentionality from the leaders; to do this systematically over time, especially with complex issues, requires a leader who understands the importance of creating the common ground where groups work best. There are several that enable a leader to unify the organizational members, and these steps are described in Chapter 6. However, the first step to mastering this skill is by discovering your values. Now you have an understanding of your personal values. This section covers the leader's work of establishing a common set of values for the members of the organization. Organizational values are part of the culture of an organization (Schein, 2004). They are the threads that support and bind members' behaviors and attitudes.

Unlike Moses coming down the mountain with the 10 Commandments, leaders do not have omnipotent powers to command everyone to come together on common ground. Today's employees want to participate in the creation of organizational values, their own unified common ground. Kouzes and Posner (1993, pp. 126–129) describe successful processes for achieving a common set of organizational values: listening, trusting, and sharing with everyone involved.

- Allow sufficient time and techniques for all who want to participate to have the opportunity.
- Establish safety by engaging with other members and the organization's leadership.
- Teach the skills of giving and receiving feedback, seeking clarification, and sharing ideas.

- Share collaboration and consensus process.
- Educate everyone on the history of the organization.
- Share the organization's vision.
- Break into discussion groups to share responses to these questions, and generate written suggestions.
  ○ How does the vision fit with your vision?
  ○ What does the vision do for you? What concerns you?
  ○ What is missing from the vision? What would you like to change?
- Engage representatives of discussion groups in discussions of group norms, values, and behavior statements.
  ○ Be certain behavior statements focus on the "how" instead of the "what."
- Achieve consensus with discussion group representatives.

Organizational Values

Below is a set of five organizational values and related behavior statements from Juniper Networks (http://www.juniper.net/us/en/company/profile/value), a company that makes routers, Ethernet connections, and network security platforms:

- Authentic
  ○ Uncommon and inquisitive thinking
  ○ Individuals cooperating as a single global company
- Trust
  ○ Acting with integrity, fairness, respect, and reliability
- Excellence
  ○ Driven by our craft
  ○ Delivering beyond expectations
  ○ Disciplined repeated effort
- Bold Aspirations
  ○ Imagine, innovate, and create solutions
  ○ Transform possibilities into realities
- Meaningful Difference
  ○ Behave in a balanced, thoughtful manner that considers every aspect and outcomes of our business decisions

Juniper Networks' set of five values was determined through a highly engaged discussion process involving members of the organization from all levels. Members of an organization want to be included in the community of shared values. They need to know how their beliefs and their jobs connect to the organization's values. Such organizations are more productive, have a more trusting environment, show increased support and sharing between members, and expend energy more effectively to achieve excellence. Pulling together in a common direction is a more successful workplace formula than having members focus on one-upping the group in the next cubicle or another agency in the community. Due to competition being a learned component of Western culture (S. R. Covey, 1989), organizations and community members must be encouraged to explore win-win thinking through common values, agendas and collaboration to succeed. Kouzes and Posner (1993) add to our understanding of competition by explaining, "When the fear of 'losing' to a teammate diminishes, the need to gain personal power also decreases" (p. 132). Competition inside the workplace, though encouraged by many organizations, is shown by several research studies to be undesirable.

Leaders and organizations must also support shared values in very visible ways. Recruitment, orientation, and training of new employees must be in alignment with the organization's values and be designed to both communicate and reinforce these values. Follow-up surveys from employees will provide vital feedback regarding the ongoing influence of organizational values in both operations and leadership behaviors. Organizations members must see a strong link between the rewards systems, recognitions, promotions, and merit raises with organizational values. Communicating values through the stories of the employees as well as the outcomes of the products and services or the organization makes values real. When shared values come alive in the organization, the culture also aligns with the direction the members' desire. When organizational values are quiet and dusty, employees start to wonder, "Are we still doing that?"

SUMMARY

A ship cannot chart its course without a rudder to guide the vessel. A leader cannot lead successfully without a thorough understanding of his or her values. When employees are connected with their own values, they are much more likely to become engaged in their work. There is common ground for organizational values and alignment with the rudder. These are the components of a successful work team, team leader, and organization.

ETHICS

"Ethics is a study of the underlying beliefs, assumptions, principles, and values that support a moral way of life," writes Robert Starratt (2004, p. 5). Ethical leadership is the act of making choices for the organization based on the study of those beliefs, assumptions, principles, and values. "An ethical dilemma can be defined as an undesirable or unpleasant choice relating to a moral principle or practice," according to John Maxwell (2003, p. 5). With the continuous disappointments and even crises created by morally bankrupt leaders as exhibited by Watergate, Enron, Penn State Athletics, and the "storm-chasing" nonprofits cashing in on disaster relief around the globe, ethics becomes a critical topic in the study of leadership.

REFLECTION: THE JUDGMENTS WE MAKE

Scan the headlines of any national news agency and more often than not you will find articles exposing the unethical choices by people in leadership positions:

- Refugees in need of food and medicine due to power-hungry dictators in war-ravaged lands
- Sexual assault of children by athletic or religious leaders
- Manufacturing plants built overseas to pay lower wages in third world countries rather than minimum wage in the United States
- Substandard manufacturing plants with few, if any, safety regulations, resulting in fires and employee deaths
- Undisclosed food additives used in processing plants from countries overseas
- Government supported cyber attacks on financial and security institutions
- Payment of bribes to government officials for the support of other governments or businesses

And yet as leaders are rightfully judged on their behaviors, people tend to judge themselves on a different scale—intent. If we intended to be a caring and humble colleague today, but did not, shouldn't we get points for wanting to be caring and humble? Should leaders be judged on a stricter scale than we judge ourselves?

Take a moment to remember what you thought this last week. What judgments, assumptions, actions, behaviors, comments, choices, and so on did you make regarding those who crossed your path? What expectations did you have of neighbors, shoppers, colleagues, friends, drivers on the road, pedestrians, drivers vying for parking, classmates, athletic referees, politicians, neighbors, instructors, parents, children, teens, family members, and so on? Were you fair? Respectful? Patient? Kind? Ask yourself, are your actions always ethical?

- ____ Always ethical?
- ____ Mostly ethical?
- ____ Somewhat ethical?
- ____ Seldom ethical?
- ____ Never ethical?

What motivated you to select the answer you did? Would others agree with you? Would selecting a different timeframe have resulted in a different answer? If so, what does that say about your consistency of actions and choices?

You are human, capable of mistakes and inconsistencies; yet, hopefully none as egregious as found in the media headlines mentioned previously. How can you minimize such inconsistencies? How can you be true to your principles and become an ethical leader?

DIAGNOSIS: DEFINING ETHICAL AND UNETHICAL BEHAVIOR

Individuals and organizations make decisions based upon the perspective of producing the greatest benefit while doing the least amount of harm. Conflicts among values held by the individual, those espoused by the organizations in which they work, and those held by society create the conflicting ethical issues you and your colleagues wrestle with each day. Sometimes ethical issues are not easy to recognize. Ferrell, Fraedrich, and Ferrell (2002) define and classify ethical issues into seven categories:

1. Conflict of Interest – Individuals must choose whether to advance individual interests or those of the group or organization.

2. Honesty and Fairness – Some may perceive the activities of organizations similar to a game with few rules, instead of expecting organizations to be trustworthy, law-abiding, and choosing to do no harm.

3. Communication – Organizations have been known to give false or deceptive descriptions, exaggerations, or even outright lies on product labels, in reports, and online and in print messages.

4. Technology – Electronic communication and social media brings issues of employee and client/customer privacy to the forefront, expansion of other laws and policies to cover this growing, popular medium, as well as the protection of intellectual property in a new world of individual open access.

5. Financial – Being good stewards of funds that support organization operations include monitoring how funds are both spent and invested, donations are managed, programs and services are priced, and grant funds are budgeted and measured toward program outcomes.

6. Employees – Organization employees can be the victims of unethical acts (intimidation, harassment or discrimination), or the victimizer by withholding information, theft, sabotage, or use of company resources. Employees may also have a key role to play as a whistleblower in the face of an unethical organization.

7. Leaders and Managers – Employee and operational excellence are the primary focus of organizational leaders who must balance duties to stakeholders above and below in the hierarchy. These leaders must be concerned with implementing policies such as codes of conduct, health and safety, discrimination, harassment, drug and alcohol abuse, community relations, sound budgets, and environmental impact.

Although this is not an exhaustive list of ethical concerns, reviewing the seven categories will remind you of personal examples that will increase your awareness and recognition regarding ethical decisions. Awareness encourages thoughtful discussion, analysis, and the engagement of others in the process. When an organization discourages discussion and ethical analysis, you should become concerned. Documenting the events to consult with a trusted member of the organization's leadership would be your next step in handling an ethical dilemma.

Why do individuals and organizations make unethical decisions? Employees learn ethical behavior through the people they interact with both at home and at work. It is the bad apple theory at work; one bad apple does spoil the whole bunch. According to Maxwell (2003), there are three reasons for making unethical choices:

1. Convenience – Do you choose the easy answer or the right answer?

2. Winning – Do you choose to do whatever it takes to win, or do you make the ethical choice and possibly lose?

3. Setting Standards That Benefit You – Do you choose standards you expect all members to uphold or standards that allow everyone to get by on their good intentions?

According to Power, Higgins, and Kohlberg (1989), people make different decisions in ethical situations because they are at different levels of cognitive moral development. An overview of Kohlberg's levels describes the early stages of development as a person interested in his or her own immediate interests, external rewards, and punishments. At the mid levels of development, correct decisions are described as conforming to the expectations of good behavior of the larger society. At the highest level, the individual sees beyond the laws and policies of groups and makes ethical decisions regardless of negative external pressures.

Ethical theories describe how people think about ethics in general: through a framework of character or a framework of conduct. You might refer to your supervisor as a person of integrity (character), or a person who acts with fairness (conduct). When considering ethical conduct, you must know the rules guiding the conduct as well as the consequences of the actions. Using the context of character and conduct helps clarify the various approaches to ethics theory.

Ethical Theories

Ethical theories focus on consequences, results, and outcomes. Are the results good or bad? In this frame, there are three approaches to ethical decision making (Northouse, 2013).

- Ethical egoism is when people choose to create the greatest good for themselves.
- Utilitarianism states that people should make choices that bring the greatest good to the greatest number.
- Altruism states that choices should be made to bring the greatest good to others and such selflessness is a moral obligation.

In a human services setting, a counseling center staff may choose to set office hours from 9 a.m. to 5 p.m. to allow staff to have the maximum time with their families. This decision is rooted on ethical egoism. Another agency may choose a utilitarian approach and select to have office hours 7 days a week, including evenings, thereby providing the greatest choice of appointment times to the greatest number of potential clients. The staff of the third agency using an approach of altruism may not only choose office hours 7 days a week, but may also choose to locate satellite offices in three other sections of the community and not expect reimbursement for mileage or overtime pay for weekends. This choice provides the greatest good since not only are the hours convenient, but also the location of service is convenient, and the staff feels a moral obligation to provide this service.

Deontological theory is focused on rules and duty. The choice rests with making the right decision, one that is good and morally correct. Returning to the counseling center example, a duty exists for counselors to be available to their clients beyond office hours for emergencies. Therefore, it is a duty and morally right decision to have an on-call schedule for the counselors, 7 days a week, 365 days a year. As the director of a counseling agency or other type of human services organization, it is not inappropriate to review all of the ethical considerations for staff, clients, and other stakeholders.

Leaders alone are not responsible for bad leadership. It is a dance of the leader and those being led that constitutes the leadership process. Kellerman (2004) studied the patterns of bad leadership and followership and uncovered seven patterns.

1. Incompetent leadership results when leaders and followers lack the will and skill to sustain effective action.

2. Rigid leadership is not flexible. Leaders and followers cannot adapt when change occurs.

3. Intemperate leaders lack self-control and are supported by followers who are unwilling to intervene.

4. Callous leaders lack empathy and respect to the majority in the organization. The needs of the group remain unknown and unfulfilled.

5. Corrupt leaders and followers lie, cheat, and steel to benefit their self-interest, maintain power, and achieve financial gain.

6. Insular leadership involves leaders and followers who minimize or disregard the needs of group members outside the smaller circle.

7. Evil leaders and followers commit physical and psychological harm through pain.

It is difficult to say which of the seven is more painful, costly, or calamitous to human life. All involve a failure in leadership and followership. Greed, arrogance, complacency, lack of checks and balances, and avoidance are some of the many reasons we find ourselves with an unethical and ineffective leadership process.

With such variation in the individual's perception of ethical behavior and the influences that create their perspective, it is the leader's concern to establish a common view of ethics for the consistent operation of the organization. Understanding the theory helps you understand the multiple dimensions of the question and consequences regarding the choices you make.

PRESCRIPTION: ESTABLISHING A CULTURE OF ETHICS

Establishing an ethical culture in an organization is the primary responsibility of leaders. The ethical climate of the organizational culture is comprised of the professions' code of ethics, previous leadership actions on ethical issues, coworkers, managers, and organization policies and procedures. Organizational culture has been cited as a significant factor in ethical decision making from studies and training conducted by the Compliance and Ethics Institute (http://www.complianceethicsinstitute .org). One tragedy frequently referenced as an example of poor decision making is the 2003 NASA Columbia accident. The Columbia Accident Investigation Board (2003) noted in their report, "NASA's organizational culture and structure has as much to do with this accident as the external tank foam." Establishing an ethical culture should not be left to chance or postponed until the first crisis occurs. It also is not enough to train employees to have good character and to be sensitive to ethical issues. The only way to have consistent decisions in alignment with the interests of all stakeholders is to develop and require compliance with the organization's ethical policies (Ferrell et al., 2002). Establishing an ethical culture happens systematically and intentionally through every organizational process.

Establishing an Ethical Culture

An organization is considered a moral agent accountable for its ethical conduct (Ferrell et al., 2002, p. 154). Since organizations, both for-profit and nonprofit, are chartered by the state, they have many of the rights and responsibilities of individuals. The Federal Sentencing Guidelines for Organizations (2013) hold organizations accountable for employee conduct as well as their leadership decisions and results. Ferrell et al. (2002) explain further that organizations have the characteristics of an agent and as such, are responsible to society rather than to the individuals employed there. Nonprofit organizations have additional codes and standards compiled into a web-based clearinghouse (see Independent Sector, 2015). Because of the special stewardship of the board of directors and employees of a nonprofit to the money raised for specific programs and services, such standards and codes include the following:

- Standards for online giving
- Standards for gifts in kind
- Standards to guide relationships between nonprofits and corporations
- Samples of a Donor Bill of Rights
- Standards for membership organizations
- Standards for grant making
- Standards for a variety of state, regional, and international organizations

Failure to comply with these standards and requirements, or lack of attention from leadership to ethical codes and policies, can result in fines or the loss of public trust for most organizations. If sentencing occurs through the Federal Sentencing Guidelines for Organizations, organizations must remedy any harm and must ensure through appropriately monitored actions that similar issues are prevented in the future. Assets may also be divested from the organization if the level of harm and neglect is severe.

Ethical Organizations

Rhoades (2011) described a quality, ethical organization as one that upholds an organization's responsibilities to society:

1. Economic Responsibility – To produce programs and services that society wants and needs

2. Legal Responsibility – To operate within the laws of the local, state, and federal levels

3. Ethical Responsibility – To make choices, behave, and act in a way that is expected but not codified by law

4. Philanthropic Responsibility – To give back to society through contributions of time, expertise, and money

In addition to an organization's responsibility to society, leaders in ethical organizations have a responsibility to their employees as well as the organization. They must provide, distribute, and monitor employee rules and guidelines. They do this by maintaining the familiarity and regular enforcement of the rules and guidelines. Leaders also conduct periodic ethical compliance audits. They establish responsibilities for specific employees at multiple levels to manage the organization's code of ethics. Leaders consider the compliance as well as the endorsement of the organization's policies and guidelines when rewarding and promoting employees. Leaders provide employees anonymous avenues to report potential problems without risk of retaliation. The CEO/Executive Director's responsibility is to model ethical conduct, speak and write about the ethical culture, highlight employee's ethical decision making, and regularly meet with employees responsible for the management of the organization's code of ethics.

Ethics training programs for employees are helpful but do not establish an ethical organizational culture. Recommended content of employee ethics training programs include the following:

- Understanding and recognition of ethical issues
- Procedures for reporting possible ethics violations
- Identification of employees who can assist with ethical concerns
- Individual and organizational responsibilities for ethical compliance
- Impact of the code of silence around ethical issues (The code of silence is an unwritten rule in some professions to never report a colleague's error.)

The profession of human services has its own code of ethical standards. It is managed by the National Organization for Human Services. (http://www.national humanservices.org/ethical-standards-for-hs-professionals). Other professions under the human services umbrella have codes of ethics as well:

- Counseling: http://www.counseling.org/Resources/aca-code-of-ethics.pdf
- American Mental Health Association: http://www.amhca.org/assets/news/ AMHCA_Code_of_Ethics_2010_w_pagination_cxd_51110.pdf
- National Association of Social Workers: http://www.socialworkers.org/pubs/ code/code.asp

SUMMARY

Ethics are practices and actions for individuals requiring focus, analysis, and the alignment of values with everyday choices. Leaders are expected to act with character and achieve positive consequences for the good of many. Organizations have a responsibility to society to achieve positive results for the greater good by establishing an ethical culture where all employees and stakeholders are committed. Such choices are pure and simple in concept but require discipline and consistency to achieve. Human services as a profession has a commitment to the betterment of their clients, communities, and society. Yet this commitment does not make it immune to human error or poor choices. Attention to ethical practices is critical for leaders in all sectors. Leaders' and organizational values are the foundation of ethical actions. Because leadership has a moral foundation, leaders must be vigilant and aware of how individual decisions affect others.

TRUST

Leadership is built around relationships, and trust is the foundation of every relationship. Trust within a relationship is a feeling of safety to be you, comfort in the ability to admit a mistake, and a willingness to share your hopes, dreams, and disappointments. In personal and professional relationships, you have an imaginary gatekeeper who helps you maintain a sense of security by using a facade, behind which you hide your true self. When you feel safe, the gatekeeper allows a relationship to start.

Trust is defined as a strong belief in the reliability of someone or something, a confident expectation (Kouzes & Posner, 1993). In the context of leadership, trust is an outcome of the ability to create an environment of acceptance, respect, and integrity. Trust is an action, ability, or competency that is learnable and measureable (S. M. R. Covey & Merrill, 2006). A trustworthy person is one who is deserving of your trust. Before one can trust or be trusted, becoming trustworthy is the first step.

REFLECTION: BECOMING TRUSTWORTHY

Trustworthy people possess certain characteristics. Consider situations where you were sizing up a new person in your life to determine how much personal information you felt safe sharing. This situation could have been with a new colleague, classmate, roommate, romantic relationship, or even with your faculty member at the beginning of a new semester. Usually the safety assessment you create follows this path (S. M. R. Covey & Merrill, 2006):

- Listen for consistency, straight talk
- Radar engaged to detect respect: topics, tone, dignity, facial expression, language of inclusion
- Listen and look for openness and transparency. They choose to share first. Both parties are seeking to find common ground, similar experiences
- Information is shared such that verification is possible

Relationships begin when common experiences and ideas are shared. As common experiences are revealed, trust increases. In the give and take of relationships, sometimes less than helpful behaviors can occur. Trust can be damaged if the error is deemed to be intentional. What reminders should you heed as the seeds of trustworthiness are being planted?

- As much as we try to avoid them, mistakes happen. Even a confused meeting time can become an early trust issue if not resolved. Apologize immediately and seek to recover the relationship.
- Do not gossip. Do not warn coworkers about another's behavior even if you believe you will spare this person future pain. Show loyalty to all.
- Give credit to everyone involved, whether a formal team or an entire department. Never take credit for someone else's work.
- Deliver what you promised, when you promised, at the quality level you promised. Be a person others can count on. Do not be afraid to ask questions to ensure commitments are kept. Do not develop a reputation as the team member who is always late with a product others will have to rework.
- Seek personal improvement. Improvement happens when you allow yourself to trust another's observations and opinions of your performance. Such feedback ensures we are current with the job and helps us not to become blinded of our own myopia.
- Be forthcoming about anticipated trouble spots. This is not gossip, but a data trend that needs to be watched. Good news is fun to share, but confronting hurdles together also builds trust. Do not ignore the elephant in the room. These are current issues that, due to not being dealt with, cause fear and reluctance of others to be open to a conversation regarding it. Due to the festering, these issues can appear to be the size of elephants. Dealing with reality when it happens is the best choice, even if it is difficult.

Being proactive in your ongoing development as a trustworthy person will include the following actions and behaviors:

- Assumptions are the first step to miscommunication. Taking the time to clarify yours and others' perceptions and expectations will build trust.
- As a leader accountability starts with you. Take responsibility, own the successes and the failures. Self-trust grows with each accomplishment.
- Leadership is built on understanding others which results from listening first. Listen for how others feel. Set your agenda aside and really listen. As a leader it is tempting to share your ideas, to give advice, and solve problems. By listening first, you will work on the correct problem as well as involve others in the solution.
- Since 1801, the motto of the London Stock Exchange is "My word is my bond." Major transactions were executed without written contracts. The foundation of this environment is to keep promises and commitments. Unlike at the London stock Exchange, some people only offer a vague commitment. Reneging on a commitment is the fastest way to break trust with others. Do not over promise on what you are able to deliver.
- When leaders extend trust to employees, they express confidence in the ability of those individuals. Trust becomes reciprocal in relationships, when it is extended to someone it is also returned to you. Extend trust to those who have earned it and conditionally to those who are vying to earn it.

Explore how the sum of the following 13 behaviors builds your credibility as a trustworthy leader.

DIAGNOSIS: TRUST-BUILDING

Rate yourself on your current performance of the 13 trust-building behaviors in Table 4.1 from Stephen M. R. Covey and Rebecca R. Merrill's 2006 book, *The Speed of Trust: The One Thing That Changes Everything* (pp. 231–232), discussed in the previous section, by using a 5-point rating scale where 1 is low and 5 is high.

Once you have rated yourself, review the feedback for problem areas. Where can you improve? Then answer the following questions:

- Which of these behaviors do you already practice?
- Are there aspects of these behaviors that will allow you to build sustainable trust in your organization?
- Which of these behaviors are ones you experience in your organization? How does that make you feel?
- Which behaviors are ones to which you might be contributing? How might you change this?

Table 4.1   Trust-Building Behaviors

Behavior	Opposite	Current Performance				
Talk Straight	Lie, spin, double-talk, flatter	1	2	3	4	5
Demonstrate Respect	Show disrespect or respect only to those who can do something for you.	1	2	3	4	5
Create Transparency	Pretend, withhold information	1	2	3	4	5
Right Wrongs	Don't admit or repair mistakes	1	2	3	4	5
Show Loyalty	Take credit yourself, bad-mouth others, sell others out	1	2	3	4	5
Deliver Results	Fail to deliver, deliver only busyness	1	2	3	4	5
Get Better	Don't invest in improvement	1	2	3	4	5
Confront Reality	Skirt real issues, ignore elephants	1	2	3	4	5
Clarify Expectations	Assume expectations, give vague or changing expectations	1	2	3	4	5
Practice Accountability	Take no responsibility, do not hold others accountable	1	2	3	4	5
Listen First	Pretend listen, speak first, don't reach understanding	1	2	3	4	5
Keep Commitments	Break or make no promises, make vague promises	1	2	3	4	5
Extend Trust	Fake or withhold trust	1	2	3	4	5

What happens when trust is broken or poorly built? Trust can break quickly or gradually erode along a continuum from major to minor, due to either intentional or unintentional behaviors (Reina & Reina, 2015). A major trust betrayal often is sudden from a significant change in the organization that causes employee discomfort with how the change was managed. It is the little daily habits of failing to attend to the 13 behaviors of trustworthiness (S. M. R. Covey & Merrill, 2006) that erodes trust. The daily accumulation of human errors in trustworthiness creates disappointment, frustrations, doubt, confusion, and pain. Workers feel hopeless, loss of passion, loss of focus, and question their place in the organization. Some become bitter, resentful, angry, and will disengage (Reina & Reina, 2015).

PRESCRIPTION: OPTIMAL WORK ENVIRONMENTS

Optimal organizational practice is a relatively new field, which focuses on optimal leadership and management practices that in turn create the best human conditions in work environments (Reina & Reina, 2015). Trust is the critical ingredient in optimal work environments. At all levels within the workplace hierarchy, trust is continuously challenged. According to Dennis and Michelle Reina (2015), when trust erodes, relationships are compromised. People shut down, pull back, and hesitate to engage. Because human behavior is inconsistent and filled with cycles of steps forward as well as missteps, the cycle of building trust is captured with this understanding and resulting roadmap. The cycle begins with building (or rebuilding) trust => then achieving trust => then betrayal of trust => and back to building trust. Incorporating this process requires a shared understanding of the steps and stages as well as the behaviors required to rebuild. Reina and Reina (2015) describe trust as an exchange, created step-by-step, and reciprocal (I need to give trust, to get trust). They identify three dimensions of trust:

The Three Cs

1. Trust of Capability
   a. Acknowledge people's skills and abilities
   b. Allow people to make decisions
   c. Involve others and seek their input
   d. Help people learn skills

2. Trust of Character
   a. Manage expectations
   b. Establish boundaries
   c. Delegate appropriately
   d. Encourage mutuality serving intentions
   e. Keep agreements
   f. Be consistent

3. Trust of Communication
   a. Share information
   b. Tell the truth
   c. Admit mistakes
   d. Give and receive constructive feedback

  e. Maintain confidentiality

  f. Speak with good purpose

Trust of Capability enables the team to work at their highest level by teaching and mentoring skills and knowledge, and then trusting people to use the new skill sets in their expanded responsibilities. Trust of Character encourages a line-of-sight among employees uniting direction and vision of responsibilities, which in turn enables teamwork. When employees are fearful and self-absorbed, they cannot see anyone other than themselves. Trust of Communication keeps information free-flowing, honest, and free from gossip and confidentiality breaches.

Rebuilding workplace trust after a betrayal, whether major, minor, intentional, or unintentional, requires a 7-step healing process (Reina & Reina, 2015, p. 147).

1. Acknowledge what occurred. Employees must believe leaders are listening to perceive them as caring and understanding. Leaders must allow employees to express their emotional pain from the loss. Failure to listen empathically will result in employees who feel diminished and discounted and rebuilding trust will be that much farther out of reach.

2. Allow feelings to surface. Create formal means of communication such as a task force or focus group to encourage employees to share feelings and ideas. Help people verbalize their pain. Due to a situational breach of trust, some employees will be reluctant to share. Leaders must assist employees to feel safe expressing feelings. Employees will not care about an organization until they believe the organization cares about them. An employee caring about the organization is vital for good customer/client service to exist. Without it, it can lead to resentment and entitlement.

3. Giving and receiving support. Employees have a high need to know the organization and how their new roles fit, especially during times of change and transition. Leaders need support in this rebuilding process, too. They both have information and relationship needs, and if met, can move forward. It is in this forward step, taking stock of the situation and reaching out to each other, that employees and leaders shift from finger-pointing to a focus on problem solving, shared responsibility, and accountability.

4. Reframe the experience. Do not ignore the details, but fill in the remaining parts of the bigger picture for the organization. Identify the internal and external threats if trust is not restored and opportunities when trust is rebuilt. Explore opportunities. Engage in sessions of asking productive questions

and creating groups to seek answers. Help employees see options to problem solve for the organization as well as their own personal behavior choices.

5. Take responsibility for mistakes. These actions must begin with the organization's leadership. After this happens, other members of the organization will follow. This is the reciprocity at work in trust building. "Trust begets trust and betrayal begets betrayal," according to Dennis and Michelle Reina (2007, p. 40). Employees who remain trapped by their emotional pain will first blame leaders and then react in a way that further contributes to the initial betrayal cycle. Leaders must break the betrayal chain by reestablishing a culture of truth telling. This must involve extensive communication to clarify expectations and negotiate team agreements. This is the beginning of new commitments with employees, which must be specific and delivered.

6. Forgive yourself and others. Forgiveness happens over time and begins with ownership of the betrayal followed by an apology. No excuses or justifications. A true apology is acknowledging the betrayal, understanding the pain, and committing to change. Forgiveness is personal and takes place after a perceived change will sustain, enduring a trustworthy environment. Leaders must resolve issues, meet needs, focus on emotions, and give the process time. Leaders should not expect employees to forget. This is neither reality nor desirable, since no one wants to repeat the same mistakes again.

7. Let go and move on. Employees will move to acceptance when they can shift their energies to a new trustworthy future. Practicing the individual 13 trustworthy behaviors and seeking the organizational behaviors described in the transactional trust model will bring every member of the organization into the cycle of rebuilding trust.

SUMMARY

Trust is the result of the work of an organization as well as its members who can identify shared values, engage in the development, and practice of ethical procedures and dialogue, and individual and organizational practices of trustworthy behaviors. Trust building is a cycle that grows and matures through building relationships that are respectful and safe. It begins by developing as a trustworthy individual who walks her talk and values others. In all relationships mistakes and betrayals occur, which require apologies and forgiveness to rebuild. Organizational cultures can be seen as ethical and trustworthy. Building such a culture requires leaders to embrace competence, contractual and communication trust. Leadership holds a critical role in all of these elements that comprise the best leadership and management practices, thus creating the best conditions in a work environment.

REFERENCES

Bennis, W. (1989). *Why leaders can't lead: The unconscious conspiracy continues.* San Francisco, CA: Jossey-Bass.

Columbia Accident Investigation Board. (2003). The accident's organizational causes (chap. 7). In *Report* (vol. 1). Washington, DC: Government Printing Office. Retrieved from http://history.nasa.gov/columbia/Troxell/Columbia%20Web%20 Site/CAIB/CAIB%20Website/CAIB%20Report/Volume%201/introduction.pdf

Covey, S. R. (1989). *The seven habits of highly effective people: Powerful lessons in personal change.* New York, NY: Simon and Schuster.

Covey, S. M. R., & Merrill, R. R (2006). *The speed of trust: The one thing that changes everything.* New York, NY: Free Press.

Dweck, C. S. (2006). *Mindset: The new psychology of success.* New York, NY: Random House.

Federal Sentencing Guidelines. (2013). *Sentencing of organizations.* Retrieved from www.ussc.gov/Guidelines/Organizational_Guidelines/guidelines_chapter_8.htm

Ferrell, O. C., Fraedrich, J., & Ferrell, L. (2002). *Business ethics: Ethical decision making and cases* (5th ed.). Boston, MA: Houghton Mifflin.

Independent Sector. (2015). Compendium of standards, codes, and principles of nonprofit and philanthropic organizations. Retrieved from http://www .independentsector.org/compendium_of_standards

Kellerman, B. (2004). *Bad leadership: What is it, how it happens, why it matters.* Boston, MA: Harvard Business School Press.

Kouzes, J. M., & Posner, B. Z. (1993). *Credibility: How leaders gain and lose it, why people demand it.* San Francisco, CA: Jossey-Bass.

Kouzes, J. M., & Posner, B. Z. (2007). *The leadership challenge* (4th ed.). San Francisco: John Wiley and Sons.

Kouzes, J. M., & Posner, B. Z. (2010). *The truth about leadership: The no-fads, heart-of-the-matter facts you need to know.* San Francisco, CA: Jossey-Bass.

Maxwell, J. C. (2003). *There is no such thing as business ethics: There's only one rule for making decisions.* New York, NY: Warner Business Books.

Northouse, P. G. (2013). *Leadership: Theory and practice* (6th ed.). Los Angeles, CA: Sage.

Power, F. C., Higgins, A., & Kohlberg, L. (1989). *Lawrence Kohlberg's approach to moral education.* New York, NY: Columbia University Press.

Reina, D. S., & Reina, M. L. (2007). Building sustainable trust. *OD Practitioner*, *39*(1), 36–41.

Reina, D. S., & Reina, M. L. (2015). *Trust and betrayal in the workplace: Building effective relationships in your organization* (3rd ed.). Oakland, CA: Berrett-Kohler Publishers.

Rhoades, A. (2011). *Built on values: Creating an enviable culture that outperforms the competition.* San Francisco, CA: Jossey-Bass.

Schein, E. H. (2004). *Organizational culture and leadership.* San Francisco, CA: Jossey-Bass.

Starratt, R. J. (2004). *Ethical leadership.* San Francisco, CA: John Wiley and Sons.

Chapter 5

Self-Management—Time, Personal Goals, and Organization

LEARNING OBJECTIVES

The student will

- create specific measurable life goals,
- adopt an attitude of thrift in relation to time,
- analyze a daily schedule of tasks to determine levels of urgency and importance,
- plan a weekly schedule of goal-related tasks,
- organize a workspace, and
- recognize loss of leaders' effectiveness when focus is lacking.

TIME

Time is the great equalizer of all humankind. No matter your standing, gender, ethnicity, education, or geographic location, we are all given only 24 hours per day. Even if you don't need all 24 hours on that particular day, you can't bank the extra hours in a "time savings account" to spend later on a busier day. Nor are you able to borrow time as a loan from a future day to study 4 extra hours for exam week. Therefore, how do you spend those 24 precious hours each day?

REFLECTION: DO YOU REALLY MANAGE TIME?

If someone questioned how you spend your money, you might respond with some of these statements:

> I made a budget and estimated the amounts I will need in each category of expenditures.

> I allow myself only so much cash to spend each day in the hopes I might have a bit left over to put toward something I want.

> After paying important bills such as food and housing, I deposit $100 into a savings account each month for a down payment on a house, car, vacation, and so on.

> I compare prices at several stores to ensure I get the best value for my money.

> I donate money to legitimate charitable causes, but I don't donate to every charitable request.

> I balance my checkbook/accounts statement each month and monitor it weekly to prevent an overdrawn balance.

However, if someone asked how you spend your time each week, would you say things like this?

> I study my to do list each week and record how much time I estimate it will take to complete each task.

> I allow myself so much time each day for my tasks in the hopes there might be some remaining for "me time" each day.

> At the beginning of each week, while making a daily schedule for each day of the week, I schedule my most productive time toward my most important goals.

> I prioritize my list of tasks each week and seek to only allocate my time to those items related to my personal mission.

> I allocate time to the most important goals first and rarely spend time on unproductive matters or abandon my plans when others tempt me with spontaneous opportunities.

> I review my weekly schedules and plans to ensure I am getting the most value for my minutes.

Can you identify the parallels between the two lists? Do you practice more items on the money list than the time list? If so, can you say you manage your time as well as your money?

DIAGNOSIS: FIND YOUR TARGET

Managing time is similar to managing money in several ways. Both are valuable and scarce resources. You "spend" each on the things you want. By spending it strategically, you hope it will bring you happiness and success in return. Each person has unique ideas regarding happiness and success; to capture those ideas as a summary statement of life goals is called a personal mission statement. In Stephen Covey's leadership book *The Seven Habits of Highly Effective People* (1989), Covey describes a personal mission statement as the summary statement of what you want to achieve in your life—your legacy. The mission statement describes the vision of a life well lived and how you anticipate others will remember you. To achieve the mission you envision, you must be intentional, take aim, identify all steps from the target to where you are now, and then allocate your time and effort accordingly to make the journey.

Life plans are not usually accomplished in a short period of time, and your attention span for long-term goals can be easily distracted (Steel, 2011). Unlike money, which people usually guard more frugally, time is easily given away. By not protecting and carefully allocating your time, you might push the attainment of your life plan even further down the road to a new timeframe and possibly a new target must be established. Without the target, it is easy to lose focus. With so many paths and distractions to choose from, you risk spending your time, and other resources, running down side streets and possibly finding yourself facing dead ends. Let's find your target by identifying the well-lived life and legacy you want to leave. The result of developing your personal mission will become your life plan. Once this is established, you will learn how to focus your time and resources on achieving your plan.

What do you hope to achieve? From the items listed in Table 5.1, select those you want to accomplish in your life.

Table 5.1 Lifetime Achievements

• Education	• Close Family Ties	• Lifelong Friends
• Strengthen the Human Condition	• Fun and Adventure	• Good Health
• Impact Local Community	• Travel the World	• Strong Faith
• Professional Success	• Loving Life Partner	• Economic Stability
• Act With Strong Moral Compass	• Create or Discover Something New	• Impact on a Global Scale

How does this achievement vision look in 5 years? In 10 years? In 20 years?

To help you with visioning achievements, use the category of education as an example.

In 5 years, you might complete bachelor's and master's degrees. In 10 years you might complete a special leadership development program. In 20 years you might be teaching in a professional development program for your professional association. Now review the items you selected from Table 5.1, review your choices and create a 5-, 10-, and 20-year vision for each achievement you selected. After creating each vision statement, narrow your list if the vision is weak and/or does not resonate with you.

Now craft a personal mission statement that captures the essence of the achievements you described. A mission statement must be memorable, so limit its length to one or two sentences.

My personal mission is _____

_____

_____.

To achieve your personal mission, goal statements must be crafted to define the route you will take to get to the desired results. Goal statements are written for long journeys (5–10 years) and the shorter journeys (1 year) necessary to achieve the bigger goals. Writing personal goals is covered here; then later in Chapter 8, organizational goals will be discussed. Writing and achieving goals is a very important skill for leaders. With paper or a computer, make a life plan goals table like the one shown below (Table 5.2). Rank in order from 1 to 10, with 1 being most important, up to 10 of the items listed above in Table 5.1 or any other life achievements you deem important.

The process of setting your goals is important; therefore, don't skip steps or gloss over details. Complete your version of the table below by responding to these three statements:

1. Spend some time thinking about your list of ranked life achievements in column 1.

2. Then determine what you will need to do to be successful in each. Describe in detail what success means for each objective. Describe what the end result of success in this achievement looks like. (Columns 2 and 3)

3. Put some timelines in place. At what age do you want to accomplish each item? How will you know you achieved success? (Columns 4 and 5)

Pause for a moment to review your work and prevent some common mistakes. Look at your table and the items in the first and second columns. When beginning

Table 5.2 Life Plan Goals

#1	#2	#3	#4	#5
List your desired life achievements. (Long-term goals)	List specific actions to take to succeed in these goals. (Short-term goals)	Describe what success looks like when achieved.	At what age/ year do you want to accomplish this?	How will you know you have achieved the result/success you desire?
1.				
2.				
3.				
4.				
5.				
6.				
7.				
8.				
9.				
10.				

this process, it is common to describe a large goal without breaking it down to the smaller specific actions that allow you to create short-term goals. Don't be discouraged by the large number of short-term goals you identified in this process. Finding the short-term goals can only mean greater success in the long-term goals. In fact, think like an architect. We are going to build more than a life plan (a house for the purposes of this example); we are going to describe its exterior, number of rooms, the layout, storage closets, flooring, roofline, windows, plumbing, electrical systems, and so on. Remember, if it is not in the plan, it doesn't get built. Let's also use an academic example. What are the differences in these three goals?

a. I will take and pass 15 credit hours each fall and spring semester this year.

b. I will make good grades in all my classes this year.

c. This 30-credit academic year, I will earn at least a B in each class, capture and file career-relevant material from the classes, and build a working relationship each semester with at least two faculty members who can write reference letters for me.

How different will the long- and short-term goals be for each of the three sample goals? Will writing statement b automatically get you the results for c? Of course not! And sadly, what students really want is goal statement c, but almost always compose a goal statement like a or b. Now toggle out of pause and think about what you really want—in detail!!! Remember, the contractor only orders the materials to build what you, the architect, describe. Don't just create the framework of your life plan goals; make each goal come alive!

Next, analyze the list of details and timelines; then select those that must be completed this year. From the timelines and specific goals, build your agenda for this year identifying those specific goals you want to accomplish. Hopefully, you will feel a sense of excitement as you see your life plan take shape. There will be some parts of your life plan that continue to be shrouded in mystery. For example, you may not know who your life partner will be, but you know you want to have one. For those goals, be as specific as you are able.

For those still unsure about committing to a life plan, try using this opportunity to practice the process. Identify a path you are considering and proceed to iron out the details as outlined in the remainder of this chapter. The effort you put into this process teaches both how to create a life plan and allows you to increase your edification regarding the path you are considering.

Review the time chart below (Table 5.3) to determine how you are currently spending your time. Recall the opening discussion of this chapter about the importance of managing our limited resources such as time and money. The next exercise will help determine how your time is spent. Look at the eight categories at the top of the time chart. These will help you sort what you did each hour into key categories. Number 7 is a category for important goals and achievements not covered in numbers 1 through 6. The *other* category (number 8) is one you will want to keep on your time chart to record those things you do daily that both don't fit under the named categories and are likely less important toward achieving goals. Tasks typically found in the other category include (eating fast food meals, naps, texting, surfing the net, playing video games, shopping, transportation time, hanging out, etc.). Make seven copies and label one for each day of the week, Sunday through Saturday. Start tomorrow and record how you spend your time for 7 consecutive 24-hour days noting specifically in each hour how you spent your time. Record the description of what you did every hour in the boxes of your table; you will likely have several things happening in the same hour and therefore, notes in each hour across several categories.

Now examine the results of how you spent your time each day.

- Did you accomplish each day what you wanted to accomplish? What did you want to accomplish but did not?
- Did you have weekly goals to accomplish?

Table 5.3 Time Chart: How Are You Spending Your Time?

Start Date _____ End Date _____

Hour by Hour	Day of the Week							
	#1	#2	#3	#4	#5	#6	#7	#8
	Family: Parents, spouse, children, siblings, grandparents	Education: In class or homework, reading, skill building	Health: Sleep, exercise, medical check-up, healthy meals	Work: Professional success	Friends, fun, recreation, and relaxation	Community: Faith, volunteer, clubs, neighbors	Additional long-term goals and short-term goals	Other: Texting, surfing Internet, fast food, commute, naps
7 – 8 a.m.								
8 – 9 a.m.								
9 – 10 a.m.								
10 – 11 a.m.								
11 – Noon								
Noon – 1 p.m.								
1 – 2 p.m.								
2 – 3 p.m.								
3 – 4 p.m.								
4 – 5 p.m.								
5 – 6 p.m.								
6 – 7 p.m.								
7 – 8 p.m.								
8 – 9 p.m.								
9 – 10 p.m.								
10 – 11 p.m.								
11 p.m. – 12 a.m.								

- What did you do each day to move long- or short-term goals forward?
- Are your days balanced or are some days saturated with to-do items while others are recovery from the never-ending list?
- What surprised you?
- Does the other category seem to capture more time than you'd prefer?
- Is there a category in need of additional time?
- Step back and look at all seven daily tables. Are you satisfied with your time expenditures?
- Are there other items to note? What are the lessons to learn?

Now that you have evaluated 7 days worth of time, you can begin to see the choices you make spending your 24-hour allocation. Ultimately, you are the one who says yes to how you spend your time. What goals are you saying yes to? Your weekly time allocation chart will identify these details.

As good stewards of time allocations, review the time allocation chart for the activities in your week and their connections to the goals you have in your life plan. Here are some tips for evaluating the importance of your activities:

1. Weekly and daily activities that connect to the goals in your life plan are important. Activities that facilitate several key life goals are the most important of all.

2. Fun, vacation, relaxation, and spontaneity are important too—to a point. Everyone needs relaxation time: time to read, go out with friends, spend time at the beach, weekend ski trips, and watch favorite TV shows. However, you know when fun time becomes a time waster. You start watching TV just because it is on. Then there is the computer or smart phone. You open and read every email, surfing through sale offers you don't need. Or you are on Facebook posting what you had for dinner. Then there are the video games ...

3. Not everything is important, and we need to learn from our past experiences and mistakes to eliminate what is not important. *It is OK to say no, especially when you are excited and committed to your long-term goals!*

4. Don't confuse other people's urgencies for your important matters. It's not appropriate to be rude, but you can offer to talk with them at a mutually convenient time.

If I were to ask you if you spent the time well, you would not be able to answer that because you have not declared your intent. In other words, what were your goals to accomplish in that week? Or month? Or year? Just like money is spent based on needs and future plans, time should be spent on needs and future plans.

Focus on Your Personal Mission

Mission statements declare the intent and direction for our lives. It is the essence of Covey's (1989) "Habit Two: Begin With the End in Mind." In other words, recognizing what success and the steps it takes to achieve it is keeping the mind focused on the end goal. A mission provides a purpose and a reason to be productive. Productivity can be defined as the ability to generate worthwhile effort, relationships, programs, services, and so on. It answers the question "What did you do today?" The personal mission statement becomes the compass for guiding the leader in how time and scarce resources are spent.

- Have you ever noticed a lack of focus in the choices you make? This might be translated as spending time on things that do not seem to be connected to your purpose. Busyness does not mean you are operating with a mission.
- Do you struggle with identifying which choices to make? You may be spending too much time in the debate about which choice to make with your time and resources. Spend a little time clarifying your purpose; then you can determine a clear choice.
- Do you simply decide not to decide and allow others to completely influence your choices? When confusion reigns, it might feel easier to let others decide how you spend your time or equally bad, even taking the first offer without weighing the options against your purpose.

A lack of purpose and focus does negatively impact your personal productivity. The process of living by a personal mission statement sharpens your focus, allows you to have clarity on the important goals you want to achieve, and influences how you spend precious time and resources. The results are not just increased productivity but personal satisfaction and a sense of balance derived from getting what you desire out of life. Like the tires on your car, your life requires alignment. Imagine having personal alignment from the choices you make to the results you want to achieve.

Review the personal mission statement you wrote earlier in this chapter. Now that you have written goals and analyzed your time, does it still describe the essence of your life's key accomplishments? A personal mission statement encompasses both the personal and professional sides of you. Does yours reflect both sides? Take a few minutes and polish this important declaration. Place it where you will see it every day. As you continue to develop as a leader, you may find that your mission needs to be adjusted here and there. Mission statements need to flex as your life journeys forward. Don't be afraid to capture it in words now. You will modify it as the roles in your life evolve. Living by a mission statement is a lifelong endeavor. To view an example that has been polished over time, the author's mission statement is below:

> I will prioritize the people in my life through my roles as spouse, mother, daughter, friend, and teacher. I will live my life in a way that intellectually challenges myself, and others, to become the servant leaders our world so desperately needs. I will commit to the habits that ensure my own well-being, as I cannot give to others if I do not take care of myself spiritually, physically, and emotionally.

Within my mission statement, you can identify my key roles and complete the what, who, and how statements outlined below. For example, writing this book aligns with my mission to teach by relaying my experience and research to you, the student.

1. What my goals are?

2. Who I want to influence?

3. How my time is allocated?

Your personal mission statement does not need to look or sound anything like mine because your experiences and life's dreams are your own. From your mission statement, can you complete the what, who, and how statements:

1. What are your goals?

2. Who do you want to influence?

3. How is your time allocated?

When you are intentionally focused on your personal mission, you will be able to allocate your time and resources without guilt in ways that bring the results you desire as well as make you feel productive. The importance of correctly apportioning your time allocations has a direct impact on your ability to achieve your goals. The only way to know if your allocation is enough is to analyze your effectiveness and progress toward goals.

PRESCRIPTION: BECOMING INTENTIONAL THROUGH PLANNING

Now that you have diagnosed weaknesses in your current methods for finding your leadership targets, how do you write a detailed and specific long- and short-term goal and allocate the time to make your mission and long- and short-term goals a reality?

PERSONAL GOALS

What are your goals? Are your goals in writing or just something you think about? You have learned you must be specific, detailed, and think like an architect. There are even more skills to learn about the topic of goals, specifically how to write one. In the world of leaders, goals are written to describe gaps, gaps between what is now and what the leader wants the target to be. An example of a goal statement written to describe a gap follows:

> In the next academic year, I will increase my academic performance from 50% final grades of B or better for 30 credit hours and no relationships built with faculty members for recommendation letters to final grades of 100% B or better and at least two relationships built with faculty members for letters of recommendation.

You will recognize this goal as one discussed earlier in the introduction to the topic of goals. Can you identify the gap in the revised goal statement? It is very clear and allows no question regarding the current versus the desired state of academic performance. The formula for writing the goal as a gap statement is as follows: From X (the current level) to Y (desired level) by Z (when the change is to be completed).

The importance of being so specific lies in the universal lack of commitment to accountability. You have been victim to a friend's or colleague's waffle words when he or she has attempted to shade a commitment by such statements as,

- I never said *when* I would complete this, or
- I didn't say I would increase grades in *all* my classes, or
- I just meant I would *try* to do that.

Using a gap statement that is specific and written to the formula prevents most of the waffle words when it is time to measure results. As a leader, you are frequently measured by your results, even for personal goals. What follows is an example of how to use a gap statement to write a specific, achievable goal.

Long-term goal: Find a life partner

Short-term goal: Increase the pool of quality candidates and the potential for meeting candidates.

Formula: Starting today, in the next 6 months, I will cease the strategy of random in-person and online introduction to potential dating partners to a strategy of determining qualities I do and do not desire, identifying locations (both virtual and in-person) where such candidates are located, and adjust my schedule to accommodate increased communication and meetings.

- Determine and write a list of attributes your life partner must have.
- Determine and write a list of deal-breaking characteristics your life partner must not have.
- Analyze where such a pool of your potential life partner candidates might congregate, live, work, socialize, and so on.
- Find opportunities to be present in such locations and activities.
- Accept or invite communications from this candidate pool.
- Accept or invite dates from new candidate pool.
- Revise list of attributes and deal-breaking characteristics as you interact with potential candidates.

This is an intentionally detailed goal statement and plan of measurable short-term goals that will increase the pool of quality candidates needed to find a life partner. To achieve long-term goals, having a thoughtful detailed set of short-term goals is the best method to succeed. Without taking the short-term goal steps and meeting those goals, the chances of finding a life partner from random opportunities, not intentional, without attributes you want and need, will likely be unsuccessful. Yes, there can be that wishful hope of a romantic, fate-driven encounter to achieve this type of goal. However, do you understand that by not creating short-term goals as a path to long-term goals, you are leaving the accomplishment of your big goals, and ultimately your mission statement, to a romantic, chance-driven encounter? Leadership demands more than chance and happenstance.

In addition to writing goals in a manner that avoids ambiguity and promotes accountability, it is important to write goals so that they can be measured and verified by multiple eyes. If a group observed the process of increasing the pool of life partner candidates, would they all agree that the steps had been accomplished, the pool was a quality pool for the seeker, and increased time was allocated to facilitate the process? Given the specificity in the statement, you would agree that those steps could be observed, measured, and verified.

As leaders, it is not enough to just complete important goals; important goals deserve to be completed with excellence. Good enough is no longer good enough. Plan time to be excellent. We often forget to schedule and monitor the time needed to accomplish what we identify as most important. It is easier to set small goals and schedule small tasks such as stop at the grocery, pay two bills, and take the car for maintenance. How will you schedule and monitor time for improved grades, improved relationships with family members, or improvement in your leadership ability? The key is to write goals using the formula, break down the large goals into short-term goals, and then schedule those action items into your week

Using a Calendar

The next step in this process is learning how to schedule and monitor a weekly plan. As you have learned in this chapter, you have the power to control your allocation of time. The week is the cycle by which you allocate your time. Successful time managers select a specific day and time each week to plan and map their weekly calendar. Select a consistent planning day and time for most weeks of the year. Choose a location to hold this weekly appointment with yourself; collect all needed materials:

- 12 month calendar with space to write, not just appointments, but also tasks for the week
- Tools to maintain the weekly and daily calendar (computer, smart phone, tablet, paper notebook, etc., should be portable and convenient to keep it with you at all times)
- Copy of your mission statement and the life plan goals you just created
- Copy of work goals
- List of personal, work, or family events (birthdays, reunions, and holidays)

Allow yourself about an hour the first time you do this; then 30 minutes is generally what it takes to maintain the weekly plan on a regular basis. Start by reviewing your mission statement and long-term goals. Determine the critical things to accomplish this year. Repeat for your work/school goals. Then ask yourself this question: "What is the one thing you can do to move your goal forward this week?" There may be more than one thing you can do this week, but just think, if you could move forward 52 steps on your goals each year, how successful you would be? The key to this weekly calendar is to allocate time to the important items from the top five of your life plan. Is that how you currently set your annual and weekly plans? Be especially clear and intentional regarding what constitutes an important classification. Most important are goal and mission-related items. Just because an item is on your to do list or sitting in an email request does not mean you should prioritize it ahead of other items. As the person in control of your time, ask the question, "Is this goal or mission related?" Rethinking priorities is always good. Stay in communication with your work-team, family, or others who may have a stake in this task. Leaders share how they choose to prioritize.

Be prepared; accept unexpected things happen. Count on it! Plan not to schedule every available minute you have; keeping at least an hour of open time each day allows you to flex for the unexpected, accommodate for a bad estimate of how long you thought an item would take to complete, or to add an additional item to complete because you have the gift of time. Learn to estimate how long a task will really take. That is a skill set that comes with awareness, experience, and practice. We all know that "just a minute" person whose minutes are nothing short of a 30 minute delay on a good day.

Calendars are not only to remind of appointments with others, but to keep appointments with yourself, allowing you to accomplish your important goals. Every task on your to do list should have a place on your weekly calendar or a planned date for the following week. It is too easy to give up commitments to yourself to tend to other people's needs. In fact, promises to ourselves are the most frequent ones we break. If you use a weekly planning system consistently, you will be more productive and find it easier to recover when life throws a curve ball.

In addition, use of a regular daily planning time to make adjustments to your weekly calendar is necessary to accommodate life's changes. Life is fluid; plan on 5 to 10 minutes at the end of each day to review the next day's agenda to see if it is still appropriate and focused on your goals and priorities.

ORGANIZATION

The average American worker loses at least an hour everyday hunting for papers, files, keys, and phones in order to complete a required task (Bruch & Ghoshal, 2002). Assuming these organization-challenged behaviors began during the college years or before, imagine how much time leaders could gain by not losing papers, files, assignments, keys, and phones and how many hours of your life that totals. If this problem could be solved, the workplace, home, or student day would have the gift of a seemingly extra hour everyday!

REFLECTION: THE PAIN OF LIVING IN CHAOS

Do you have organization systems in place to prevent these frustrating, time consuming delays from happening to your day?

For example, you know you saved your presentation to a thumb drive last night, but there are six of these mini memory sticks in your backpack and they all look alike. It is going to cost you about 20 minutes to search for the presentation document. You are going to look so unprofessional in front of your new boss. Or you have the leader of the study group's phone number on the post-it note she gave you last week now stuck to your bathroom mirror. You are late for the meeting, and you failed to enter her number in your cell phone. Will they wait for you before disappearing into the depths of the library? Or there was a guest speaker in class last semester who mentioned the possibility of summer jobs in your field and you even got a business card, but there are about a dozen dog-eared business cards from various strangers in the bottom of your computer bag and you have no idea who any of the contacts are. Or you received a very nice email from an adjunct professor three semesters ago regarding a paper you wrote. It would be a great recommendation for graduate school. Unfortunately you can't remember the adjunct's name, you didn't file or print the email, and a key word search isn't turning up anything relevant.

Organization is the challenge that plagues everyone. You can be very organized in some aspects of your life and disorganized in others. What can you do to get organized and save time?

DIAGNOSIS: WHERE ARE YOUR ORGANIZING TROUBLE SPOTS?

The focus of this section is school and work organization. First let's determine what you tend to lose or misplace and how frequently. Use this list to check off the item and select a letter to show how often you are looking for it. D = daily; W = weekly; M = monthly; O = occasionally/a few times a year.

	D	W	M	O
Keys (house, apartment, office, car)	D	W	M	(O)
Cell phone	(D)	W	M	O
Glasses	D	W	(M)	O
Pen/pencil	(D)	W	M	O
Library book/text book	D	W	M	(O)
Handouts or notes from class/meeting	D	W	M	(O)
Current paper project files	D	W	M	(O)
Bills	D	W	M	(O)
Important email	(D)	W	M	O
Computer document or file	D	(W)	M	O
Important "snail mail"	(D)	W	M	O
Business cards/new contacts	(D)	W	M	O
Clear desk work space	(D)	W	M	O
Empty file space	(D)	W	M	O

If you have nothing on this list that registers at the D, W, or M levels, you are doing very well and are encouraged to email me with any tips or practices you have adopted. However, it is likely this list has touched at least one trouble area for most of you. Missing items is a signal you have not created a home or a station for where these important items reside. Organizing is not only about neatness but also about whether your space functions well (Morgenstern, 1998). When items reside where you use them, they are easier to find and then put away. If there is little storage near your work surfaces, then you must be creative about storing things in boxes or drawers based on functions.

Morgenstern (1998, p. 15) states that clutter occurs for three reasons:

1. Technical Errors – Failure to arrange work surfaces and storage by function.

2. External Realities – Inability to resolve the lack of storage issues inherent in the design of the space.

3. Psychological Obstacles – Internal forces that sabotage systems you create.

Morgenstern makes several recommendations for fixing these trouble spots in the following section.

PRESCRIPTION: TAMING THE MESS

First, begin with the overall amount of stuff you keep in general. This is not news to you. Clean out and throw away unnecessary items. In your planning schedule, set aside 2 or 3 days semiannually to complete this task. Most individuals try to accomplish this over the winter holidays, in the spring as taxes are compiled, or at the end of the school year. Clean out frequency is actually needed more than once a year. Otherwise, it becomes too large a job and is avoided. Combining a clean out with holidays, taxes, or end-of-school-year activities is also overwhelming. Because those other events have so much stress surrounding them, the clean out is what usually is eliminated. By setting a more frequent clean-out schedule, not affiliated with other high-stress events, the activity doesn't become the dreaded weeklong cleaning marathon.

Is your desk a mini office supply store? Growing up in the public schools, the student desk was where supplies were kept in the younger grades. Lockers and backpacks became that storage place during middle and high school years. In many home offices, study spaces or workplace desks/cubicles continues those same views of a desk as a supply cabinet carrying forward. In fact, the most effective desk holds only the bare minimum of office supplies (one of each essential item) and uses the majority of its drawer space to hold the various project files that are active and current. Once a project is complete, it should be filed, not in your office, but in a filing space away from your workspace. If you are using electronic files, you should move the folder(s) away from the active files and clearly label for ease of retrieval, key word searches, and so on. What do you really need on the surface and at your fingertips? The more decorative bins, tins, and cups you collect, the more clutter will be stored on the top of your desk. This always results in less workspace. How many pens and pencils do you really need? How many of those on your desk even write? Can you contain all those technology cords with electrical ties to keep the trail of wires at bay? How many old cell phone chargers or digital camera cords are stashed in a drawer for technology you don't own or use any longer? How old is the phone book on your desk? Do you use it or Google it? Then there is that stack of technology manuals for the old version of Windows you stopped using in 2005. Recycle what you can, and throw away the rest. To get rid of old electronics, many communities and universities host technology disposal days. Your office filing cabinet should be purged regularly for items no longer active or useful. When you make a label for a file, put a date on it. That will be your first clue as to the age of the file's contents. Keep an index at the front of each file drawer to itemize its contents.

A project is never complete until the related files (paper and electronic) have been reviewed, duplications and draft documents removed, and other nonessential items tossed. If you own a scanner, paper files can become electronic, requiring as soft copies almost no space. Always include this clean-out activity as part of the project plan. If you are a student, school folders and notebooks should be purged as well. Create folders or notebooks for important research papers, notes, or handouts that might prove useful in later classes or your career. Do keep names and contact information for faculty members, class speakers, and internship supervisors who might become references or future job contacts.

Labels, titles, legibility, and a filing system with input from all the users are keys to the ability to retrieve older files. Work with your colleagues to create a mutually agreeable filing system. Multiple employees may need access to current or older documents given the team approach of so many workplaces. Agree on the title of the file and documents, include a date, and if there are hard copies—you may choose to color code. If a paper file is removed for use, agree on what is left in its stead so others can find the folder if there are simultaneous needs. Determine how long a folder is allowed to be checked out or who is allowed to have paper or electronic copies. Determine the life span of the contents. Some offices have legal or policy concerns that determine how long a file must be maintained.

Contact information for your growing network of professional colleagues is important to keep current. Several computer software programs save contacts and provide places for you to note when and why you last contacted that person. This can be very helpful for clients, vendors, community collaborators, and other stakeholders in your organization. Business cards are a common way for colleagues to quickly share contact information at meetings and conferences. Computer programs can scan an electronic business card and input the information to an electronic contact list. That is very convenient. However, there are still many paper business cards making the rounds and handling that data is important. There is a three-step process for handling the paper business card. (1) Write on the card when and where you received it and another detail about why this person or the organization could be important to you. (2) Establish a place in your wallet, purse, computer bag, and so on where such business cards will be housed. (3) During your regular weekly planning session, record this person's contact information into your computer's contact list. Syncing your smart phone contacts at this time is also a good idea.

Keeping up with notes can be challenging as well. Practiced habits of keeping up with school notes do not seem to carry over to workplace notes. Those three–ring binders and spiral notebooks are not so commonly used in the workplace. Generally, those organizers tend to corral class notes for the duration of a semester. In the workplace, meeting notes are a different issue and their longevity expands beyond a semester. Employees can go to meeting after meeting with a legal pad in hand. Notes can get buried as pages are turned to reveal the next clean sheet of paper. Or notes are taken on tablets and never connected to the project file. Time to organize or transcribe the notes is not allocated in the weekly calendar, which results in stacks of legal pads on employee desks with a myriad of notes over the course of several weeks. The chance of finding anything when you need it in that sea of paper or computer files is slim. As electronic tablets become more sophisticated, pen and paper notes may soon become antiquated. However, note-taking technology is evolving via script software but is adequate only if using a stylus or typing skills are good. Even electronic notes require systematic file names and the ability to store with the overall project file.

Last but not least, turn your attention to the briefcase/bag you take back and forth to work everyday. It is easy to fill it with good intensions every evening and then not even open it. The file, tablet, or jump drive sits there enjoying the ride each day until it is wedged between other files, binder clips, and miscellaneous items. "What's in your bag?" Morgenstern (1998) strongly recommends cleaning out your workbag weekly and adopting an ironclad rule: "Never take work home unless you have scheduled the time to complete it into your daily and weekly plan."

Finding objects you have misplaced is aggravating. Study your patterns to determine which rooms in your home you inhabit just prior to departure for work or school as well as when you come home. Establish a limited number of places you are "allowed" to put your keys, cell phone, and so. By adhering to a short list of locales, you will greatly reduce the number of potential places such items might be located.

SUMMARY

Learning the self-management skills of personal mission statements, goal setting, planning, organizing, and the discipline of focus are important to everyone's success. They are especially important to leaders. How can you expect the members of your team to use their time wisely, take deadlines seriously, demonstrate accountability, and create a work environment all can respect if the leader does not role model those same behaviors.

A favorite supervisor once said, "A deadline is not a guideline." In the world of serving clients, collaborating with community organizations, and requesting funds from government and other sponsors, time is a critical factor. No one wants to learn this lesson the hard way. A colleague's performance review score was lowered because her boss expected an "on time" assignment to be submitted at least a day early. Another friend has a supervisor who locks the door 5 minutes prior to the start time of a staff meeting. No one enters late.

Just what is the focus of your time priorities? Have you put those goals and your personal mission in writing? Do you look at them weekly or even daily? Spontaneity is wonderful and has a good place in your life, but focus on mission and goals enables you to achieve at your highest level. All leaders are expected to achieve with personal excellence.

Finding your notes and other important documents as well as keeping an office space that you can actually work in is a minimum expectation in most work sites. When your mother asked you to clean your room, little did you know she was preparing you for the world of work and leadership. Clean up, clean out, and find a home in your office for the things you use. Time and space are too valuable to waste. Time, focus, and organization in the working world are serious business.

REFERENCES

Bruch, H., & Ghoshal, S. (2002). Beware the busy manager. *Harvard Business Review*. Retrieved from http://www.hbr.org

Covey, S. R. (1989). *The seven habits of highly effective people: Powerful lessons in personal change.* New York, NY: Simon and Schuster.

Morgenstern, J. (1998). *Organizing from the inside out: The foolproof system for organizing your home, your office, and your life.* New York, NY: Harry Holt.

Steele, P. (2011). *The procrastination equation: How to stop putting things off and start getting things done.* New York, NY: HarperCollins.

Chapter 6

Organizational Management—Team Building, Management, and Motivation

LEARNING OBJECTIVES

The student will

- evaluate the importance of team building in today's workplace,
- describe leadership actions that build teams as well as leadership actions that impede teams,
- differentiate the roles and processes of responsible managers,
- explain the procrastination equation, and
- compare and contrast intrinsic and extrinsic motivation and determine which is most influential in workplace engagement.

TEAM BUILDING

Working in teams has become the way of the 21st century workplace. Search committees interview potential employees about their accomplishments in a team environment to ensure, if hired, the candidate's integration into the team will be seamless and the new hire will collaboratively drive the team in a positive direction. In 2006, the Center for Creative Leadership conducted their annual leadership survey, which revealed that 91% of top-tier managers believe teams are central to the success of organizations (Martin & Bal, 2007). FranklinCovey's (2012) ongoing study of workplace productivity uncovered that teams contributed 35% of the effort toward the organization's goals. Work teams, committees, advisory groups, task forces, cross-functional teams, and so on are prevalent in all sectors of the workplace.

Lean budgets, a by-product of a tightened economy, continue to force organizations to operate with leaner staffs that can meet the organizations' diverse needs, eliminating the need for specialized departments. The quantity and quality of programs and services required in today's marketplace demands an "all hands on deck" approach. The old adage, "two heads are better than one," becomes real through cross-functional work teams comprised of employees with diverse skill sets and experiences. Organizations face complex problems; therefore, it is not uncommon for groups comprised of several locally, nationally, or globally based organizations to work together in search of solutions.

REFLECTION: YOUR TEAM EXPERIENCES

You work as a member of a team in all facets of your life, from work, to school, and in your community. In spite of this daily interaction with groups and teams, it is not uncommon for you to feel uneasy engaging in these experiences. Rest assured, your feelings are not uncommon. Maybe you had to deal with an unpleasant group member, believed the group leader was inefficient or ineffective, felt "stuck" doing all the work, or saw the team leader take all the credit. Conversely, maybe your group experience was energizing. Everyone pulled his or her weight, great ideas flowed, and the end result not only garnered a solution to the original problem but also left you feeling inspired and prepared for your next group project. Lencioni (2002) describes true teamwork as rare and difficult to achieve, but not impossible. Lencioni and others encourage us to achieve this state of true teamwork because it is so powerful and can make a measurable difference for team member happiness as well as the success of the organization. Answer these questions from the "Team Leadership Questionnaire" (Morgeson, DeRue, & Karam, 2010) regarding your last experience working in a team:

1. What was the purpose or mission of the team? Was the mission clear to everyone on the team? Did everyone agree on the mission?

2. Was the selection for the team based on people's talents and skills? Were the members of your team aware or made aware of your talents and skills?

3. Were you aware, or made aware, of the others' talents and skills? How were the team's roles assigned? Were the decisions based on talents and skills?

4. Did the team have the talents and skills needed to accomplish the goal(s)? Was training provided or offered?

5. Did the team establish goals, expectations, and a work plan (sometimes referred to as a team contract)?

6. Did the organization leader meet with the team? Did the leader provide support or assistance with group identified challenges?

7. Was progress monitored and feedback provided to team members?

8. Were new ideas welcomed?

9. Were adequate resources provided?

10. Did the team leader promote the work of the team within the organization? With outside stakeholders? Was credit given to the team leader, the team, or individuals?

11. Based on your assessment, was it a good group work experience? Why or why not?

Now, reflect beyond the quality of the work experience; did you feel part of a team? Maybe you were just part of a work group but were hoping to be part of a team? How important is the sense of belonging in a work team? How important is feeling that your ideas are important to the group? What is the difference between a team and a group? Can a group transition into a team?

How does leadership play a role in work groups and work teams? Does the leader's role change between the two? If you want to lead a work team, what steps should you take? How will you help your group transition to "team" status? What does it mean to be a successful team leader?

DIAGNOSIS: WORK TEAM OR WORK GROUP

Susan Wheelan's (2010, p. 2) definition of work groups and work teams:

> A work group is composed of members who are striving to create a shared view of goals and to develop an efficient and effective organizational structure in which to accomplish those goals. A work group becomes a team when shared team goals have been established and effective methods to accomplish those team goals are in place.

It would seem obvious for organizations to want to rally around the success of work groups given the importance and size of the workload most groups carry in the workplace. Those who study and coach work groups have found otherwise. Wheelan's (2010) 35 years of experience as a research analyst and writer focused on work groups and teams revealed that only 46% of 700 work teams, in existence for 6 months or longer, were capable of contributing to their organization's goals. Only 17% were what she considered to be high performing teams.

Wheelan (2010) also identified organizational support for work teams as a key factor in their success. Yet upper management rarely invests in actions that will make the difference in group performance. It is like planting seeds for a harvest in poor soil. Without a quality growing medium, fertilizer, sun, and rain, the seeds will not produce a harvest. Likewise, work groups will not produce their intended results if the organization's leadership does not become a student of successful work teams. Below are Wheelan's recommendations to positively influence group performance by organizational leadership:

- Clearly define the organization's mission.
- Support innovation.
- Expect success.
- Value superior quality and service.
- Pay attention to detail.
- Value group recommendations.
- Set clear expectations for group output, quality, timing, and pacing.
- Reward group and teamwork rather than individual performance.

Using a meta-analysis, Morgeson et al. (2010) report a perspective about team leadership concerning the source of leadership. Their report also outlines key leadership processes that result in increased team performance as well as the phases of team activity. Their findings indicate team leadership is not from a single source but from many sources. Work teams today address complex problems and have many needs that are best met from multiple sources of leadership, both internal and external to the group. These leaders may have formal roles such as project managers, team advisors, or department managers. However, not all work team leaders are assigned a formal leadership role within the organization. Examples of informal leadership include a team member leading through a shared leadership approach or stakeholders who emerge as champions of the team and have no direct responsibility for the group's performance. Team leadership functions consist of two phases of team activity: first, a transition phase and then an action phase. The list in Table 6.1 details the various functions team leaders play in each phase.

Wheelan (2010, pp. 26–31) also identified phases in work group to work team development and transition. She compared the growth of a group to the growth stages of human development from children to adults.

Table 6.1   Team Leadership Functions

Transition Phase	Action Phase
Compose team	Monitor team
Define mission	Manage team boundaries
Establish expectations and goals	Challenge team
Structure and plan	Perform team task
Train and develop team	Solve problems
Sense-making	Provide resources
Provide feedback	Encourage team self-management
	Support social climate

Source: Morgeson F. P., DeRue, D. S., & Karam, E. P. (2010). Leadership in teams: A functional approach to understanding leadership structures and processes. *Journal of Management*, *36*(5), 10. doi: 10.1177/0149206309347376.

Wheelan's (2010) stages 1 and 2 are comparable to Morgeson's et al. (2010) transition state and Wheelan's stages 3 and 4 are comparable to Morgeson's et al. action stage. All groups go through these stages as they develop into teams. Some groups move through these stages several times as the growth to become a team is not linear, but cyclical. Teams will also cycle back into previous stages as membership changes, organization goals evolve, and external demands impact strategic plans.

Using the columns that outline each stage's characteristics in Table 6.2, you should be able to determine the growth stages and organizational support needed of work groups you encounter. Facilitating the transition from work group to work team requires engagement from all stakeholders of the team. Team members, leaders, and the organizational leadership team all play an important role. It is when the group develops as a team that effectiveness increases exponentially.

PRESCRIPTION: HIGH PERFORMANCE TEAMS

As with any change process, becoming an effective group member requires understanding what behaviors are associated with effective team members and effective teams. Knowing what high performance team behaviors look like gives team members a target for change. Again, Wheelan (2010) details these attributes in Table 6.3.

Some organizations believe it is helpful to gather the troops for an outing: bowling, rock climbing, intra-office softball, or building a float for community parades. These social events are important in establishing esprit dé corps,

Table 6.2 Work Group to Work Team Phases

Stage 1 Dependency and Inclusion	Stage 2 Counterdependency and Fighting	Stage 3 Trust and Structure	Stage 4 Work
Members concerned with personal safety	Emerging conflicts about values	Goal clarity and consensus increase	Members clear and agree on group goals
Need for acceptance and inclusion by others	Disagreements about goals and tasks	Roles and tasks of members adjust to increase likelihood of goal achievement	Tasks require team, not individual effort
Fear rejection	Feelings of group-member safety allows dissent to occur		Members clear about and accept roles and status
Communication is tentative and polite	Dissatisfaction with roles	Communication structure more flexible	Role assignments match talents and skills
Members want dependable and directive leadership	Members challenge leader and each other	Leader's role less directive, more consultative	Delegation is prevailing leadership style
View leader as competent and benevolent	Subgroups and coalitions form	Communication content more task oriented	Communication structure matches demands of task
Expect leader to provide direction and personal safety	Attempts at conflict management begin	Pressures to conform increase	Open communication structure, all members participate, are heard
Do not challenge leader	Goal clarification begins	Helpful deviation tolerated	Appropriate ratio of task and supportive communication
Group's goals are not clear to members, nor do they try to clarify	Member engagement increases	Coalitions and subgroups continue to emerge	Team gets, gives, uses feedback about effectiveness
Do not express disagreement with initial goals	Group intolerance of subgroups and coalitions is evident	Tolerance of subgroups and coalitions increases	Spends time defining and discussing problems and decisions
Initial role assignments not based on members' talents and skills	Deviation from emerging group norms begins	Cohesion and trust increase	Uses participatory decision making
High member compliance and conformity	Conflict resolution increases trust and cohesion	Member satisfaction increases	Implements and evaluates decisions and solutions

Communication tracks through leader	Conformity decreases	Cooperation more evident	High voluntary conformity
Engagement limited to vocal few	If conflict resolution efforts are successful, consensus about group goals increases near end of this stage	Individual commitment to group goals is high	Task-related deviance tolerated
Minimal conflict		Greater division of labor	Team expects success
Lack of group structure and organization		More conflict, but managed effectively	Team encourages innovation
Group commitment based on identification with leader		Group works to clarify and build a group structure facilitating goal achievement	Team norms support high performance and quality
Subgroups and coalitions are rare			Members pay attention to details
			Team accepts subgroups as well as coalition formation; integrated into team
			Team contains smallest number members to accomplish goals
			Subgroups work on important projects, rewarded by team
			Tasks contain variety and challenge
			Members are cooperative, team is cohesive
			Periods of conflict frequent but brief due to effective communication and conflict management strategies

Source: Adapted from Wheelan, S. A. (2010). *Creating effective teams: A guide for members and leaders* (pp. 26–31). Thousand Oaks, CA: Sage.

Table 6.3 High Performance Teams

High Performance Team Members	High Performance Teams
Don't blame others for group problems.	Members are clear about and agree with the team's goals.
Encourage the process of goal, role, and task clarification.	Tasks are appropriate to team rather than individual solutions.
Encourage adoption of an open communication structure in which all member input and feedback is heard.	Members are clear about and accept their roles; role assignments match member's abilities.
Promote an appropriate ratio of task and supportive communication.	Leadership style matches team's development level.
Promote the use of effective problem-solving and decision-making procedures.	Open communication structure enables all members to participate.
Encourage the establishment of norms that support productivity, innovation, and freedom of expression.	Team gets, gives, and uses feedback about its effectiveness and productivity.
Go along with norms that promote group effectiveness and productivity.	Team spends time defining and discussing important problems and decisions.
Promote group cohesion and cooperation.	Team uses effective decision-making strategies.
Interact with others outside the group in ways that promote group integration and cooperation within the organizational context.	Team implements and evaluates solutions and decisions.
Support the leader's efforts to facilitate group goal achievement.	Subgroups are integrated into teams as a whole.
	Team members have sufficient time together to develop a mature working unit and to accomplish the team's goals.
	Team norms encourage high performance, quality, success, and innovation.
	Periods of conflict are frequent but brief, and the group has effective conflict management strategies.

Source: Adapted from Wheelan, S. A. (2010). *Creating effective teams: A guide for members and leaders* (pp. 71–76). Thousand Oaks, CA: Sage.

as well as achieving interpersonal understanding, friendship, and fun in the workplace. However, they do not replace the best practices and behaviors for high performing teams.

Leaders must exercise patience, be supportive, coach, as well as be able to let go (become less controlling) as the needs and maturity of the group evolve. Although each work group is different, allow approximately 6 to 9 months for a group to begin to approach stage 4. Help the group members learn to manage the group themselves and understand the four stages of group development. Understanding the process helps everyone work through the stages instead of assuming the conflicts are inappropriate and interpreting the disagreements as personal attacks. In fact, Wheelan (2010) suggests three productive forms of group intervention if a group becomes stuck in a stage:

- Goal setting – helps refocus the group on why they exist
- Feedback – course corrections are accepted more readily if delivered as regular feedback
- Attention to group development issues – keep the future team informed on their progress as a team as well as the tasks and goals

Lencioni (2002, p. 97) describes five group dysfunctions that impede their ability to function as a team. The diagram in Figure 6.1 shows the five issues in a pyramid structure. They are not to be treated as linear stages but instead as an interdependent chain of qualities that prevent a group from achieving high performance. One broken link creates a problem that touches all levels of the model.

Although a simpler model of team development, Lencioni (2002) emphasizes similar recommendations as Wheelan's (2010) detailed framework. Lencioni (2002) describes several group-member behaviors and leader actions to avoid the five

Figure 6.1   Five Group Dysfunctions

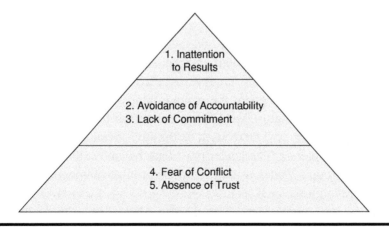

Source: Lencioni, P. (2002). *The five dysfunctions of a team: A leadership fable* (p. 188). San Francisco, CA: Jossey-Bass.

dysfunctional levels. Achieving trust (level 1) requires shared group experiences over time. It also requires a leader who shares authentic vulnerability and creates a work environment that encourages and does not punish vulnerability among the group. Only when you are a part of a group that has established a level of trust, will you allow yourself to be vulnerable by admitting your mistakes and weaknesses. Trust makes conflict (level 2) possible. All relationships require productive conflict to make good decisions and be able to grow. Conflict regarding ideas and priorities should be welcomed as opposed to personal attacks, back stabbing, and office politics. Therefore, it is imperative for the leader to create a safe environment for group members to be honest when sharing their opinions. To do this, group members will have to resolve previous disagreements to prevent old animosity from contaminating the group's dynamics. Fear of making a decision due to risk aversion or fear of conflict is common for groups at level 2.

Healthy debates lead to buy-in and commitment from group members (level 3). Knowing your opinion was heard and considered enables you to feel committed to the group's proposed solution, even if it was not your first choice. Lack of commitment can occur when a group practices consensus as their ideal decision strategy. Groups unable to resolve controversy and who believe that 100% agreement is necessary for a decision will bring the forward motion of any group to a standstill. Consensus does not require 100% agreement about the decision but instead requires 100% agreement that all members felt heard and thus able to support the decision. Leaders can facilitate this process by bringing clarity to the issues and decisions. Then the leader can compile the information and decisions in time-lines, which outline the group's goals and their plan for execution to all the group's members. Holding everyone accountable to the decisions and the time-line becomes infinitely less challenging when everyone has a clear understanding regarding the expectations. Accountability (level 4) of the group to the group's goals is sometimes lost to members prioritizing their own advancement instead of the advancement of the group as a whole. This is a common mistake made by group members focused on their own self-interest. When commitment is higher to individual goals than group goals, members of the team do not hold themselves or each other accountable to the group's goals. If there is no accountability for the collective goals, the group is unable to focus on the results. If individual rewards and status (level 5) are connected to the group's achievements, then group members will be focused on the advancement of the group rather than their own self-interest. The leader must look beyond self-interest as well. A key role of the group's leader is to develop the group's members into future leaders and the group into a team.

The level of commitment from the group's leader is imperative not only to the success of the group but also to the dedication of its members, leading by example and design. Focus and rewards on the collective goals must become the mantra of the leader.

SUMMARY

Teamwork is a much desired state of working together, but least understood in the process of leading a group to this level of ability. A work group and a team are not one and the same. Not every work group needs to become a team and not every project needs a high functioning team. Teams require time to develop as well as attention and resources from the leaders and other stakeholders of the organization. Teams are also subject to the changes within the organization and need time to adjust to new members, new leadership, or strategic goals. Learning to lead and coach a team to its highest functioning level is a desired skill set. There is nothing more effective and productive in an organization than a high functioning team.

MANAGEMENT

Employees who rise in the ranks of the organization are soon asked to be responsible for supervising the work of others in a department or work group. Such employees become known as team leaders, supervisors, managers, or bosses. What is the job of a supervisor or manager, and how do you successfully transition from being a colleague and friend to the boss?

REFLECTION: EARLY LEARNING EXPERIENCES ABOUT MANAGING

At one time or another, you have imagined yourself as a manager, either living up to or exceeding the example that was set by a previous manager in your career. Maybe you had a manager who led in a way that exhibited the characteristics you now believe managers should possess. You observed this person and since have modeled your behaviors after theirs. Conversely, maybe you had a manager who made you feel micromanaged or expendable and thus taught you about the type of manager you did not want to become. When tapping employees to serve as managers, many small- to mid-sized organizations offer little in the way of training for new managers. Too often it is the observations of other managers that fully informs manager behaviors.

The word *boss* is an older Dutch word that means *overseer*, a word that Americans preferred to the aristocratic term master (http://www.etymonline.com). Over time, other terms, such as supervisor and manager, were adopted and deemed to be more favorable. However, these additional terms also carry some negative connotations. The word supervisor can elicit visions of someone who is authoritative or domineering. The word manager paints a picture of administrative work, someone who is in the middle hierarchy of the organization. For the purposes of this chapter, we will use the term manager. Today that role has expanded to include both supervisory and administrative functions.

As a manager, you are responsible for monitoring the processes of the organization, delegating responsibilities to team members, monitoring employee progress, and reporting the results to the executive director. Yet, as the manager, you have a responsibility to do so much more. Think of yourself as the conductor of the orchestra. The conductor doesn't only show up for tryouts, dress rehearsal, and the performance. There are an array of responsibilities that comprise a high performing orchestra. The conductor serves as the catalyst, coaching and pushing each musician to ensure all performances are error free and high quality. The conductor monitors pitch, sets rhythms, and seeks audience response. To be a manager, first, you must picture yourself on the platform holding "the baton."

When was the first time you experienced having responsibility for someone else, when your words and actions had a significant impact on others? Was it your first time babysitting, after the parents' departure, and you realized you were in charge of the kids? Maybe it was the summer you were a lifeguard at the community pool, where you enforced the pool's rules to ensure the safety of everyone under your watch? Or possibly it was when you were elected to a leadership role for your college student group, and it was your responsibility to ensure the success and longevity of the organization? How did you approach this responsibility? Were the experiences successful? Do you remember making decisions in advance about how you were going to interact with others in the new role? These are examples of your early experiences managing others and how you might have been influenced as a new manager.

Consider a time when you were new to a work situation and wanted ongoing assurances as you stepped through your first day. The good manager at Organization X spent time with you to demonstrate your job, answer questions, introduce you to colleagues, and even got to know you. This good manager touched base with you the first several days of your employment and provided encouraging feedback at the end of each day. Conversely, the manager at Organization Z took you to your work site, made a few general comments, and said you would figure it out. Discreetly, you watched others performing the same task and mimicked their every move. As your day progressed, you even hoped someone would become a friendly face, ask about you, and you would find something in common, maybe even a friend. At the end of the day, you wanted someone to say you had done a good job and wanted you to return. You are remembering situations when time and attention from a manager was both wanted and needed. Good managers (Organization X) make a positive difference in the daily work of an organization and its employees (Buckingham & Coffman, 1999). What are other manager actions and choices that add value and enable people of highly productive organizations?

Diagnosis: Manager Responsibilities

The question contents below are considered responsibilities of good managers. Think about your current or most recent work experience. Check yes or no as you answer the following questions.

Workplace Measures

1. On your first day as well as into your first week, your manager worked with or met with you for at least 50% of your workday?
   ___yes   ___no

2. You know what your manager expects of you?
   ___yes   ___no

3. Your manager is visible in your work area at least once a week?
   ___yes   ___no

4. Your manager taps stakeholders beyond the leadership team for input on major decisions?
   ___yes   ___no

5. Your manager demonstrates interest and care for you by knowing your name and several interesting facts about you, such as but not limited to your spouse/children's names, hometown, college/high school attended, favorite snack, favorite sports team, favorite leisure activity, career goals to which you aspire, and so on?
   ___yes   ___no

6. Your manager encourages your development?
   ___yes   ___no

7. Your manager shared with you the importance of the organization's mission, vision, and values and outlined how your job impacts the accomplishment of all three?
   ___yes   ___no

8. Your manager communicates with you frequently and clearly?

___yes   ___no

9. Your manager provides the tools and resources you require to do your job?

___yes   ___no

10. Your manager clearly communicates the measurements by which your work performance is evaluated?

___yes   ___no

11. Your manager expresses appreciation/praise at least weekly for your contributions toward the organization's goals?

___yes   ___no

12. Your manager appears to communicate with and support all employees equally within his or her team in an equitable fashion?

___yes   ___no

Source: Questions adapted from Gallup's *Measures of the Workplace*, Buckingham and Coffman (1999).

Were you able to identify managers from your employment history represented in the 12 questions? In what areas were these managers strong? What were their challenges? Can you derive from this question set the types of manager actions and behaviors that might be desirable in the eyes of both the employees and organization? Organizations need engaged employees, leaders with vision, and managers who are able to identify, hire, and coach the new employees so that they become successful members of the team. Buckingham and Coffman (1999) call it the organization's power supply, the catalyst role. It's like a chemical reaction between the employee's talents and the organization's goals.

PRESCRIPTION: THE JOB OF A GOOD MANAGER

A good manager is the alchemist of the organization. Buckingham and Coffman (1999) identify four core stages within the catalyst role for managers:

Manager Catalyst Roles

1. Select a person

2. Set expectations

3. Motivate the person

4. Develop the person

Buckingham and Coffman (1999) believe too few large organizations see value in the expert deployment of these four catalyst roles by a manager. Many large organizations have deferred these responsibilities to human resources (HR) and training departments who respond with assembly line-like precision. The on-boarding and training processes become carbon copies for every employee in every department. For an initial orientation to the organization, this may be efficient. To provide professional development for employees beyond the orientation, it requires a more individual approach guided by the department manager responsible for the employees. However, in smaller organizations, the chief executive officer carries out the leadership and management functions. Many times this results in a CEO who has difficulty carving out time for all the many hats she wears. The hat of manager includes the HR roles including supervision, coach, training, evaluation as well as monitor of the internal workings of the organization. Balancing the leader and manager roles is difficult in a small organization. Returning to the orchestra example, the manager/conductor knows all of the musicians in each section, their strengths and weaknesses, who are the principles, who is cross-trained in other instruments, each individual's style of play, and who has untapped musical capabilities. The manager/conductor works hard to interpret the musical piece so that it highlights the strengths of the players in that orchestra while remaining true to the composer. It is an important job, and when done well, is successful for both the orchestra and the individual musicians. In addition to the catalyst responsibilities, the manager/conductor must also perform leadership responsibilities to ensure the orchestra meets all of its goals. For these roles, I might refer to her as the leader/conductor. The leader/conductor is focused on comparing success strategies of nearby orchestras, interests of donors, coming trends for orchestras, long-term planning, community support, guest musicians' availability, the musical selection interests of the audience, and which musical selections would expand the ticket-holder demographics. Both manager and leader roles are very important to the organization's success. Unfortunately, it is the manager roles that tend to be given less priority or are ignored as today's workplace has evolved into a task- and time-oriented environment with a focus on external growth as opposed to internal development.

Based on the four catalyst roles, there are six important processes for managers to deploy:

Management Processes

Process 1 – Hiring and On-Boarding

Employee Need: Comfort and competence in the new role of an organization.

Organizational Need: New employee needed to start quickly, HR paperwork completed, and the new hire trained to perform error free.

Most organizations have rules and policies regarding hiring practices. If you have questions regarding your organizations' policies, inquire to the executive director or human resources department to ensure you are in compliance. The first part of the hiring process includes writing and reviewing job descriptions. Consider how you would write a job description that emphasizes both relationships and results. Job descriptions that overly prescribe methods decrease employee innovation and the new perspective that comes with a new hire. The upcoming section in this chapter on motivation will help you understand more on this topic.

The tendency in the workplace is to overlook the employee's need for comfort and job competence, a tendency that results in a rushed training with little more than a review of the employee handbook. Instead, show the employee the work-site and his or her office or location. Let him or her shadow you and others for a defined period of time. Let the new employee practice the job then observe him or her in action. Immediate, helpful feedback is imperative. This is the time to coach for your expectations as a manager. (In Chapter 11, you will learn more about feedback skills.) Abandoning this employee after the first hour of training and instructions will cause them to feel like an outcast and further delay their ability to bond with the team. Do not overlook the employee's need to have someone to go with on break, to lunch, or even be invited to an office happy hour. As the manager, plan your schedule to include blocks of time for several days over the course of a week or two to orient, train, monitor, and mentor the new employee. You are building a working relationship, demonstrating you are trustworthy, approachable, a dependable resource, and that you want her to succeed. Investing your time during her initial days pays huge dividends later in a very loyal, well-trained employee. Quality client services and relationships between employees and clients/customers are rooted in the relationship between the employer and employee. Employees give what they get. If they work in a high quality, relationship-oriented environment, that behavior is what they will mirror and deliver.

Process 2 – Monitoring Results and Appreciating Success

Employee Need: To see you in his or her work space seeing the job through his or her eyes; noting and relaying appreciation for good work as well as to provide helpful feedback for improvement.

Organizational Need: To spot-check efficiency and effectiveness at the point of client/customer contact, noting observable results, and to provide "course correction" where needed to ensure results are on schedule and aligned with the organization's goals. To enable employees to practice state of the art methods.

The manager's tendency is to look for and comment on the negatives they observe and make no notes of average or above average work until the annual evaluation. One of the top five employee complaints is the manager's inability to express appreciation for good work. Establishing a culture of appreciation is important to sustain positive employee motivation. This is different than rewards, which, you will see shortly, are not always a motivator. A note, kind word, or office celebration when an employee or work team is "caught doing good" is key to a giving, team-oriented, and supportive work environment. Another management tendency is to see the improvement the employee needs to make and saving the feedback for the annual review. Sharing current feedback is helpful not only for the employee but also for the organization. Who can remember what really happened last week much less 3 months ago? Withholding helpful information makes the employee feel set-up during her annual performance review and is harmful to your relationship as well as the overall work environment.

Process 3 – Attract, Value, Develop, and Retain Human Capital

Employee Need: To feel valued and respected, to give skills and talents to the organization, to grow and develop increased capacity and new skills, to network at professional meetings, and to know that there are opportunities for advancement within the organization if they so choose.

Organizational Need: To attract and retain the top-tier employees, to provide the resources for training and development, and to establish a positive organizational reputation in the community and related professional associations to continue to attract talented candidates.

Organizations become unhealthy and weak due to a lack of investment in their people. Low employee motivation, high turnover, increased number of complaints and backstabbing, high absenteeism, poor communication, and low productivity are signs of a weakened organizational state (Maxwell, 2011). Organizations need to grow their people. Employees need to know they will have adequate resources provided for professional growth and to continue meeting professional standards. It is the responsibility of the managers to advocate for the professional development of employees. To say one belongs to a profession or hires professionals implies employees are certified, qualified, proficient, and authorities in their fields. When employees help managers create plans for learning and professional growth, employee motivation to carry out the plan is high. The Center for Creative Leadership's (CCL) research study on future trends in leadership development explores improved practices in teaching and learning leadership. In the report, Petrie (2011) emphasizes the importance of employee involvement in their professional development plans and describes it as key to organizational success. The CCL also recommends employees think about their development in two directions—horizontally and vertically. Horizontal growth is the set of learning skills that help employees expand responsibilities within their current role. Vertical growth is when employees develop the skills to take on new roles in the organization or even in another organization (Petrie, 2011). Too often organizational budget cutbacks consistently attack employee development funds first. Yet studies reveal (Maxwell, 2011) that the organization's quality and capacity will deteriorate when investment in employee development and organizational capacity is eliminated. If this inability to stay current continues, programs and services will soon fail to meet the needs of clients and constituents. The reputation of the organization will decline and donors and other sources of funding will redirect resources to competitor organizations.

The most common mistakes managers make in supporting employee development and organizational capacity is (1) the lack of planning and purpose for the training followed by (2) the failure to apply the training. Unfortunately, it is not common for organizations to ask employees for perceptions on their own skill needs and the coming capacity needs of the organization. Selection of training for professional employees is generally made based on self-selection to attend predetermined, annual meeting-themed programs of professional associations or marketing efforts of consulting firms. Rarely is the effort focused around training to meet a specific organizational or individual need. Even more troubling is the frustration of the employee who attends a training program, yet has no mechanism to incorporate the new skills or share what they learned with their manager or other employees. And worse, the manager provides zero support or appreciation for the employee to implement the new skills. Yes, even when the organization pays to send employees to training, most treat it like a weekend excursion. Alternately, when managers develop learning goals for training sessions collaboratively with employees and connect them to the employees' overall learning goals and development plan, the level of learning and achievement increases dramatically. The employees' new knowledge is not only valued, but the time and effort to apply and share their new skills is important and worthy of the organization's investment.

Process 4 – Clarity About Mission, Vision, and Goals

Employee Need: Meet expectations, to feel that he or she matters to the success of the organization, and to have less confusion regarding goals and priorities.

Organizational Need: Meet goals, engage employees, and realize measurable results.

A mission statement (discussed in Chapter 8) serves as the compass for the organization, guiding the manager's direction to employees. The manager must talk the talk in addition to walking the walk of the mission statement. He or she must understand it, be able to state it, and educate employees regarding the essence of it. The manager must insist all employee tasks advance the organization's mission. Use of the mission statement is the key to success for all leaders and managers in an organization.

While a mission is the long-term look at the organization's direction, goals are the short-term victories that help achieve the larger mission. Too often organizational goals are set at a staff retreat by upper leadership with little input by entry-level employees or mid-level employees or managers. Many times the resulting goals have no plan to ensure their achievement. Goals are infrequently discussed with the team, which over time, results in employees prioritizing other tasks and asking, "Are we still doing that?" It is the management's role to communicate and monitor the goals, implementation plans, and results. Goals, plans, and results should be discussed frequently and posted in a central place for everyone to reference and see the progress. Some organizations call this their "dashboard" because the information is usually displayed as pie charts, tables, or graphs much like the dials on the dashboard of a car. The organization dashboard also gives key information on the organization's progress and current status; even a warning light if a system is not working.

Managers should provide systems to keep employees informed about progress on goals. The dashboard is such a system. If an employee cannot see how her job connects to the organization's goals, she feels disconnected and unimportant to the group. As such, she is less likely to give the same level of effort as the employees who can see "the needle move on the charts of the dashboard" as they complete their tasks. Humans feel part of the group/community when what they contribute matters to the results of that group. Employee motivation is connected to this concept called mattering (Schlossberg, 1989). All employees should know specifically what their role was in the accomplishment of each organizational goal.

Process 5 – Performance Appraisals

Employee Need: Fairness; no surprises; coaching, feedback, and course correction; and appreciation and recognition.

Organizational Need: Connection to organizational goals, opportunity for course corrections, and employees who want to achieve.

Performance appraisals are annual events that all too often both employees and managers dread. Employees fear the year of unknown/missing feedback and are forced to wonder if the organization has been happy with their work. Adding to the dysfunction of the process, the organization requires the manager to complete a generic, one-size-fits-all organizational evaluation form that does not describe any specific or unique features of the employee's job, nor does it mention the mission or current goals of the organization. The manager does not have employee observations or data on results, so he or she is writing general remarks about employee collegiality, general leadership skills, and adherence to company policies. Good performance appraisals are processes driven jointly between employees and managers with mutually agreed upon targets and goals, and quarterly meetings to discuss progress made toward the established goals. Such progressive evaluation methods are least common in government, public service, education, and nonprofit sectors.

To develop a quality performance appraisal, the manager should consider setting meetings with each direct report.

- Meeting 1: The manager discusses with the employee the mission and goals of the organization. It is important that during this process the manager outlines how the employee's job contributes to the overall big picture for the organization. Even if the employee is an entry-level employee and entrusted with limited responsibilities, this will help her understand that they are important and integrated into the team. The manager then asks the employee to take some time to develop individual goals that will advance the organization's mission and an action plan to achieve them.
- Meeting 2: The manager will review the employee's individual goals to ensure they are measurable and aligned with the organization's goals. The manager will also review the action plan to ensure the pre-set deadlines are realistic. In this action plan, the manager and employee agree to quarterly meetings to review the employee's progress. It is important for the employee to know that additional meetings are welcome, but will be scheduled at the discretion of the employee. This process prevents the annual feedback surprise and assures that asking for feedback is encouraged.
- Meeting 3: The meeting's focus is to review with the employee the agreed upon goals and timeline. It is during this meeting that the manager and employee also discuss the employee need for additional resources to be successful. This could include trainings, conferences, or even new technology. The manager should seek to create opportunities for their employee's growth.

Process 6 – Grow New Leaders

Employee Need: Guidance and support to grow professionally, to transition from a colleague to a manager/leader, to have a mentor from among other managers and leaders, and to expand capacity to manage and lead the organization.

Organizational Need: To have a viable leadership succession plan and organizational growth and to create a pool of new managers and leaders who are ready for new responsibilities

The best managers and leaders are always learning and helping others to learn. The highest function of organizational leadership is to produce new managers who can lead as well (Maxwell, 2011). Mentoring is a strong component in new manager development. An established manager transfers wisdom, experience, and skills in an effort to mold a new manager. Maxwell (2011) explains the established leader must demonstrate a commitment to the new leader's success by adding value through constant encouragement. When an organization grows managers and leaders, the organization also grows. An organization that does not identify new management and leadership talent, support mentoring programs for potential leaders, or provide formal and informal leadership development will be relegated to mediocrity, or worse, closing their doors. The leadership circle will become a closed group with no new blood. Talented employees will leave the organization as soon as they realize there are no potential openings at the top or no developmental path to get there.

Managers who facilitate and encourage members of the leadership team to serve as mentors are especially helpful in the development of a pipeline of future leaders for the organization and a succession process. Mentoring is neither an accidental process nor a scripted assignment. It takes commitment from both the mentor and the protégé to develop the relationship. Larger organizations may have formalized programs that invite employees to participate in such relationships. Some of the strongest mentoring relationships are formed at the request of the protégé. It is flattering to be asked to serve as someone's mentor: therefore, it is unlikely an invitation to be a mentor will receive a negative reply. Multiple mentors early in a career are very beneficial, one inside the organization and another who works outside of it. Each can provide insight to guidance through the many decisions made in career advancement. If your manager is a helpful resource and guide, invite him or her to serve as your mentor. Plan to meet with each of your mentors several times a year, more often if you have a specific need. Be sure to tap him or her for recommendations for important books or articles you should read, as well as identify professional meetings and training opportunities you should attend.

Promoted to Manager

Being selected, groomed, and promoted to a manager/leader position speaks to the potential and confidence your manager sees in you. Many times promotions are given based upon success in an individual entry-level role in the organization. Too often, the organization does not support the newly promoted employee in the leadership role. According to Carol A. Walker (2011, p. 78), new leaders fail to realize "that their jobs are no longer about personal achievement, but instead about enabling others to achieve, that driving the bus can mean taking a back seat, and building a team is often more important than cutting a deal." Walker continues, "Organizations of rookie managers assume management skills will be learned by osmosis. The rookie manager's boss plays a key role by engaging in intensive coaching and training" (p. 78). Walker (pp. 80–81) recommends five key skills needed by rookie managers:

Delegating – You can't do it all yourself. Empower your direct reports to become a trusted, talented team. Everyone wins.

Getting Support from Above – Engage your boss in yours and your direct reports' success at the beginning. Don't wait for problems, and don't be afraid to ask for assistance. This is a partnership directed to the success of all. Even if you have the same boss as before, expectations are different and new ways of communicating need to be clarified.

Projecting Confidence – Confidence is neither arrogance nor spouting the organization's line. Direct reports need to see a manager who is both capable and considerate.

Focusing on the Big Picture – Don't let the organization's strategy get lost in fighting the daily fires. Plan time in your day to work on the important goals, not just the urgencies that erupt. Guide your direct reports to do the same.

Giving Constructive Feedback – Managers who avoid giving feedback to direct reports cost them their credibility as managers. Practice giving positive and negative feedback to direct reports. Ask them to provide feedback to you. This is part of the job of being a manager.

The next important relationship to strengthen (Eikenberry & Harris, 2011) is with your direct reports. Arrange a meeting and carefully plan and prepare. Know what you want to take away from the meeting as well as what you want them to take away. There will be additional dynamics if you were a former peer within the group you now supervise; heed Eikenberry and Harris' suggestions (2011, p. 16):

- Acknowledge the transition. Be genuine. Share that this is an adjustment for you as well as the group.
- Talk about the changing relationships. Share your hope the changes will be positive and that some changes might be different for different people and individual needs will be taken into account. Your goal is for a smooth transition.
- After you have clarified your new role with your boss, share that description with the group.
- Outline your expectations for them. Preparing ahead of time for this conversation will give you the opportunity to have clarity regarding what you plan to help them accomplish.
- When you are finished, ask for their feedback. What are their expectations for you? Listen carefully, take notes, and clarify their meaning. You can ask for clarification regarding their suggestions, but do not negotiate about what they share—maybe later. For now, understand your starting point with the group.
- Ask for their help and patience. Even the best leaders do not know all the answers. If they did, why would they need a team of direct reports? Likewise, you do not know all the answers, even if you have good ideas.

Give yourself time to have these conversations, to allow the transition to evolve, to reflect on its progress, and to make an action plan with input from your boss and your group. Following this process as a new boss you will grow into the position with an increased likelihood of support and receptivity.

SUMMARY

Whether the role of manager is in a separate position or part of a CEO leadership position, developing and enabling your staff and teams to perform at their highest level is a key component of your job. It is likely role modeling good management behaviors was not part of your previous experience in the workplace. Sadly, today's workplace overloads managers and leaders with administrative tasks that create unhealthy time compromises. Only by reevaluating your important roles as a manager, evaluating what your staff needs from you, and setting priorities that allow you to invest time in beneficial ways for your team and the organization will you change the cycle of limited staff and team support.

MOTIVATION

The American Psychological Association (http://www.apa.org) defines motivation as the process of starting, directing, and maintaining physical and psychological activities, including mechanisms involved in preferences for one activity over another and the vigor and persistence of responses. As managers and leaders, it is your job to motivate your work group and at the same time, feel motivated by your manager as well. How do you create a motivating workplace? As a leader, what influence do you have? How do you keep yourself motivated?

REFLECTION: MOTIVATION THEORY AT WORK

Studies of workplace psychology were first recorded in Frederick Taylor's research published in the 1910s. In it, he described methods of improving efficiency within the manufacturing workplace. He believed if management rewarded positive behaviors and punished negative ones, the manager would motivate the workers to produce in the correct manner (Pink, 2009). Daniel Pink (p. 18) refers to this motivation method as "carrot and sticking." In the 1940s, psychologist Harry Harlow studied motivation in primates and discovered that carrots (or raisins in the case of the monkeys) were not enough to induce a repeat of primates' problem-solving behaviors he had observed earlier. This led him to hypothesize primates and humans are motivated by things other than extrinsic motivators (raisins and carrots). Therefore, he proposed, internal motivators might also be an unexplored driver in human behavior (Pink, 2009). Harlow influenced the research of Abraham Maslow, the psychologist most recognizable for his 1943 study, "Theory of Human Motivation," which was based on his humanistic perspective of psychology. He did not see humans as sick, dysfunctional creatures, or cogs in an assembly line. He believed humans have an ascending order of needs, the lower-level ones (needs based on survival, safety, and belonging) that must be satisfied first before meeting the higher-order needs such as learning, having confidence and self-esteem, and reaching their full potential. Researchers McGregor and Herzberg expressed a similar philosophy regarding human motivation. Herzberg wrote *The Motivation to Work* in 1959, which described a framework of workplace and job characteristics. Some characteristics met a few basic needs and satisfied workers while others motivated and pushed them to do more. McGregor wrote the *Human Side of Enterprise* in 1960 in which he described the behaviors of management in relation to employee behaviors. One set of behaviors is Theory X, which described employees as shying away from responsibility and as such required their managers to micromanage them. Conversely, Theory Y stated employees do seek responsibility, possess self-direction, and are dedicated to the organization's mission. McGregor observed management in organizations that employed either Theories X or Y to determine which was more successful. He discovered managers who acted using Theory Y were more successful than mangers using Theory X. Equally important to the successful task results; he learned that employees were happier and more loyal in a Theory Y environment.

Consider previous jobs or even classes in which you have been an employee or participant. Were you happier and more motivated in some situations over others? Answer the questions in Table 6.4.

DIAGNOSIS: EXTRINSICALLY OR INTRINSICALLY MOTIVATED?

You just finished describing how you felt in a workplace environment that was either autocratic (Theory X) or student/employee empowered (Theory Y). Build on those ideas by answering the following questions.

- What motivates you on the job?
- What motivates you in the classroom?
- What motivates you while working on a favorite activity?

In fact, when you are working on a favorite activity, does it feel like work? Does the motivation for favorite things come almost automatically? If so, describe how this feels?

Table 6.4 Environmental Motivation Theories

What did you experience? Think about a recent/current workplace or classroom experience.		
• A Theory X environment • Employer/teacher behaved as if you were a number, allowed you to do mostly low-level activities, was demanding, no thank-yous, one-way communication	• A Theory Y environment • Employer/teacher knew you as a person, had high expectations of you, and challenged you with work and learning when you requested	• Describe your environment, is it X or Y?
What did you do in this job/classroom?		
Check the boxes below to describe how you responded/felt in the situation above:		
Did what I had to	Was caring and committed	No knowledge of results
Couldn't wait to get started	Boss received the credit	Took initiative
Result was good enough	Gave my best effort	Resented feedback, received only if there was a mistake
All shared the credit	Celebrated success	Withheld my best effort
Felt energized	Became a clock-watcher	Asked why we were doing this
Felt like quitting	Lost interest	Wanted to do/learn more
Didn't trust others	Looked for excuses to not go	Shared with anyone who would listen how good/bad it was

Let's explore why in some cases you feel very motivated and not so much in others. Leaders want to influence their teams to be a motivated force. Here's what you need to know about motivation.

The earliest research observed that motivators came from human biological needs. Because humans don't live alone, researchers observed additional motivators that came from the environment. Volunteering is a good example to use when studying motivation. You experienced enjoyment going to a nonprofit agency to volunteer because the volunteer coordinator greeted you with a smile, talks happily with you, and thanks you profusely for your assistance. You might be presented with a certificate annually at a reception printed with the number of volunteer

hours you contributed. The smiles, attention, statements of appreciation, and certificates are all extrinsic rewards. But what if there was a budget cutback and the
agency had to reduce the work hours of the volunteer coordinator and could not
purchase certificates. Would lack of certificates and interaction with the volunteer
coordinator curtail your interest in volunteering? There may be a few individuals
who are only motivated by extrinsic rewards, but most all humans have an inner
drive that is motivated by intrinsic rewards. These are the internal drives that bring
satisfaction and delight when you solve problems, create an idea, or master a new
concept. The enjoyment comes from performing the task (Pink, 2009). The act of
volunteering at the agency continues because of the intrinsic satisfaction you get
from knowing you are making services available to members of your community
who are in need.

Self-Regulation and Choices

Motivation is more complex than the feelings of satisfaction from a task. It is
also about self-regulation and choices. What motivates you to make choices about
how you spend your time? In their 2006 meta-analysis on the theory of motivation,
Steel and Konig defined motivation using this formula:

$$\text{Motivation} = \frac{\text{Expectancy x Value}}{\text{Impulsiveness x Delay}}$$

Decode the formula through the definitions of each value in the equation:

- Expectancy – the confidence in your ability to complete the task with excellence.
- Value – your perception of the worthiness of the task (can also be influenced
  by your perception of how others see the worthiness of the task).
- Impulsiveness – your sensitivity to delay, loss of focus, and distractibility.
- Delay – length of time until feedback, reward, and appreciation are received.
  (Longer time frames impact motivation negatively.)

According to the formula, the ability to stay focused on a high value task that will
be accomplished with pride is diminished by things that distract us as well as the
length of time it will take to see the task to completion. The path to big important
mission-driven goals is difficult to keep in focus unless there is a deliberate effort
to break it down into smaller steps that can be achieved in short time blocks so
participants can feel short-term success and progress regularly.

Several drivers influence how we make choices to spend our time and maintain
our interest. Opportunities that meet our need to be liked and to affiliate are important drivers in humans. Those drivers impact our desire to have friends and a friendly

work environment. Your desire to feel self-confident impacts your ability to begin the task as well as the belief you will do a good job (expectancy theory). Therefore, the interests you value are placed in a higher position on your list of priorities such as the list of goals you created in Chapter 5 when you framed your life plan. Wanting a high grade-point average while in college is both desirable and valued, but the length of time until graduation (delay) can diminish the likelihood you might choose to spend time studying or writing a paper when the immediate opportunity for fun and affiliation are present. Knowledge of these motivational drivers highlights how easily you might choose to spend your time at a social event with friends rather than writing a paper in the library. You might refer to that choice as a procrastination behavior. Procrastination behaviors are major impediments to achievements and productivity.

Surfing the Internet, playing with your pet, cleaning or other tasks seem more appealing than the prioritized items needed to be completed to reach your long-term goal. Piers Steel and Cornelius Konig and (2006) report that procrastination affects 50% of children and 25% of adults. To be an effective leader, you need to know how to locate and keep your focus. It not only affects your personal or organization's goals, but also impacts your employees. Your leadership should drive others' decisions in how they make their commitments and allocate their time for the success of the organization. What will motivate you and your employees to change established negative behaviors? The final chapter of this book will offer some ideas about changing personal habits.

PRESCRIPTION: FINDING AND MAINTAINING YOUR FOCUS

Researchers have written about motivation in regard to general psychology, the workplace, education, volunteerism, economic choices, and the behaviors of consumers (Steel & Konig, 2006). Many times the language is different, but people are still people and require something either intrinsic or extrinsic to drive them forward. Since 2005, researchers from many disciplines began to compare notes and connect ideas and concepts to develop one basic descriptive theory of motivation. Motivation is complex to identify and describe, yet you know when you feel motivated. You might describe this feeling as being "in the zone." In his book, *Flow: The Psychology of Optimal Experience,* Mihaly Csikszentmihalyi (1990) described motivational experiences as follows:

- Framed by purpose and achievement
- Challenging to one's mental and physical state (just enough)
- Transported to a focused state of being where one's sense of time, place, and self melt away in the accomplishment of an audacious goal

Find Your Focus

We will begin by outlining how to find your focus. Identifying your goal is the first step, staying focused on the goal is the more difficult second step. Everywhere you look, there is something or someone jockeying for your attention. Your motivation drivers are cued to satisfy your important needs. Unfortunately, those needs do not have a separate gatekeeper looking at your long-term goals, making decisions for you. That hard work is up to you. This is the work we call self-regulation, having the ability to say no to an immediate need (such as impulse shopping) when there is a long-term goal at risk (such as saving money). You have already begun part of the journey to understand self-regulation in Chapters 3, 4, and 5 when topics were covered on understanding individual style, values, time management, life plans, and organization. Your roles and how time was allocated were analyzed for effectiveness. (In Chapter 9, you will learn more about connecting the vision of where you are going to the specifics of a measurable goal.) The following list provides tools for improving self-regulation:

- Organizing
- Identifying and protecting your peak productive hours (10 a.m. to 2 p.m. for many)
- Allotting appropriate time to the task
- Planning, prioritizing, and calendaring
- Using a quota, target, or benchmark to accomplish so many (pages, miles, hours, etc.)
- Self-control and the elimination of distractions and temptations
- Ability to start a task
- Ability to stay on task
- Ability to finish a task

The ability to master the skills of self-regulation is key in the ability to overcome procrastination and maintain a motivated state. When focus is lost, we must make another decision to focus and start again. As you can see, multiple decisions to start and refocus drains energy and risks a future focus decision never getting off the ground.

The second question to address is how to lead others to make commitments and follow through with their best effort for the purposes of the organization. If you were to quiz a group of employees and ask what motivated them to come to work every day, the most probable initial response is the paycheck. Remember, the paycheck is an extrinsic motivator and provides the means to cover people's basic needs of food, water, and shelter as is outlined by Maslow's lowest rung of human needs.

Intrinsic and Extrinsic Motivation

"But wait," you say, "how can the paycheck be the motivator if I've just spent the past two pages singing the praises of intrinsic motivators?" To help you understand, Herzberg's research on motivators and hygiene factors (1959) as well as the model of employee motivation developed by Nohria, Groysberg, and Lee (2008) will illuminate the relationship rewards have with motivation. Herzberg referred to rewards, such as paychecks, as hygiene factors. In reality phrases such as "necessary but not sufficient" are better descriptions. Humans need a salary that meets their basic needs, buys a few extras, and is equitable to the salary of others in the field. Salary becomes part of the web of hygiene factors and when considered together, become a foundation or launching pad to motivation in the workplace. Other hygiene factors forming this foundation include the following:

- Status
- Security
- Relationship with others at work (subordinate, peers, supervisor)
- Work conditions
- Supervision
- Policies and administration

The external motivators Herzberg identified include the following:

- Personal growth
- Advancement
- Responsibility
- The actual work
- Recognition
- Achievement

External motivators are the engine of motivation according to Herzberg (1959). Once our needs for financial support are met, it no longer motivates, and the intrinsic motivators drive us to commit and achieve. If financial needs are not met, employees feel taken advantage of and become resentful and bitter.

Nohria et al. (2008) explained their employee model of motivation through a model built around four drives: to acquire, to bond, to comprehend, and to defend. Employees need to fulfill one of the four emotional drivers. If an organization wants to motivate an employee, the organizations leaders must identify the driver and have created a work environment that creates a conduit to the employee's work motivation drive. Each of the four drives is identified with the conduit described and related actions the organization can take.

1. Acquire – an organizational reward system with a pay scale equitable to competitors as well as performance accountability and rewards.

2. Bond – a supportive and collaborative work culture valuing teamwork, sharing, and friendship.

3. Comprehend – a workplace and specific job that emphasizes competency and expertise in a role that is critical to the success of the goals of the organization.

4. Defend – a workplace led with fairness, transparency, and colleagues who build trust.

Impact of Managers on Motivation

Nohria et al. (2008) also reported how important employees' perceptions of managers were to motivation. Employees believe their managers have a responsibility to provide a positive work environment and control over company policies to enable them to meet their four drives: acquire, bond, comprehend, and defend. If even one drive is not fulfilled, the manager is rated poorly. In this model, it is a combination of the direct manager and organizational factors that influence employee motivation. Just as you have expectations about your manager maintaining a motivating environment, your employees have expectations for your role as a leader that include enabling motivational factors.

SUMMARY

Motivation is not something you can do to someone else. Instead, leaders and managers set the stage by enabling and influencing the organization to establish a motivating work environment for all members of the team. Coach employees to find what activates their internal motivating choices. Lead consistently in how the four drives are fulfilled for employees. Set compensation packages to be competitive and equitable. Organizations should reward teamwork, not just individual accomplishments. Your team has expectations of you as a leader to create a work environment that empowers and encourages them to stay focused and energized on goals that really matter. However, building and sustaining your own motivation are also integral to creating a positive, motivated work environment for others. Therefore, you must role model skills of self-regulation, organization, and maintaining focus. These skills will help you create and maintain an empowered team.

REFERENCES

American Psychological Association: http://www.apa.org/research/action/glossary.aspx

Buckingham, M., & Coffman, C. (1999). *First, break all the rules: What the world's greatest managers do differently.* New York, NY: Simon & Schuster.

Csikszentmihalyi, M. (1990). *Flow: The psychology of optimal experience.* New York, NY: HarperPerennial.

Eikenberry, K., & Harris, G. (2011). *From bud to boss: Secrets to a transition to remarkable leadership.* San Francisco, CA: Jossey-Bass.

FranklinCovey. (2012). The five choices to extraordinary productivity: Two-day seminar facilitator manual. Salt Lake City, UT.

Hertzberg, F. (1959). *The motivation to work.* New York, NY: Wiley.

Lencioni, P. (2002). *The five dysfunctions of a team: A leadership fable.* San Francisco, CA: Jossey-Bass.

Martin, A., & Bal, V. (2007). The state of teams. *The Center for Creative Leadership White Paper.* Retrieved from http://www.ccl.org

Maslow, A. H. (1943). Theory of human motivation. *Psychological Review, 50,* 370–396.

Maxwell, J. C. (2011). *Five levels of leadership: Proven steps to maximize your potential.* New York, NY: Center Street.

McGregor, D. (1960). *The human side of enterprise.* New York, NY: McGraw-Hill.

Morgeson, F. P., DeRue, D. S., & Karam, E. P. (2010). Leadership in teams: A functional approach to understanding leadership structures and processes. *Journal of Management, 36*(5). doi: 10.1177/0149206309347376

Nohria, N., Groysberg, B., & Lee, L. E. (2008). Employee motivation: A powerful new model. *Harvard Business Review, 86*(7/8), 78–84.

Petrie, N. (2011). *Future trends in leadership development.* Greensboro, NC: The Center for Creative Leadership.

Pink, D. H. (2009). *Drive: The surprising truth about what motivates us.* New York, NY: Riverhead Books.

Schlossberg, N. (1989). Marginality and mattering: Key issues in building community. *New Directions for Student Services, 1*(48), 5–15.

Steel, P., & Konig, C. J. (2006). Integrating theories of motivation. *Academy of Management Review, 31*(4), 889–913.

Walker, C. A. (2011). Saving your rookie managers from themselves (pp. 77–90). HBR's 10 Must Reads: On Managing People. Boston, MA: Harvard Business Review Press.

Wheelan, S. A. (2010). *Creating effective teams: A guide for members and leaders.* Thousand Oaks, CA: Sage.

Chapter 7

Organizational Management—How to Run a Meeting and Make Decisions

LEARNING OBJECTIVES

The student will

- examine purposes to hold a necessary meeting,
- observe a meeting and determine if it was effectively planned,
- create a fishbone diagram to illustrate a decision-making process,
- describe four methods of decision making and select the method most appropriate for multiple situations, and
- demonstrate the use of four tools that gather and organize data for decision making.

HOW TO RUN A MEETING

Meetings consume the majority of hours in the modern workday. An employee in a "knowledge worker" type position in any job sector can expect to have several meetings during the workweek and at least one a day. Higher level positions require even more meetings on the daily calendar. And as you will see in Chapter 10, technology has enabled meetings to happen without everyone being in the same location. If you are engaged in organizations and activities outside of work, meetings are part of those environments as well. Family meetings, faith group meetings, community meetings, and club meetings can easily consume one's week. If you have children or a spouse, add their group meetings on top of your own, and you can see how quickly your meeting time adds up. It seems today's lives are surrounded by groups attending to a never-ending stack of meeting agendas.

REFLECTION: YOUR MEETING EXPERIENCES

Meetings take place to accomplish information sharing, problem solving, and decision making so that key stakeholders can participate efficiently and effectively. Recall the meetings you have attended in your many experiences at work and in other types of organizations. Did you feel your time was well used? Was your voice heard? Respond yes or no to the questions below to assess your experience at the most recent meeting you attended:

- I received adequate notice of the meeting time and location?
  ___ yes   ___ no
- I had the opportunity to submit items for the agenda?
  ___ yes   ___ no
- The meeting had a purpose and an agenda?
  ___ yes   ___ no
- The meeting started on time?
  ___ yes   ___ no
- Location, time, and date were conducive for maximum participation?
  ___ yes   ___ no
- All stakeholders appropriate to the meeting purpose were invited?
  ___ yes   ___ no
- Meeting space was comfortable with appropriate seating, technology, adequate lighting, and a minimum of distractions?
  ___ yes   ___ no
- Ground rules were established or previously agreed upon?
  ___ yes   ___ no
- Meeting facilitator was skilled in running an effective meeting?
  ___ yes   ___ no
- Agenda items were addressed with few distractions?
  ___ yes   ___ no

- Appropriate decisions, actions, and votes were recorded and shared with participants in a timely fashion?
  ___ yes   ___ no
- Meeting ended on time?
  ___ yes   ___ no
- I felt my time was well used?
  ___ yes   ___ no
- I had opportunity for my voice to be heard?
  ___ yes   ___ no

Based on your answers, give the meeting planners a grade: A if efficient and effective; B if moderately efficient and effective; C if you felt your time was wasted; D if all agenda items were not accomplished; F if nothing was accomplished.

DIAGNOSIS: MEETING PLANNER AND PARTICIPANTS

Meetings can become unpleasant, ineffective, dreaded time wasters due to the following pitfalls:

- Unclear views of meeting outcomes
- Personal agendas
- Misunderstandings between participants
- Inability to make decisions

Be wary of hastily planned meetings. When meeting organizers do not attend to the needs of participants, fail to communicate clearly, behave as if the meeting were their own personal gathering, and do not facilitate the actual operation of the meeting, the participants become unhappy, communication turns into gripe sessions, and the organization may suffer from lack of trust, indecision, and little or no forward motion on goals.

In addition to the meeting planner's lack of skills, be aware of participants who also lack the skills to work in a group. Learn to recognize the person in the meeting who has an ax to grind by behaviors such as being a poor listener, using insider jargon, and asking repetitive questions about the same issues. If you are a newly elected or appointed leader of the group, be aware of participants who have past loyalties to the previous leaders. They lack trust, exercise power and domination, and make personal accusations. They work to turn everyone's attention to the problem they have. They question everything and usually threaten to "take their toys home" if they do not get their way (Pew Foundation, 2001).

PRESCRIPTION: PREPARING FOR AN EFFECTIVE AND EFFICIENT MEETING

Tips for Meeting Planners

The first step to avoid confusion is to determine the purpose of the meeting. Is the group having a meeting mostly out of habit, such as weekly staff meetings? What needs to be accomplished at this meeting? Typical reasons for workplace meetings include the following:

- Brainstorm new ideas
- Strategic planning
- Professional development retreats/training
- Resource allocation
- Decision making
- Client case review
- Budget review/approval
- Policy making/review/update
- Performance review/promotion review
- Goal achievement follow-up
- Disseminate news that is critical for all to hear simultaneously
- Work team plan/feedback

For a successful meeting, first communicate the meeting purpose and be a gatekeeper in determining what will be placed on the agenda. Accept agenda items based upon the purpose of the meeting. After items for the agenda have been agreed upon, decide what would be the best method to work through it. What environment would be more conducive to reaching the goal: such as through an online forum, in a learning environment, in a relaxed setting, in a structured setting, or one-on-one? Be judicious in the request for the time of your colleagues. If an agenda can be organized so that some participants can leave early, come later, or attend online your consideration of others shines through. Once in the meeting, start on time, stay on the agenda, and end on time. This will result in participant respect for this and future meetings. Meeting attendance and attitude will rise when participants' time is respected.

Second, are the participants clear on the goals and desired outcomes? Are they aware that there is an expectation of a discussion and decision? Were materials provided to participants in a timely fashion so they can read, research, and review the items on the agenda and be prepared for a discussion and decision? Some group members are process thinkers and need more time and details, while others are expedient thinkers who require a reason to review the information (remember Chapter 3). Do not let your lack of meeting planning skills or assumptions about participants' need for decision time prevent the meeting from a successful conclusion. How will the group make the decision? Is there agreement and understanding about this process? Are there group-created processes and ground rules to stay focused and provide the members with tools to return the discussion to the established purpose? Ground rules can be helpful if there are hidden agendas or if office politics surface. Below is a list of suggested ground rules for the group to agree upon:

- Stay on point. (It is everyone's responsibility to point out distractions.)
- Do not interrupt those who have the floor.
- Provide a reasonable balance of "air time." Have time limits for discussion.
- Share your opinion; don't make assumptions for other's thoughts. Speak for yourself.
- Don't take disagreements personally.
- Discussions are not fodder for tomorrow's gossip mill.
- Treat all with respect.

By setting clear goals and having a specific agenda that involved opportunities for others to have input to the agenda, you have conveyed a message of respect as well as focus on the business at hand (Pew Foundation, 2001).

Third, does the agenda contain old business? Was the research for necessary additional information regarding the old business completed since the last meeting? This action item should be at the top of the meeting planner's list so that decisions and action can prevail in the upcoming meeting. Like the information for new agenda items, this too must be shared in advance. Have all the stakeholders in attendance at the previous meeting indicated attendance at this meeting? Some members will be reluctant to make an important decision if key stakeholders are absent. Meeting reminders and stakeholder follow-up is recommended. As a rule, groups tend to make riskier decisions than individuals. Having key stakeholders present will allow for adequate discussion of facts and data. Think of the time spent in meetings as critical for strategy and communication time to address issues and plan accordingly (Pew Foundation, 2001).

Too many times group leaders assume they must facilitate their meetings. Certainly they can if they choose, but the duties of a meeting facilitator are to maintain neutrality, ensure the process is fair, and to record agreements. It may come as a surprise to many that the meeting facilitator's job is not to push an agenda item or the process. Showing favoritism, criticizing, debating, arguing, or talking too much is also not appropriate. Given those parameters, why not choose another team member to facilitate the meeting. It might even be appropriate to rotate the facilitation duties. The list below includes additional tips for the assigned meeting facilitators:

- Prepare for the meeting; know expectations, attendees, and issues.
- Remind the participants of your neutral role.
- Review and use ground rules.
- Explain decision-making method to participants (leadership chooses decision-making process).
- Confirm participant agreement to goals, objectives, and agenda.
- Be inclusive.
- Keep the group focused and the process moving forward.
- Restate discussion summary and key points, and seek clarification if necessary.
- Record decisions or appoint a recorder.

Accurate recording of important decisions made in meetings is critical. As most police officers will tell you, three eyewitnesses to the same incident will not give the same description of the event. It is not that they are dishonest or have a visual disability; it is that we all see and focus on different things in the same situation. Therefore, what we see and remember is different from someone else. It is best to have a neutral third party, someone who is not also trying to facilitate or participate in the meeting, serve as a recorder or secretary for the meeting. Recording ideas and projecting the comments on a screen or recording on a whiteboard for all to see is useful beyond the historical record. Here are the benefits:

- Participants feel heard by the group.
- Participants can check remarks for accuracy during the meeting.
- Discourages repetition.
- Holds ideas for use later in agenda.
- Encourages sense of accomplishment.
- Easy to catch up latecomers or participants whose attention strays.
- Increases accountability.
- If someone was unable to attend, it provides an unbiased account of the meeting.

(Pew Foundation, 2001)

Research by social scientist Robert Putnam, author of *Bowling Alone*, a book on declining civic engagement published in 2000, continues to support the Pew Foundation's premise that organizations and communities of all sizes have difficulty gathering all the stakeholders around the table. Encouraging key stakeholders to remain committed to the work of the organization and its decision-making processes is a hallmark of good leadership. Stakeholders are impacted by the organization's actions; therefore, they have important information to add to the deliberations of a group. Organizations cannot afford to exclude their representation and thus their perspectives. The more varied the ideas and experiences at the table, the stronger and more innovative the solution (Jonas, 2007).

Tips for Enabling Meeting Participants

Meeting planners can do many things to enable the participants to be effective:

- Securing meeting times and locations convenient to participants
- Allowing time for participants to learn about each other
- Providing adequate notice for meetings
- Sharing agendas and supporting materials for meetings in advance
- Sharing expectations about the type of work to be done in the meetings
- Starting and ending on time
- Showing genuine appreciation for the participants' work at the meeting

Essentially, all suggestions described in the first part of this chapter are actions that enable meeting participants to work at their best and create a desire to want to attend the meeting. Everyone wants to be part of an effective group that accomplishes what it sets out to do.

DECISION MAKING

Decision making is one of the most important actions groups can take. Before a group determines a course of action and the related action items are assigned, the participants first need to have clarification on the necessary related issues, must be able to provide input, and engage in discussion to forecast each possible solution. Only then can the group make effective decisions and take action. This process seems logical and simple on the surface. The complexity multiplies with each person, viewpoint, set of experiences, and leadership of the group.

REFLECTION: YOUR EXPERIENCE WITH GROUP DECISION MAKING

Every day, you make a series of decisions such as selecting an outfit, your route to work, or the items that make up your lunch. These are choices you usually make alone, using your own judgment and experience on style, traffic patterns, and nutrition. Imagine adding one more person to the decision-making process; the amount of dialogue and feedback required has increased exponentially.

Now let's consider a work team or whole organization. The decision-making process becomes even more complex due to the number of people now participating in the process.

Have you participated in a large (five or more) group decision-making process? Describe the decision the group was charged to make.

- Was it simple or complex?
- Was it a short or lengthy process?
- Did everyone in the group work together respectfully? Did you feel heard?
- Was data collected and then used to inform the team's discussion?
- What method was used in the decision-making process? Did group members vote? Did the senior member of the group make the decision?
- Did the group support the final decision? Did you support the final decision? Did others support the decision in the organization?
- Who decided how to make the final decision? If you were doing this again, would you use the same process?
- Were the different possible solutions reviewed in detail during the decision-making process before the group decided on one? Did you understand what made the selected solution superior to the other options?

Whether your previous experience using group decision making was positive or negative, the question set reveals a number of actions leaders and groups should take to achieve a quality decision-making process and outcome.

DIAGNOSIS: THE STEPS IN DECISION MAKING

There is a logical set of steps groups frequently fail to follow in the full decision-making process. First, they must determine how they will make the final decision. Second, they must describe the problem as clearly as possible. Third, they must explore possible solutions and related issues by gathering and organizing data. Last is using the process identified in step 1 to make the decision. Beginning with step 1, if a leader or organizational authority figure is in the group, he or she should determine the decision-making process. This is part of the leader's responsibility. However, when the line of authority is not clear (as frequently happens in nonprofit and community collaborations), group members jointly decide. This fuzzy line of authority is also common in educational and human services organizations, especially in dealing with family situations and service providers from many departments.

When deciding on the decision-making process (Patterson, Grenny, McMillan, & Switzler, 2002), there are four questions to consider:

1. Who cares? Choosing participants for the process should come from those who care and are affected.

2. Who knows? Experts on the situation are always important to include on the team.

3. Who must agree? This is a question about stakeholders, those individuals who might enable the service to take place, or bring helpful influence and approval at a later stage.

4. How many people should be involved? Do we have enough or too many people to make a good choice and give the decision momentum to carry it through the action stage?

In step 2, the group facilitator/leader must help the group achieve clarity about the problem itself. In haste to hurry a decision or to take control, leaders can cause critical errors at this step when the group is excluded from or eliminates problem clarification. It is easy to allow previous patterns of experiences to steer the leader to ignore small differences and make assumptions (Campbell, Whitehead, & Finkelstein, 2009). Everyone must be on the same path toward solving the same problem.

In step 3, the group must decide how to incorporate and sort through the many types and quantity of ideas and data in the decision-making process. There are some helpful tools used in the quality management profession that can be very useful for all kinds of organizations when sifting through the data. You will see several examples later in this chapter.

In step 4, the actual act of making the decision becomes a "fait accompli" for the group by having successfully worked through steps 1 through 3. Too many times groups become stuck in the process and never actually make the choice. Frustration ensues and participants and stakeholders withdraw. Clients soon look to other organizations to meet their needs.

PRESCRIPTION: THE TOOLS OF DECISION MAKING

According to Patterson et al. (2002, pp. 164–173), the four basic methods of decision making are command, consult, vote, and consensus. Each of these options, from command to consensus, brings increased degrees of involvement from the group with the level of commitment increasing in tandem. Moving from command to consensus also tips the scales toward a much more process-oriented and time-consuming procedure. The four methods are described with details about their rules for use as well as their weaknesses.

Command decisions usually come from external sources, such as government mandates, professional requirements, and safety standards. Organization leaders simply convene their groups to make the decisions work. In a few other command situations, leaders may choose to let someone else make the decision because it is a low-stakes decision or one leaders in the organization do not care about. However, leaders should be cautious when using the command method. The current generation of employees expects to be involved in the decision-making process. Rules when using this method include the following:

1. Don't allow command decisions to become as frequent as the daily coffee break. Find ways to incorporate choices or flexibility.

2. Explain the "why" of the decision. This generation does not follow blindly. The more people who understand why the decisions are necessary, the more likely they are to buy in to its implementation, facilitate the implementation, or follow the decision.

Consulting is a good way to gather lots of data for a decision when the decision makers are not the experts on the subject. Maybe an organization is building a new facility, and the leader selects a committee to investigate and visit facilities built during the previous 3 years for organizations similar to yours. Large amounts of data will be collected, including the experiences of each of the new facility's users. Using this method, the organization's leader will need to specify whether or not the facility designers and data collectors will be invited to participate in the decision-making process. The leader must be very clear at the beginning of the process on the parameters for participation. There are suggested rules for when and how to use the consulting method:

1. Many people will be affected by the decision.

2. Large quantities of information must be gathered.

3. People care about the decision and the impact it will have.

4. There are many possible solutions, some of which could be expensive or controversial.

5. Communicate who will participate in the data collection and decision-making processes as well as why these people were chosen.

6. Do not pretend to consult with a team if the leader has already decided. Doing so will cause group members to distrust the leader for disrespecting the time, effort, and information contributed.

Voting is helpful when efficiency is needed and there are several good choices from which to select. However, voting creates winners and losers. Organization leaders will want to consider the reaction of the losers. Rules for selecting a voting method are as follows:

1. The choices are not weighty matters.

2. There are many good choices.

3. Participants care more about not spending too much time on the choice.

4. It is useful to *reduce* a long list of possible solutions so that a different decision-making process can be used to select from the shorter list.

5. Voting should never be the "cop-out" method when participants cannot achieve a choice through other decision-making processes.

Consensus is a dialogue among participants that allows all to share thoughts, ideas, and arrive at a common choice everyone supports. This process can unify a group and generate high quality solutions. Consensus is about choosing what is best for everyone. However, this process can be overused and implemented poorly. Participants of an overused consensus method could lose patience and the focus needed on complex issues. Leaders must maintain patience and help the group stay focused. The consensus decision-making process should be used under the following circumstances:

1. With high stakes and complex issues.

2. When choices are not equally liked.

3. Everyone cares and is affected by the issues.

4. Everyone in the group must have adequate time to devote to the consensus process.

5. Group members participate in healthy discussions by respecting everyone's ideas and opinions. Disagreements must not become personal.

6. Group members must not lobby for a solution nor give in to others' ideas.

7. Everyone must support the final solution; all participants own triumphs and failures.

Gathering the Data for Decision Making

Gathering and organizing data are important initial steps in the decision-making process. The methods used to analyze the data can profoundly affect the decision-making process in regard to clarity, group members' feelings of contribution, and buy-in. Brassard and Ritter, authors of the book *Memory Jogger 2* published in 2010, describe four techniques that can be added to the leader's repertoire of group tools used in decision making.

Tool #1

Brainstorming is a common group technique used for creating an unlimited number of ideas that can generate solutions to problems and spark new program ideas. Brainwriting 6-3-5, as described below, is a different approach that might generate breakthrough ideas and new excitement from the team.

Why use Brainwriting 6-3-5?

- Provides a time and structure for teams to thoughtfully generate a large number of ideas as well as to find unusual connections and combinations among the listed ideas

What is Brainwriting 6-3-5?

- Provides a worksheet for team members to record ideas
- Combines the group's energy of exchanging ideas in a thoughtful written process
- Diffuses emotional issues that may reduce participation and creative flow among team members
- More likely to build synergy among the team than brainstorming

How should Brainwriting 6-3-5 be used in a group?

- Involve the whole group to clarify the topic and then write it as a problem statement.
- The target size group for this technique is four to six individuals. If you are in a larger group, divide the larger group into smaller groups of four to six to maintain the suggested range.
- Give each participant a Brainwriting 6-3-5 worksheet as shown in Figure 7.1. Each person records the problem statement at the top of the worksheet.
- The object is to take 5 minutes to write three ideas (one per box beginning in row 1) that could lead to a solution. Group members should not talk during the writing time. Use a six- to ten-word sentence to describe your idea. If you are unable to think of three ideas, leave the other box(es) blank.
- After 5 minutes has passed, send the worksheet to the person on the right in your group. Group members are then instructed to read the previous person's ideas. Once everyone has done this, 5 more minutes are on the clock for another round of three ideas. Use the previous person's thoughts to build on, write a variation of, or to stimulate a new idea.
- Circulate the worksheets until everyone has added three ideas to each sheet. For each round, the same rules apply. Group members are to read the previously listed ideas before they contribute their own. As more rounds are completed, it may take a bit longer to read all the ideas and write. Add a little time as needed.

- Review all the ideas as a whole team. Eliminate duplicates. Clarify others as needed.
- Sort the ideas using an Affinity Diagram or the Nominal Group Technique (described after the sample Brainwriting 6-3-5 form in Figure 7.1).

Figure 7.1   Brainwriting 6-3-5 Format

Problem Statement:			
	Idea #1	Idea #2	Idea #3
Round 1			
Round 2			
Round 3			
Round 4			
Round 5			
Round 6			

Source: Brassard, M., Ritter, D., and Oddo, F. *Memory Jogger 2: Tools for Continuous Improvement and Effective Planning.* (2010). Goal/QPC.

Tool #2

An Affinity Diagram organizes a large number of creative ideas. Why use an Affinity Diagram?

- Gives the team a technique to cluster the ideas into natural groupings that provide clarity about the problem and can lead to breakthrough solutions

What is an Affinity Diagram?

- Encourages creativity in all stages of the process
- Breaks down communication barriers in the team
- Encourages a nontraditional look at connections among ideas
- Allows breakthrough thinking to occur naturally
- Encourages ownership of ideas and results since the team is actively involved in both
- Overcomes team paralysis brought on by an overwhelming array of options and a lack of consensus

How should I use an Affinity Diagram?

- Record ideas on large sticky notes in an ink and letter size that are seen from a distance. Use phrases with a noun and verb. Most Affinity Diagrams have 10 to 40 ideas on sticky notes to group in clusters.
- Invite all group members to participate. On a wall, whiteboard, or flipchart and without talking, the group members move the sticky notes into clusters where the ideas seem to belong together. Sorting will slow or stop when each person feels comfortable with the groupings. Silence is important at this stage so groupings do not appear because of history or emotion. If one or two items travel frequently among clusters in the process, consider making a duplicate to temporarily put ideas into two clusters. (Be sure to label those as duplicates.) It is also okay for some notes to stand alone.
- Gain team consensus on a theme for each cluster, write it on a sticky note, and place the different themes above or centered in each cluster. Then working a bit more slowly, go back and rename each cluster with a concise statement that captures the grouping's central idea being sure each note in the cluster still connects. You may choose to edit the summary statement or move that idea note to another cluster or to stand alone. If the cluster of ideas is too large to summarize with a concise statement, you may also choose to create two smaller clusters from the large one. It is during this process of creating the concise summary statements that breakthrough ideas occur.

Figure 7.2 is a final Affinity Diagram arranged with the summary statements at the top of each column of sticky note ideas.

This is a small example of an Affinity Diagram from staff discussions for improvements to follow-up call procedures. If the group chose not to use an Affinity Diagram, you might instead use the Nominal Group Technique (NGT).

Tool #3

NGT provides groups a way to rank choices for a consensus discussion.
Why use the nominal group technique?

- Allows groups to include the individual importance of issues by ranking each idea

What is the NGT?

- Builds commitment to the group's choice through equal participation in the process
- Allows every group member to rank issues without pressure from others

Figure 7.2   Affinity Diagram of Client Follow-Up Services

Problem Statement: Issues Associated With Clients Receiving Follow-Up Calls		
Summary: Providers' Issues	Summary: Members' Issues	Summary: Outreach Issues
Staff too busy	Client's lack of awareness that call is provided	Unable to contact due to inaccurate intake information
Staff's lack of training in follow-up procedures	Client's lack of understanding of follow-up call benefits	Outdated files showing who is due for follow-up

- Puts quiet group members on an equal footing with more dominant members
- Makes a group consensus or lack of it visible and allows the major causes of disagreement to be discussed

How should I use the NGT?

- From previously generated (using brainstorming, brainwriting, etc.) lists of issues, problems, or solutions to be prioritized by the group, statements are written on a white board or flipchart.
- As a list is created, group clarifies meaning of each item, and duplicates are eliminated.
- Record final list so all can see using letters as identifiers (since numbers will be used in the ranking process).
- Each participant records the identifying letter associated to each idea of the list and gives each letter a number indicating its rank or preference.

Example:
Issue: Why does intake paperwork have errors?

A. Lack of staff training

B. Unclear directions for client

C. Clients do not allow enough time to complete paperwork before appointment

D. Clients do not bring data needed to complete paperwork

Participant ranking sheet

A. 3

B. 4

C. 1

D. 2

Then combine the rankings of all team members. Such a process can reveal the sentiment of the group or at least eliminate a suggestion or two. In this example in the Figure 7.3, idea B is not a highly valued suggestion by the group. Although there is a top-ranked item (Danielle rated it #1), its ranking is still close in value to the A and D ranked ideas. Although C looks to be the runaway contender for most highly ranked reason, it will be important to share the thinking for the rankings in the group. The discussion to achieve consensus will likely have a higher degree of success because of each participant's engagement in the ranking process.

Instead of or in addition to sorting ideas generated by a group, there may be a need to identify root causes of a problem so that the group works to solve the actual problem instead of a surface symptom.

Tool #4

The Cause and Effect Fishbone Diagram is a tool that enables a group to identify and explore the possible causes of a problem that can lead to undesirable or desirable results.

Figure 7.3   Nominal Group Technique

Ideas	Maria	John	Danielle	Stephen	Amy	Total
A	3	2	4	3	4	16
B	4	3	1	4	2	14
C	1	1	2	2	1	7
D	2	4	3	1	3	13

Why use the Cause and Effect Fishbone Diagram?

• Enables a group to discover root causes and not just treat symptoms.

What is the Cause and Effect Fishbone Diagram?

• Enables the group to focus on the content of the problem, not the history or personal connections.
• Creates a snapshot of the collective knowledge around a problem and builds support for resulting solution.
• Focuses the group on causes not symptoms.

How should I use the Cause and Effect Fishbone Diagram?

• Write a problem statement as specifically as possible. Establish group's agreement with statement.
• Brainstorm a list of causes for the problem statement.
• Select cause categories. Common labels for these cause categories include management/leadership; measurements; materials; people; processes; machines/equipment; technology; sources; products, programs, and services; and environment/location. Some fishbone diagrams will have four ribs, others six or more. Use only the categories that make sense for your group's problem. Determination of the categories is a group decision.
• Draw the diagram that will sort and arrange the current work of the group. The diagram (Figure 7.4) resembles a basic fish shape: head, backbone, and ribs. The problem statement in the fish diagram appears as the "head" of the

Figure 7.4 The Cause and Effect Fishbone Diagram

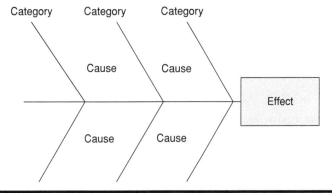

fish and is referred to as the effect. The problem is seen as the result of the root cause.

- Draw a backbone horizontally from the head, or the problem statement, that connects the lines representing the ribs. (See Figure 7.4.) Each of the ribs of the fish is labeled as a category of causes. The smaller lines joining the ribs represent the range of possible causes in that category. Arrange the causes already brainstormed. It is possible you may have to add or eliminate a rib/ cause or brainstorm additional ones to complete a forgotten category.
- Once the drawing is labeled and the data/ideas sorted in the fishbone framework, causes become easily identified for group discussion, decision making, and problem solving.

SUMMARY

Effectively running meetings and making decisions are much overlooked "soft" skills that leaders and managers take for granted. Given the amount of time spent in meetings as well as the impact of meeting environments on participants' effectiveness, sharpening meeting skill sets is important to the group's and organization's success.

Planning and facilitating a thoughtful, organized, and effective meeting solidifies the trust you have worked toward with your team members and shows you value their knowledge and experiences. It also sends a clear message regarding productivity and accountability expectations when you exhibit those same behaviors during meetings where the key planning and report outs take place. Bad attitudes quickly develop when the team members believe the leadership wastes their time in meetings when their input was neither requested nor valued. Become the host of meetings and decision making in which group members want to participate.

Avoid the do-nothing reputation of some groups who can't make a decision. Intentionally take each step in the process and choose the best method for the situation. Deciding how to decide establishes trust through transparency in the decision-making process. This is why the government in the Sunshine Act of 1976 became vital to the public regarding public institutions. Teams and citizens both want to know how and why decisions are made. Be a champion of keeping the communication channels open so everyone has access to the information. Leadership in the sunshine puts the office grapevine out of business.

REFERENCES

Brassard, M., & Ritter, D. (2010). *Memory jogger 2: Tools for continuous improvement and effective planning.* Salem, NH: Goal QPC.

Campbell, A., Whitehead, J., & Finkelstein, S. (2009). Why good leaders make bad decisions. *Harvard Business Review, 87*(2), 60–66.

Jonas, M. (2007). The downside of diversity. *The Boston Globe.* Retrieved from http://www.boston.com

Patterson, K., Grenny, J., McMillan, R., & Switzler, A. (2002). *Crucial conversations: Tools for talking when stakes are high.* New York, NY: McGraw-Hill.

Pew Foundation for Civic Trust. (2001). Module 4: Making meetings work better. *Leadership Plenty.* Charlottesville, VA: Civic Change, Inc.

Putnam, R. (2000). *Bowling alone: The collapse and revival of American community.* New York, NY: Simon and Schuster.

Part III

Development of Organizations

Chapter 8

Organizational Management—Vision, Mission, and Strategic Planning

LEARNING OBJECTIVES

The student will

- define and explain the impact of organizational culture;
- complete, analyze, and draw conclusions from a SWOT (strengths, weaknesses, opportunities, and threats) analysis;
- explain the value of the organization vision, mission, and goals to leading strategically;
- examine organizational mission statements to determine fit and alignment with organizational goals and strategy; and
- use a root cause analysis to determine core business purpose of an organization.

PANORAMIC VIEW OF AN ORGANIZATION

In Chapter 3, you completed self-assessment exercises to learn more about yourself, your behavior style, and how your perceptions influence your choices. This chapter is the organization's version of the in-depth look through the lenses of its culture, vision, mission, and strategic plans. These four pictures define the organization for the stakeholders by telling them why it was founded, what will always be true, and the direction it is going. In this chapter, you will also see that in successful organizations, there is a direct link, called alignment, between an organization's culture, vision statement, mission statement, and strategic plan. The pictures come together like a panoramic view of the organization as opposed to four distinct pictures.

The culture of an organization consists of the visible and invisible behaviors, attitudes, and beliefs that influence how an organization does its day-to-day business. It provides a set of social norms for how employees interact (Schen, 2010). According to Schen, there is no conclusive research demonstrating the performance of certain culture characteristics at the highest levels; research does support the necessity of an organizational culture supportive and in alignment with the vision, mission, and goals. Like individual leaders, organizations must have the integrity to walk their talk.

Other leadership books will define the vision, mission, and strategic planning processes, but in this chapter, you will experience participating in the steps of preparing each. Many leaders use these skills both in the workplace, as well as in school and community organizations. These are important competencies for leaders. The vision statement is not just an enjoyable process that provides a catchy sentence for the organization's marketing brochure; it is the organization's North Star, and it creates the starting point for the important alignment system of organizational development.

VISION

Just as you have hopes and dreams for your future, so does an organization. Individuals who work and volunteer with an organization share a common idea about what is important, and they believe this idea will collectively guide them into the future. Writing down and coming to a unanimous agreement regarding the organization's vision might be a new idea for you. You might have seen a vision or mission statement hanging in your boss' office or the employee lounge. This section will define the vision statement, why it is important, the difference between a vision and a mission statement, and how you can help an organization write one. A vision statement describes the values and purposes the organization will always stand for (Nanus, 1992). This means no matter what changes in the community, the marketplace, or the leadership of the organization, the organization's vision remains unchanged.

REFLECTION: THE ROLE OF VALUES IN A VISION

Working and becoming a part of a profession requires knowledge of your values, as well as those of the professional association and the place of employment. Building a movement based on values ignited the colonists and played a large role in the development of our country. The US Declaration of Independence illuminated key values that motivated the 13 colonies to separate from Great Britain by its emphasis on basic truths and values necessary for basic human rights of the people of this new nation: "We hold these truths to be self-evident, that all men are created equal, that they are endowed by their Creator with certain unalienable rights, that among these are Life, Liberty, and the pursuit of Happiness." In addition to the swell of pride felt when these words are spoken, the pictures in the collective minds of citizens then, and even now, create a vision defining the heart of this new nation. These core principles have endured over centuries, through social changes, and changes in national leadership. Our leaders continue to look to these values, which helped define the Constitution, Bill of Rights, and other federal laws. Although your profession and place of employment will likely not have such a dramatic start, nor ask you to lay down your life to work there, you will be a most unhappy employee if there is little truth in the principles and values on which the organization is founded. It is the principles and values that support the vision of the organization.

What are the principles and values of your place of employment? Your university? What are the visions of these organizations in your life? Do you feel part of it, or are they just words you had to research on a website?

DIAGNOSIS: VALUES, THE FIRST POINT OF THE CONSTELLATION OF EXCELLENCE

You probably have dreams about the difference you want to make in the world and have imagined yourself in your career accomplishing those changes. Your dreams to change the world are built on your values. In Chapter 4, you identified which core values were important to you. Through reflection, you observed how those values impact your daily life. In addition to your core values, the human services profession expects all practitioners in the field to endorse and live up to the standards of its values and code of ethics. Find the lists and completed exercises from your work in Chapter 4—you will need them for the upcoming exercise.

Starting with the list of principles you developed in Chapter 4, make a list of the core principles, values, and purposes that guide you. Consider those guiding principles and values shared by parents and grandparents, your faith, your community, as well as those things you want to pass on to your family now or in the future. From that list, identify which are your core values:

a. 1.

b. 2.

c. 3.

d. 4.

e. 5.

Gut check: Will these principles continue to guide your future if you had to give up something precious—such as a special friendship—to retain them? Which principles would you let go to be able to keep the friendship? Which ones would you retain? This exercise, while it may seem harsh, helps you eliminate the "fair weather" values on your list. It is important to identify those select few that are truly your core. (*Few* is defined as three to five core values and purposes.)

Compare your core values to the values and code of ethics in the human services profession (see http://www.nationalhumanservices.org/ethical-standards-for -hs-professionals). Do you see any connections? Review your core values to learn whether you have alignment with the core values of your future profession. Alignment is a relationship of parts coming together, to agree with a cause, to find similarities of purpose. Using a 10-point scale (1 is low, 5 is moderate, and 10 is high), rate the alignment between your core values and the core values of the human services profession (National Organization for Human Services, 2015) below:

- Appreciation for human beings in all their diversity; treating all clients with respect, acceptance, and dignity
- Protection of the client's right to privacy in both the helping relationship and records of services
- Service as an advocate for clients by keeping current on breaking research and policies
- Engagement as an active member of the network of human services professional in order to provide the highest quality options for client services
- Leadership for the improvement of client services, the growth of the organization, the collaboration with other colleagues and agencies, and the resulting community that embraces all its citizens

A score of less than 25 should give you pause as you explore and prepare for a career in human services.

Alignment is not only important for vision, mission, and strategic planning, but also it is important for the members of a profession to have alignment between their personal values and the values of the profession. This alignment is a significant factor in the sense of "fit" an individual feels within his or her profession. Dym and Hutson (2005) constructed a model showing the many facets of alignment between leaders and organizations (see Table 8.1).

Dym and Hutson (2005) assert that the fundamental challenge of leadership is the alignment of three components: the leader, the organization, and the community (p. 93). Now imagine an alignment with organizational, leader, and follower values. That is the core of an organization's strength, according to Jim Collins and Jerry Porras (1994). Their book, *Built to Last: Successful Habits of Visionary Companies*, studied successful companies and found evidence of the three-way

Table 8.1   Alignment Between Leaders and Organizations

	Leader	**Organization**	**Community/Market**
Basic Nature	Character and Style	Organizational Type	Patterns and Norms
Underlying Principles	Personal Values	Organizational Vision	Larger Culture
Means Available	Means Available	Organizational Resources	Economy
Purpose and Direction	Personal Objectives	Mission and Strategy	Community Needs and Market Demands

Source: Adapted from Dym, B., & Hutson, H. (2005). *Leadership in nonprofit organizations.* Thousand, Oaks, CA: Sage.

alignment of values as well as outperformance of the general stock market by a factor of 12 since 1925. Creating and building the vision on values is what inspires the employees and leaders and provides the first point of alignment in the constellation of strategy, goals, and decisions. It is the practice of setting a vision you must now master.

PRESCRIPTION: WRITING A VISION STATEMENT

Collins and Porras (2011, pp. 79) state, "There are two major components to a vision statement":

- Core ideology – defines what we stand for and why we exist
  - o Core values – guiding principles
  - o Core purpose – reason for being
- Envisioned future – what we aspire to become, achieve, create and will require significant change and progress to attain.

Nanus (1992, pp. 46–51) described a successful process to write a vision statement for an organization. It begins with an exploration of the organization's core values and purpose by asking the following:

- What value does the organization provide to society?
- What is the character of the work sector in which the organization resides?
- What is the organization's unique position in the institutional structure?
- What does it take for the organization to succeed?
- What values govern behavior and decision making?
- What are the operating strengths and weaknesses?
- What is the current organizational strategy and is it still valid?

Senge (1994, pp. 228–230) recommends using similar questions worked through earlier in this section as you begin the discovery of core ideology by arriving at core values for the constituent group:

- What values do you personally bring to your work?
- What would you tell your children are the core values you hold at work?
- Would you continue to hold this core value if it became disadvantageous to you in the workplace?
- If you were to start a new organization tomorrow, what core values would you build into it?

Creating a vision statement is a collaborative process of discovery that begins by starting with the individuals in the organization. If it is a large organization, you may need to establish a constituent group to begin the process. Once core values are uncovered for this smaller group, they are communicated to the larger group of employees. If the smaller group is representative, there will likely be alignment with the larger group. If not, the smaller group may need to be expanded, and the discovery process is repeated. It is not uncommon for the organizations core values to have originated from the founder, according to Schen (2010). While the organization developed, some values evolved over time as additional leaders and employees influenced the organization's culture.

Before moving from values to a vision statement, look at this nonprofit vision statement. It is not difficult to postulate the core values from a vision statement. Using the vision statement of the United Way of America, we will work backward to determine the organization's core values: "United Way envisions a world where individuals and their families achieve their human potential through education, income stability, and healthy lives" (http://www.unitedway.org).

Core values for the United Way:

1. Focus on individuals and families

2. Share a global vision

3. A belief that education, successful job skills, and health care should be part of the common good of the world's social and economic system

Core purpose is the second half of determining the core ideology. It helps answer the question, "Why do you perform the organization's work?" Asking the "why" question once generally gives a surface answer and we are after the core purpose. Similar to the process of root cause analysis, asking the "why" question five times will bring you to a root cause/core purpose.

1. Why does United Way fund this set of services in my community?
   Ask Why? Why? Why? Why? Why?

2. Why do children need tutoring and after school care? Why do families making minimum wage need support for health care?
   Ask Why? Why? Why? Why? Why?

3. Why are children unable to finish high school? What health risks do children face that could lead to them dropping out of high school?
   Ask Why? Why? Why? Why? Why?

4. Why are good paying jobs important for all young adults? What health habits impede successful workplace habits?
   Ask Why? Why? Why? Why? Why?

5. Why is the Gallop Organization so interested in its study on well-being and how it impacts education, health care, and job success as well as the individual and family's ability to thrive?
   Ask Why? Why? Why? Why? Why?

Core purpose of the United Way of America: Seek to uplift human potential.

Once you have worked through the five whys to arrive at a core purpose, you will want to test the statements using questions suggested by Collins and Porras (2011, p. 90).

- What would be lost if your organization ceased to exist?
- If you woke up tomorrow with enough money to retire, why would you continue to work at this organization?
- Why should people give full measure of their effort to this organization?

Core ideology is discovered, not created. It speaks with meaning and passion to the people inside the organization.

It is possible for two organizations to have the same core values and purpose; the differences will be established in how they choose to achieve their purposes. Managers must spend time communicating to all their staff about the organization's core ideology. It is what keeps them proud and excited about their organization. Students call that "school pride" when referring to student accomplishments in the classrooms and on the athletic fields. It is what keeps alumni making donations and returning for reunions. In organizations, members feel a sense of connection and pride as a result of the core ideology.

The second part of the vision statement is the envisioned future. It too has a two-part writing process. The first part is a compelling goal that will take 10 to 30 years to accomplish (Juran & De Feo, 2010). The second part is a detailed description of what it will be like when the goal is achieved. Starting with the compelling goal, the organization is seeking to identify a major stretch, a goal that everyone can point to with excitement, one that will take hard work and strong commitment from everyone. It is a goal that might make you step back and take a deep breath to say, "Can we do this?" It stretches the current capabilities of the organization and elevates the gaze of the leadership team to look toward the future at their North Star. It is also a goal that is connected to the first point in the alignment constellation, core ideology.

Again, Collins and Porras (2011) give guidance on the key questions to create a compelling visionary goal—is the visionary goal related to the following:

- A quantitative or qualitative target?
  - Become the organization providing the highest quality online training in job skills.
  - Become the most far-reaching international children's health organization.
- A common enemy?
  - Cancer will be a disease read about in history books.
  - The program will eliminate childhood obesity in the nation.
- A role model?
  - We will become the Smithsonian of the Southwest.
  - We will become as focused on improvement as SAAS/NIATx (State Associations of Addictive Services).
- An internal transformation?
  - Transform this organization to be the first choice partner for collaboration in behavioral health care.
  - Transform this institution to be the most respected provider of after-school child services.

The second part of writing the envisioned future is to describe it in such a way that everyone pictures the same goal. The organization wants to know what the goal looks like, sounds like, feels like, and maybe even tastes like. It will have to paint a picture for all the senses. This description (although not part of the vision statement) will become part of the organization's story, and it must communicate passion and conviction. As a story, it needs to be repeated often and used in many communications with staff, donors, community partners, and board members. Stakeholders must not buy in; they must enroll in the process to achieve the vision as well as know and tell the story themselves (Senge, 1994).

Juran and De Feo (2010, p. 236) warn against some common pitfalls in creating vision statements:

- Think that once a strategic plan is written, the vision will be carried out with no further work.
- Fail to explain the vision as a benefit to all stakeholders.
- Create a vision too easy or too difficult to achieve.

- Fail to consider the effects that rapid changes in the global economy will have 3 to 5 years in the future.
- Fail to involve key employees at all levels in creating the vision.
- Fail to benchmark all competitors or consider all sources of information on future needs, internal capabilities, and external threats.

SUMMARY

A vision statement that lights the way to the future of the organization also lights the way for a work team to become passionate about working toward the vision. As you craft the organization's vision statement, Juran and De Feo (2010) issue a warning to be careful in confusing core purpose with the compelling goal. Keep in mind, with each step taken, the core purpose gets closer but is never quite achieved. It will continue to serve as the organization's North Star, guiding decisions and creating targets for stretch goals. Remember also that the first part of the vision writing process is a discovery process, while the second part is a creative process. Avoid using an analytical approach, and the vision will emerge from the process instead of become forced. The expiration date for a vision statement is when the compelling goals are achieved or when rapid changes in society bring new service needs and clientele. Following a recommitment to the core ideology, the vision statement process repeats, followed by new compelling goals. Remember the core ideology does not change, ever.

MISSION STATEMENT

If a vision statement captures the core essence and the optimal desired future state of the organization's achievements, an organizational mission statement defines the present purpose of the organization.

REFLECTION: CONFUSION AND INCONSISTENCY IN THE WORKPLACE

Running in 10 directions at the same time is how some employees describe it. Flavor-of-the-month is another common description. Employees are frustrated and feel they have no control over their everyday purpose. Or employees are disillusioned because they believe that no matter what they do, it will all change or be forgotten tomorrow. Here are a few employee comments from an organization without direction:

- Have you ever felt a lack of focus in the task and meeting topic choices of your work group? This week one topic seems critical and the next week it feels that the group is off on something totally disconnected to the previous discussion.

- Do you struggle with identifying which task choices to resource? They all seem important.
- The CEO sends a memo on a concern, your group spends time planning a new solution, and the approval for resources to the plan is denied.
- Do you simply decide not to decide and let others influence your choices? When confusion reigns, it might feel easier to let others choose how you spend your time or even taking the first offer. Things change too quickly in your work environment.

These are employees struggling to have purpose in a workplace that has no clearly defined purpose. Frustration and disillusionment reign supreme followed by job hunting to find organizations that have a purpose. And of course, the purpose must align with the employees' purposes, their personal mission statements.

Now imagine the importance and power of a mission statement for an organization of many people. Picture the employees confident in their task choices, contributing to the team's goals, and proud of their work and their organization.

DIAGNOSIS: DEFINING THE ORGANIZATION'S PURPOSE

With the power and significance of an organizational mission statement so clear in our minds, writing the statement itself becomes a high priority. First, let's begin with the end in mind: What will an organizational mission statement look like when complete? Since you are familiar with the United Way of America's vision statement, let's use their mission statement as an organizational example:

Example 1: "United Way improves lives [key output] by mobilizing the caring power [verb] of community around the world [by whom] to advance the common good [key output]" (http://www.unitedway.org/pages/mission-and-goals).

What is the business of the United Way of America? From their mission statement, we can identify the organization's three major roles:

1. Improving lives

2. Mobilizing caring citizens in communities

3. Advancing the common good

These statements clarify the "what" component. The "how" component is defined by the organization's methods of mobilizing caring power. This simple sentence is mobilizing volunteers all across the country and around the world. We can recognize that United Way does not provide direct services, but is instead a catalyst in communities to improve lives and provide for the common good. As a catalyst, the organization raises monies and awareness to community needs. They do not have clients or customers; therefore, the "who" component is missing, although implied by the phrase "communities around the world."

Here is another example of a human services organization mission statement; however, this is a direct service provider:

> Example 2: Tennessee Department of Human Services: "To offer [verb] temporary economic assistance, work opportunities, and protective services [key outputs] to improve the lives of Tennesseans [Clients]" (http://www.tn.gov/humanserv).

The department's major roles are as follows:

- Temporary economic assistance
- Work opportunities
- Protective services

How they perform is by offering their programs to individuals and agencies. Many of their clients come by referral or are mandated to come by policies and rulings of other agencies. They also have offices across the state in many Tennessee communities, enabling them to deliver their services to their clients, "improving the lives of Tennesseans."

When starting to write a mission statement, notice that the examples above are memorable. That means they are short and to the point. A mission statement is useless if you have to look it up each time it is used. Consider an organization you work or volunteer for or even the school you attend. Begin the process of writing an organizational mission statement by describing the purpose of the organization; a mission statement provides clarity to these three basic statements:

1. What an organization does (These are the roles/functions.)

2. Who the organization does it for

3. How the organization does what it does

To start the statement, we will use a formula to identify the major components of the statement. Then you can create the full statement from the components, adding a bit of flair and passion. Review the list of statements and find the verbs you used. These are listed under (b). What are the key outputs (c) of the organization? These should be in the lists you generated when answering question 1. Question 2 addresses who the key customers (d) are.

a. To (opening word)

b. Verb (1 or 2)

    c. Key output (1–3)

    d. Key customer (1 or 2)

Draft the formula mission statement: To _____

_____

_____

_____

As an organization leader, having buy-in for the mission statement is mandatory. This requires involving all members of the organization, or if very large, having representatives from all levels, departments, and locations. You know you have an excellent candidate for the mission statement when it does the following:

1. Is the focus of everything you do

2. Everyone can relate what they do as the best way to accomplish the mission

3. Is short and can be memorized

4. Is used to help make decisions and guide actions

PRESCRIPTION: WRITE IT, PUBLISH IT, AND USE IT

What can a mission statement do for you? It can't do anything until it is deployed. That starts by leaders and employees knowing it and memorizing it. Distribute copies to employees and organization stakeholders; post it on the website and in high traffic areas of the organization facilities. Using it in decision-making meetings sends a clear message about purpose and focus as does including it as a part of leaders' and employees' performance reviews:

1. Have all employees/volunteers able to relate everything they do to the mission statement

2. Align goals based on which of them have the most impact on the mission

3. Eliminate activities that have the least impact on the mission

As a leader, how do you know if the organizational mission statement is at work?

1. Can all employees/volunteers recite the mission statement?

2. Can all employees/volunteers relate all of the important functions of their job to the best methods of mission accomplishment?

3. Is it used to make decisions at every level of the organization?

4. Is it used for alignment and prioritization of resources?

Think back to Chapter 6 and the discussion regarding managers and motivation. When employees know how their jobs connect to the organization mission and they can see they are critical to achieving successful results, employees work harder and are more engaged. An organization cannot establish an environment of positive employee engagement and commitment without an active and up-to-date mission statement.

With a clear mission statement, employees better understand organization decisions, changes, and resource reallocations, thereby reducing employee dissatisfaction. Employees also understand how their job connects to the organization's results and feel a sense of pride for being part of the success. The workplace that tries to be everything to everybody ends up being second-rate in most everything and ineffective in the clients' minds. Although most human services organizations are not hoping for a lifetime of "repeat business" as a for-profit organization might, they are looking for lifetime loyalty. Community supporters and advocates are who return when a human services organization achieves excellence. Too often government and nonprofit organizations mistakenly believe they will offend constituents if they focus their purpose and resources. What is most in demand is excellence, no matter the type of organization. Excellence requires focus.

SUMMARY

A mission statement is the second point in the constellation of alignment that guides the organization and its leaders. Like the basic definitions in geometry, the two points of vision and mission establish a line defining the purpose of the organization. For leaders, it provides navigation to chart a course for success and tells stakeholders what can be expected. This line provides the anchor for future action and direction from strategic planning.

STRATEGIC PLANNING

The third point in the constellation of navigation and alignment are the strategies for action and growth of the organization. Strategic planning is a process that enables leaders to analyze the organization internally as well as the future opportunities externally and determine a course of action that improves the chances of success. In the world of athletics, it is called a game plan. Every organization must have a game plan, which establishes its goals, objectives, scope, and competitive advantages. Each organization's strategy is unique and accounts for what is happening both inside and outside the organization. The process of developing the strategy involves a vision and mission, data collection, and planning with involvement from all key stakeholders. The actual planning part of the process typically involves one or two fully focused days, depending on the complexity and size of the organization.

REFLECTION: GETTING ADVICE TO ACHIEVE A GOAL

Your classmate, Sonia, shares a vision of developing a nonprofit that provides remedial education services for elementary school children. Sonia knows that to establish such an organization will require a college degree, so she enrolls in college with the mission and expectations of graduating with the knowledge and skills to create this dream job. If you were a college advisor to this student, check off all the items on the list in Table 8.2 that you might consider important, even strategic, to graduating with a path to this vision.

As you read through the list of 18 advisor suggestions, did the behaviors seem well advised and likely to propel Sonia toward achieving her mission? As Sonia's advisor, how many of the suggestions did you check? Were there others you might add to the list? Would you say this list could be a strategy? Without having a strategy, what do you think is the likelihood for a college graduate to achieve the vision of creating a nonprofit organization with the necessary business plan and leading it to become a successful enterprise?

Do you develop strategies for goals you want to achieve? Is comprehensive the adjective you would use to describe your strategy? What is a comprehensive strategic plan?

DIAGNOSIS: SWOT ANALYSIS THINKING

Returning to the previous example about Sonia, you will find the advisor's suggestion list consists of the beginning pieces to a comprehensive strategic plan. The creation of a strategic plan involves collecting facts and data that relate to the desired results. It is the facts and data that will lead us to create comprehensive strategies. Gathering the facts and data requires several methods. First, we have to look at both internal and external data. When reading the list of actions to help Sonia achieve her career plan, did you notice a pattern in the items on the left and the items on the right? The items on the left are totally in the control of the student. We describe those as internal to the student. As such, it is the student's choice regarding how she

Table 8.2   Advisor Suggestions

• Determine your academic strengths and weaknesses	• Investigate process of starting a nonprofit by talking to directors who started their own nonprofit organization
• Ascertain your ability to pay for all college costs each semester utilizing part-time work, financial aid, scholarships, monetary gifts, and budgeting	• Explore skill sets, experience, and grade point average expectations in demand by current employers in the human services and nonprofit sectors
• Dedicate study time to achieve grades required for employers or leave undergraduate school	• Explore employment locations and community needs for the education nonprofit idea
• Dedicate time to seek relevant work experience needed by the nonprofit sector	• Determine work experience required by nonprofit directors
• Dedicate time to overcome academic weaknesses relevant to key coursework	• Recruit references who can write strong letters of recommendation
• Maintain healthy habits for sustained energy to become a high achiever	• Learn to craft a competitive resume and cover letter
• Decide on an academic major and focus on completing its requirements	• Establish a career network of professionals who might become future partners in your vision
• Achieve and maintain a high grade point average	• Build a mentoring relationship with a faculty member
• Dedicate time to learn leadership skills	• Demonstrate leadership skills in campus and community groups

spends her time and if she maintains healthy habits. The items in the column on the right are not completely within her control; they are external. A student does not set salaries or requirements for jobs.

1. Review the internal capabilities to be assessed as noted above.

- Academic abilities for success in the classroom and in subjects related to the major and career choice
- Annual budget and ability to live within a budget that provides for college costs
- Ability to keep a schedule
- Available time to study
- Available time to participate in an internship or other relevant work experience
- Ability to make decisions from data

- Ability to maintain health throughout the college career
- Ability to master course content as measured by course grades

Brainstorm two additional internal capabilities useful for the student to assess.

2. Review the external capabilities to be assessed as noted above.

- Explore process of starting a nonprofit
- Analyze relationship of directing a nonprofit to related work experience, grade-point average, skill sets, leadership, and other college related experiences
- Identify potential locations for nonprofit and related community needs
- Research format of influential resumes and cover letters
- Request reference letters from respected faculty, employers, and community leaders
- Build network of professionals in the nonprofit sector
- Build mentoring relationships with knowledgeable leaders in the nonprofit sector

Brainstorm two additional external opportunities useful for the student to assess. Items in the left column (Table 8.2), if determined to be positive, are called internal strengths—those characteristics that enable us to perform well. Positive items in the right column (Table 8.2) are called external opportunities—trends, events, and forces you can capitalize on (Harvard Business Essentials, 2005). The gathering and analysis of facts and data must also include personal weaknesses and outside threats. Were there many weaknesses and threats detailed in Sonia's vision or in the advisor's suggestions to start a nonprofit? (Weaknesses: Characteristics that prohibit you from doing well and need to be addressed; Harvard Business Essentials, 2005).

3. Consider these weaknesses:

- Academic weaknesses in required courses or important skill set areas
- Inadequate resources to complete college curriculum
- Inability to set priorities and manage time according to priorities
- Behavior and health concerns
- Poor study habits
- Career interests in an area other than nonprofits
- Inability to craft requisite resume or cover letter
- No time to invest in leadership development

(Threats: These are possibilities outside of your control that you need to plan for or determine how to mitigate; Harvard Business Essentials, 2005).

4. Potential threats include the following:

- Unpredictable economy, which could lead to few start-up loans for a new nonprofit
- Career locations unacceptable to student or future/current spouse
- Unable to build a career network, reducing opportunities to establish non-profit sponsors
- Mentoring relationship is not genuine
- Other graduates with better grades, networks, resumes, skill sets, and leader-ship ability will seek to establish a competing organization

What other weaknesses and threats are missing? Add them to the appropriate list. Are the weaknesses and threats internal or external?

This method of analyzing data is called a SWOT Analysis:

S = Strengths	W = Weaknesses	Internal
O = Opportunities	T = Threats	External

Still serving as Sonia's advisor, look at the analysis of the four suggestion lists and related data. What strategies would you advise Sonia to follow? Do you have enough data to be specific? Can you prepare the data analysis in a way so Sonia knows exactly what to do? Can it be used to drive her initiative forward? Although this is a good sampling of the thought process in a SWOT analysis, a full strategic planning session for an organization includes much more.

PRESCRIPTION: THE STRATEGIC PLANNING PROCESS

The organization leader and executive team determines which stakeholders will be invited to participate in the strategic planning process. Involving more employees representing multiple functions is preferred if the space and facilitation process will allow. Engaging more employees in the process enriches perspectives and discussion. It is not uncommon for an outside consultant to facilitate the strategic planning meeting. A skilled consultant can ask deeper questions without offending the organization's employees and leadership. Hiring a consultant does not absolve the leader from knowing how to prepare for the event or how to best work with the results when the process is complete.

Dates are set and participants are invited. A list of organizational facts and data categories are assigned to key staff and leadership to collect, assemble, and distribute. In a human services agency, such items might include the following:

- Latest client needs assessment
- Community population demographics
- Budget and revenue statements from the current and previous years
- Regulatory rules, laws, and policies
- Local economy data
- Local health care statistics
- Current population potential for volunteers
- Competitors (other agencies in your delivery area who deliver similar services)
- Map of your organization's delivery area
- List of current programs and services with related results, measures, resources required

It is important that each strategic planning discussion participant have copies of the data in advance of the strategic planning session. Decision making is much simpler when everyone is working from the same data set.

The first phase of an organization drafting its strategic plan begins with the creation (or reexamination) of its vision, mission, and values. If these statements are being created, it will require the involvement of the staff. If it is a reexamination, the working group may be smaller. In most cases, a vision statement is not changed as part of this process. (See the first section of this chapter.) However, a mission statement is typically updated every 3 to 5 years. These are helpful questions (McClaskey & Owens, 2010) when updating a mission statement:

- Define the problem your organization seeks to solve.
- Describe the organization as the solution to the problem.
- What would be undone if your organization did not exist?
- Offer a solution (why and why now?)

The second part of the data and fact collection process is called the SWOT Analysis. This analysis gives us an environmental scan of the organization. Each of the four areas (Figure 8.1) is completed and then evaluated describing the situation as it is and what the desired state needs to be. Returning to the example with Sonia, an internal strength to Sonia's dream might be graduating with honors or personal leadership development skills. An internal weakness might be flaws in her plan to start the non-profit or failure to complete the college degree. External opportunities might be meeting a mentor to guide her journey to start the nonprofit. An external threat might be discovering several other nonprofits who are poised to provide the same service. This process is in many ways a gap analysis between the current situation and the desired situation. Studying and discussing the data gathered in preparation will provide indicators of opportunities or threats in relation to clients, the market, benchmarking against competitors, technology, and society trends.

Figure 8.1 SWOT Analysis

Internal Strengths	Internal Weaknesses
External Opportunities	External Threats

The outcome of the strategic development phase is to identify the organization's strategic objectives. Many times a strategy is built on a strength or core competence of the organization. Collis and Montgomery (as cited in Harvard Business Essentials, 2005, p. 21) recommend the following test to determine if the core competency is the basis for an effective strategy:

- It must be valued by the clients.
- It must be difficult to duplicate by your competitors.
- It must have a reasonable length of time in its stay as a competency (not expire too quickly).
- It is sustainable; cannot be replaced by a substitute.
- It is really superior to your competitors?

The leader is seeking a limited number of ideas (maximum of four) to modify the course of the organization to accomplish the mission (new or reaffirmed) and make progress toward the vision. Each strategy is described so that it is quantifiable and has a target, leader, team, and project plan. Strategies are tracked regularly (quarterly is preferred) to ensure progress and make any necessary adjustments (McClaskey & Owens, 2010).

The next two phases of the process are detailed in succeeding chapters. Phase 2, strategy deployment, and phase 3, strategy implementation, will be described in Chapter 9, which includes goal setting, execution, and project management. The fourth phase, evaluate and improve, is described in Chapter 10, which teaches performance excellence, measures, and assessment. Don't be surprised if you meet Sonia again.

SUMMARY

The alignment of the constellation is brighter now that the organization's strategic objectives are in place. From vision to mission to strategies, you have built a strong foundation of success. Involve those who lead, want to lead, and those who care about the organization. Share the preparation data. Look internally and externally at strengths and weaknesses as well as opportunities and threats. Seek to develop no more than four new strategies. This is not the time to do less than your best in growth and development. Next year is a great time to add more new strategies.

These skills are also applicable for student and community organizations, faith-based organizations, individuals, as well as families. Take them for a test drive. The more you use this skill set, the more focused you will become and the more likely you are to achieve the organization's goals.

REFERENCES

Collins, J. R., & Porras, J. I. (1994). *Built to last: Successful habits of visionary companies.* New York, NY: HarperCollins.

Collins, J. R., & Porras, J. I. (2011). Building your company's vision. In *On Strategy* (pp. 77–102). Boston, MA: Harvard Business School Press.

Dym, B., & Hutson, H. (2005). *Leadership in nonprofit organizations.* Thousand, Oaks, CA: Sage.

Harvard Business Essentials. (2005). *Strategy: Create and implement the best strategy for your business.* Boston, MA: Harvard Business School Press.

Juran, J. M., & De Feo, J. A. (2010). *Juran's quality handbook* (6th ed.). New York, NY: McGraw Hill.

McClaskey, D. J., & Owens, D. (2010). *Introduction to quality management.* Milwaukee, WI: American Society for Quality.

Nanus, B. (1992). *Visionary leadership.* San Francisco, CA: Jossey-Bass.

National Organization for Human Services. (2015). Ethical standards for human service professionals. Retrieved from http://www.hationalhumanservices.org .ethical-standards-for-hs-professionals

Schen, E. H. (2010). *Organizational culture and leadership.* San Francisco, CA: John Wiley and Sons.

Senge, P. M. (1994). *The fifth discipline: The art and practice of the learning organization.* New York, NY: Doubleday.

Chapter 9

Organizational Management—Strategic Goals and Project Management

LEARNING OBJECTIVES

The student will

- compose a specific strategic goal using the SMART (specific, measurable, attainable, relevant, time bound) framework,
- explain in order the steps of the project management planning stage,
- explain why projects fail,
- list and describe constraints of a project and how to mitigate the constraints,
- list and describe five reasons why a project is not fully executed, and
- list and describe four uses of data measures in project management.

STRATEGIC GOALS

Strategic goals are the end product achieved when an organization completes a strategic planning process. After all the effort by the team of stakeholders involved in the planning process, the success of your organization, and your own leadership initiative, executing on the strategic goals is a priority. The process of writing and committing to individual goals has been shared. Those skills will be called upon as the team's strategic goals are readied for action.

REFLECTION: HOW EXCITING NEW STRATEGIC GOALS BECOME FROZEN

Goals are announced frequently by organizations after a planning process. Here are a few examples of organizational planning goals:

- The county health agency will reduce costs by 10%.
- The childcare centers in the city will collaborate to deliver the most comprehensive services in the region.
- We will raise $100,000 to benefit organizations that help eliminate childhood diseases.
- We will put all employee training programs online.

On the surface, these statements seem like worthy initiatives, but as a student of leadership, you already know they are not well written. Recall the process of writing goals as gap statements. Using this formula—from the current state X to the desired result Y by a deadline Z (when)—helps the organization stay focused. Using the acronym SMART is an additional lens to review the written goals. Writing a goal: From X to Y by When

S – Specific

M – Measurable

A – Attainable

R – Relevant

T – Time bound

Are declarations of goals enough to initiate the achievement of the desired results? Maybe you participated in a group or organization meeting creating exciting plans and ideas, and as time passed, with little notice, the goal became one more item in the long archive of meeting minutes while the leaders' energy diverted to something new and urgent. Some group members may even ask, "Are we still doing that?" only to see puzzled looks from colleagues regarding the forgotten plan. How successful are you in setting a plan to accomplish an organization's goals? How does a leader prevent the excitement and forward motion in a goal planning process from ending after the planning meeting?

Far too often, the forward progress on organization goals tends to stop once the organization's planning retreat is over and the goals are announced. Setting the goal is good start, but what is the likelihood you will achieve the goal if you do not act on it? When you return to the reality of your job and the to do list already burning a hole in the top of your desk along with the 300 plus emails that arrived while you were away, who even remembers the excitement of new goals for the organization? Recent studies on productivity and procrastination describe three major impediments to the accomplishment of new goals: (1) distractions; (2) visibility, the inability to see next steps; and (3) the difficulty of choosing to allocate time toward a long-term goal are major contributors to the failure of achieving goals. Distractions are those other tasks on your work desk that are easier, more fun, or that you perceive to be on fire and needing immediate attention. Visibility is the level of detail available to the task owner of each succeeding step in the action plan for goal accomplishment. If you are unclear as to the next step, you will not move forward. No one wants to risk a mistake. Choice of priorities relates to how the day becomes absorbed with "busyness" instead of time intentionally allocated to top priority items. Deterrents and distractions prevent leaders and their teams from achieving goals within their organization. Setting strategic goals after a session of strategic planning is energizing and motivating for participating employees of most organizations. Unfortunately, the synergy built during the planning retreat is rarely sustained; therefore, the goals lose momentum, and the forward motion comes to a grinding halt. Leaders and organizations are weary of reinventing the same new ideas each year. Are you tired of making excuses for goals not achieved? The question is, will it come to life or be doomed to the graveyard of good ideas? A 2008 study of employees from over 1,000 organizations in 50 countries said their workplace was weak when it came to execution of new ideas (Neilson, Martin, & Powers, 2008).

DIAGNOSIS: EVALUATING A STRATEGIC GOAL FOR ORGANIZATION IMPACT

As part of the strategic planning session, you and your team analyzed historical and current data, reviewed the organization's internal strengths and weaknesses, as well as identified external threats and opportunities. You determined what it is that sets your organization apart, meets evolving client/community needs, and continues fueling the fire and commitment of the employees and other stakeholders. You built momentum with the team. Strategic goals were generated to position the organization for the future over the next 3 to 5 years. The strategic planning team was engaged by your leadership to make those careful decisions.

After the strategic goals are determined, it is necessary for the team to assess both the cost and return on resources for each goal. Having a safe and trusting organizational culture (Chapters 4 and 8) where participants feel their feedback and contributions are valued and key questions can be addressed is essential. It is much better to have "weigh-in" than to have to go back to ask for buy-in. By using a solution matrix for a strategic goal analysis, like the example shown in Table 9.1 below, you can involve the team in evaluating strategic goals.

Step 1: List the strategic goals being considered by the leadership team.

Step 2: Create key criteria for each of the five categories.

Step 3: Rate each goal for its impact in each category on a scale of -2 to 3 using zero as a no impact score. Negative numbers imply a negative impact and positive numbers are a positive impact.

Step 4: Total your score. Collect the team score.

Practice using Table 9.1 by analyzing a strategic goal involving an organization where you work or volunteer. You could also analyze a strategic goal involving family or friends. You could analyze possible locations for an upcoming trip, plans for a holiday or a family reunion.

Table 9.1   Strategic Goal Analysis

Strategic Goal Analysis					
Strategic Goal #1:					
Categories of Organization Impact	**1. Financial Impact**	**2. Customer & Community Need**	**3. Staff & Volunteer Impact**	**4. Unique Contribution**	**5. Mission Alignment**
	Criteria #1	Criteria #1	Criteria #1	Criteria #1	Criteria #1
	Criteria #2	Criteria #2	Criteria #2	Criteria #2	Criteria #2
	Criteria #3	Criteria #3	Criteria #3	Criteria #3	Criteria #3
	Criteria #4	Criteria #4	Criteria #4	Criteria #4	Criteria #4
Select a Goal Rating for #1	−2 −1 0 1 2 3	−2 −1 0 1 2 3	−2 −1 0 1 2 3	−2 −1 0 1 2 3	−2 −1 0 1 2 3
Your Score #1					
Team Score #1					
Strategic Goal #2:					
	Criteria #1	Criteria #1	Criteria #1	Criteria #1	Criteria #1
	Criteria #2	Criteria #2	Criteria #2	Criteria #2	Criteria #2
	Criteria #3	Criteria #3	Criteria #3	Criteria #3	Criteria #3
	Criteria #4	Criteria #4	Criteria #4	Criteria #4	Criteria #4
Your Score #2					
Team Score #2					
Select a Goal Rating for #2	−2 −1 0 1 2 3	−2 −1 0 1 2 3	−2 −1 0 1 2 3	−2 −1 0 1 2 3	−2 −1 0 1 2 3

Strategic Goal #3:					
	Criteria #1 Criteria #2 Criteria #3 Criteria #4	Criteria #1 Criteria #2 Criteria #3 Criteria #4	Criteria #1 Criteria #2 Criteria #3 Criteria #4	Criteria #1 Criteria #2 Criteria #3 Criteria #4	Criteria #1 Criteria #2 Criteria #3 Criteria #4
Your Score #3					
Team Score #3					
Select a Goal Rating for #3	−2 −1 0 1 2 3	−2 −1 0 1 2 3	−2 −1 0 1 2 3	−2 −1 0 1 2 3	−2 −1 0 1 2 3

Use the feedback and discussion to create an open dialogue on each strategic goal. You will discover the process of goal evaluation keeps the momentum from the strategic planning session, communicates goals as priorities, and increases commitment by the team. Once the goals are evaluated, a decision will then be made regarding which to adopt and resource as well as which to eliminate or postpone. Be wary of taking on too many new goals. On one hand, no one has added new staff positions or off-loaded your day-to-day work responsibilities. But on the other, these are wonderful ideas and could really make a difference for the clients and community the organization serves. One to three new goals are the recommended maximum to take on annually. Having too many goals can easily create a loss of focus to determine what is important and instead cause employees to become overwhelmed. To accomplish your regular work requirements, along with additional and equally important responsibilities, as well as to deliver these programs and services with the same high-level quality, requires strategic decision making in the personal planning process (as outlined in Chapter 5). Regular accountability process meetings with the team and your supervisor help everyone stay on track. Good strategic goals can be held over for a resource development initiative, the next fiscal year, or a future planning cycle if the resources required are not available. The key to maintaining the momentum from the strategic planning retreat is to dedicate time for evaluating the strategic goals with the team. This momentum will be much needed for implementation. Although it is ultimately the executive director of the organization who is both accountable for the organization's strategic direction and the progress made to get there, the leader cannot do it alone. Your job is to set a course for the team that will strategically position your organization for future growth.

PRESCRIPTION: LEARNING FROM KEY QUESTIONS IN STRATEGIC GOAL IMPLEMENTATION

Like many quality methods studied in leadership, there is a recommended process that greatly increases the probability of leading a team to reach strategic goals. The eight key questions below are questions you must be prepared to answer. Utilize the recommendations of the leadership coach to create a prescription for successful strategic goal implementation processes.

1. Strategic goals were identified during a strategic planning process (Chapter 8) to move the organization forward. What is the future forecast (community benefit, core competencies) for this organization? Will the strategic goals as written position the organization for what it will face in the future? **Leadership coach #1:** The data collected for the strategic planning session was extensive and should not be filed away. Rather, identify those key indicators that led to the new strategy and assign monitoring responsibilities. These indicators become excellent baseline data for the new strategic goals.

2. Were identified strategic goals the most important goals to devote resources? What was the potential return to the organization and community on the investment of member/employee time and resources? **Leadership coach #2:** Human services organizations in particular must monitor this carefully. It is called mission creep. Because the purpose at hand is to serve those in at-risk situations and return them to a state of wellness, it is common to want to provide more. Let the mission guide these decisions. Use the goal evaluation process discussed in the previous section. Don't be afraid to measure return on investment even in a nonprofit, government, or for-profit human services organization.

3. Achieving a strategic goal requires effort from many members of the organization on top of their day-to-day workload. How many goals did the organization adopt? Were employees stretched too far? Do the goals tap the talents of the current employees? Is the leader prepared to lead a team through new methods and new responsibilities? **Leadership coach #3:** Take a realistic approach to the new workload. What can be off-loaded or postponed? Who is interested in stretch assignments? Where are untapped talents? Engage the employees responsible for accomplishing the tasks assigned to each goal. Hester (as cited in Blanchard, 2013) advises leaders of the opportunity this provides to communicate about the readiness and commitment level of the employees for the new tasks and how best to

achieve them. Situational leadership basics and management skills (Chapters 2 and 6) emphasize the importance of leaders choosing their role and level of interaction with the team based on their employees' competence (skills to accomplish the task) and commitment (clarity on task and belief in the organization).

4. Achieving a strategic goal requires the identification of short- and long-term targets. Was each of the goals broken into smaller steps? Is each step clear to all who will carry it forward? Could everyone describe with similar terminology the goal and its successful completion? How will everyone know when the goal is completed? **Leadership coach #4:** Not only must members of the organization be able to write the organization's goals clearly, but also they must be able to understand and uniformly describe them. They must be able to have the steps broken down in such a way that the path forward has not a moment of hesitation. They must also be able to describe the target, which is how members know they arrived at the same destination. Are we there yet? Does everyone see that picture clearly and describe it using a similar language? This level of clarity maintains the organization's trajectory by ensuring everyone is navigating by the same compass. Setting a strategic goal is a long-range initiative, usually measured in years instead of months. Because lengthy initiatives require a sustained effort, it is best to break the strategic goal into long-term and short-term goals.

An example of a 2018 strategic goal is outlined below. It is written as a gap and demonstrates the SMART concepts with long-term goals for the full timespan and short-term goals detailed for the first long-term goal.

2018 Strategic Goal: To establish online group counseling services and change program delivery from 0% to 50% online services of scheduled group counseling services for adult clients in 5 years.

Year 1 Goal: Identify, contract, and install secure audio and visual communication software for selected members by November 2018.
    Short-Term Goal 1.1a: Identify all needed software specifications by February 2018.
    Short-Term Goal 1.2a: Release bid for software purchase and determine vendor by April 2018.
    Short-Term Goal 1.3a: Purchase and install software by July 2018.
    Short-Term Goal 1.4a: Test software use by August 2018.
    Short-Term Goal 1.5a: Train all staff in software use by October 2018.
    Short-Term Goal 1.6a: Select and train pilot client groups to use software by November 2018.

Year 2 Goal: Establish and monitor two pilot adult counseling groups using online delivery from January to December 2019.

Year 3 Goal: Increase from 5%to 20% of online group counseling services for adult clients by the year 2020.

Year 4 Goal: Increase from 20% to 35% of online group counseling services for adult clients by the year 2021.

Year 5 Goal: Increase from 35% to 50% of online group counseling services for adult clients by the year 2022.

5. Was there a champion identified for each goal? Who rallied members, helping them to resume their focus and energy toward the goal during times of chaos? **Leadership coach #5:** Every new initiative for the organization requires a champion. A champion is the person who monitors progress regularly, cheerleads for the priority level the new initiative holds, keeps the initiative in key leadership conversations, and serves to keep the staff motivated and actively engaged in tasks leading to its completion. Champions may or may not hold formal leadership positions, but the champion must be respected and trusted both horizontally and vertically within the organization. Without such a spokesperson, strategic goals are at great risk of failure. "We" translates as "nobody" in group speak. The team may be responsible, but without a champion, no one is accountable or monitoring progress.

6. Were leaders fully committed to the goals? Were decisions, resources, and staffing in full alignment with the plan for goal accomplishment? Did the leaders regularly discuss progress toward the goal? **Leadership coach #6:** A strategic goal requires commitment from the top of the leadership hierarchy. Even though leaders were involved in the strategic planning process, staying committed to the strategy and related goals is a challenge. New interests and ideas from various stakeholders are constantly submitted for the leaders to review, crises emerge, and new government regulations are passed that affect the ebb and flow of the organization. When this happens, it is easy to lose focus or even doubt earlier decisions. If circumstances become significantly different such that a SWOT (strengths, weaknesses, opportunities, and threats) analysis would yield different results or an emergency drains staff and monetary resources, it is best to cancel or postpone efforts on any new goal. Short of emergency situations, leaders must visibly demonstrate their support toward the new goal. They must discuss it in board meetings, with staff, in budget and fundraising planning meetings, as well as include it in speeches, websites, and newsletters. If employees do not see or hear the leadership's support for the new goal, perceptions of no importance will quickly emerge.

7. Were expectations clear at all levels within the organization? Were time-frames for the short- and long-term goals in place to monitor progress? Did members and work groups have new goal-related responsibilities officially incorporated into job descriptions? Were responsibilities and accountabilities communicated clearly? **Leadership coach #7:** Account-ability starts with ownership of new goals. It is important for ownership to be felt at both the organizational and individual levels. Many of the actions I outlined in this chapter previously contributed to ownership: inclusion of others in decision making, visibility of leadership involvement, organiza-tional trust of the champion, as well as ongoing communication and clar-ity. Ownership of the goal should not only reside with the organization's leadership but also with the project team. Ongoing interest and support by managers and leaders creates a sense of "we" that is recognized by all members of the organization as more than lip service. When goals and their related tasks are assigned, it is important to encourage team members to determine "how" they will accomplish the goal (Blanchard, 2013). When employees decide on the "how," they will then assume ownership of the process to accomplish the goal. Returning to the SMART goal description, Hester (as cited in Blanchard, 2013) references the letter M as represent-ing both measurable goals and motivating goals. Motivation begins when employees know they matter and what they contribute to the organization has value. The marriage of ownership and motivation is where account-ability begins. Accountability is sustained when the team's work rhythm is engaged in executing the goal. The next section will describe this process in greater detail.

8. Were organization leaders actively engaged in discussions to identify and implement changes to sustain the new goal's success? **Leadership coach #8:** Sustainment of a new goal requires all members of the organization embrace the work of the team. Even though the strategic goal is new, if it is truly stra-tegic, it will be connected to the pre-existing goals of the organization. The organization's leadership must articulate these connections as well as provide support and encouragement for all members to integrate the new effort. This might involve modifying processes and systems to make room for the new goal to operate smoothly and not make it feel as if a new program was tacked on with duct tape.

Explore the actions and interactions of leaders and employees as they relate to the strategic questions. As you learned in Chapter 8, employees working on established strategic goals will be more willing and able to buy in to the goal if they are involved in the decision-making process (weigh-in leads to buy-in).

SUMMARY

Setting a strategic goal involves a SMART process. Writing specifics means leaving very little to the imagination. It means describing every detail as if you were drawing a blueprint. The goal must be measurable, or how will you know if you achieve it and can continue to achieve it. To be attainable describes a goal an organization can resource on a sustainable basis. To be a relevant goal is to be in alignment with the organization's mission and vision as well as positions the organization for a successful future. Achieving this goal must have time targets and deadlines, which require discipline and accountability from the team. Engaging the team in a discussion of goal selection using criteria to analyze the added value of the goal leads to motivation, discipline, and accountability. As you have likely guessed, the next section on project management skills are essential to the accomplishment of tasks involved in achieving strategic goals. Project management is especially helpful when the plan is complex in scope. With your attention on goals and readiness for the next skill sets, your invitation to project management is just a paragraph away.

PROJECT MANAGEMENT

A project is defined as a series of tasks to create a product, program, or service. It has a defined beginning and end, and the tasks are not part of your regular work requirements. Projects are both large and small; some you will work on alone, and others will be completed in a group. Human services projects could include the following:

- Developing an afterschool support group for troubled teens
- Initiating a professional development association for patient advocates
- Creating a community website to provide information and support for parents regarding reducing childhood obesity
- Creating a theatrical performance or video to help students deal with bullying in schools

Project management is a systematic method to guide a project. The project management profession was developed in the engineering and manufacturing fields. However, it has become one of the most desired skill sets by senior management, according to Harold Kerzner (2009), a project management expert and senior executive director at the International Institute for Learning, Inc. In his blog, Kerzner (2009) describes it as a strategic competence necessary for the workplace. The skills of project management have great relevance to the human services sector bringing both resource management and value management to the table.

REFLECTION: WHY PROJECTS FAIL

In the workplace, projects frequently involve teams of colleagues from several different departments who must learn to work together and carry out the assigned tasks. This process is much like the group projects you were assigned in classes. Instead of colleagues who may share a supervisor, you were working with classmates and being graded by the same faculty member. Most student experiences with group projects are not positive.

Why Some Group Projects Bring a Negative Experience

- There is short preparation and planning time and little time for the group to build much of a working relationship.
- Students have little influence with their peers.
- Student motivation and consequences for lack of accountability vary widely.
- Accountability for responsibilities is not clarified or well supported in the project design.
- Students are not taught how to manage the project or lead the group.
- Typical results find that a portion of the group actually works on the project, yet all receive the same grade.

If this was your first experience to managing or participating in a group project, rest assured, this chapter will ease your fears and enable you to have a more productive experience on a project.

Human services professionals keep very full schedules of direct client contacts, programs, and services. Adding a new project to the regular day-to-day schedule can become that extra load sending your workday into chaos. Add to that the community leadership role of human services organizations and the complexity of community collaborations. Group projects can become complex and time consuming among human services professionals.

Whenever you receive a project assignment from your manager, it arrives at the door of your already busy and committed schedule. The first questions commonly asked in this situation are "What do I have to do, how am I going to fit this in my schedule, and how can I get this off my list quickly?" For many, work habits have been formed by what is the easiest and quickest way to check this project off the to do list. It is common for individuals and groups to push their personal "go" button immediately upon receiving a project. Their work mantra is "Just get it done." As you study the process and steps to project management, you will see that engaging a different button is the choice of project managers. It's time to find the "plan before go" button. How much planning time do you spend on a project before you assemble the group? How much planning time do you spend with the project group? Rein in your habit to push go and lead your team to plan the project before implementation.

If you shared with others that you were reading about project management, you might have received a question regarding new project software. Some have a perspective that project management is a software program that manages projects for you. In fact, there are such software programs available, but they are essentially useless if you do not understand both the steps of the process to managing a project and what potential problems those planning steps help you avoid. To understand the planning steps, we must first diagnose the missteps we have experienced up until now in our experience with projects.

DIAGNOSIS: ANALYZING YOUR LAST GROUP PROJECT

Take a minute to remember your last group project (as a volunteer, intern, or employee), and answer the questions below. Describe the details you remember regarding how the project went.

1. Did all the parts of the project evolve as you wanted? Yes ___   No ___
   - program
   - project group attendance
   - organization members' and leaders'
   - attendance and support
   - project leader's skills
   - project results and evaluation
   - advertising
   - facility
   - participant attendance
   - project group effort and reliability
   - target dates and timeline

   Describe the project and the parts that did not work well:

   In Questions 2 through 6, answer the question and then ask yourself why you think that result occurred.

2. Did members of the group do what they committed to do and in the timeframe requested?

   Describe:

   Why?

3. Did the project take longer, cost more, and have to be reworked or finished with less quality than the group planned?

   Describe:

   Why?

4. Were there surprises along the way, challenges that did not come up in the planning discussions?

Describe:

Why?

5. Did the project group learn from the planning process, and did they evaluate the project as well as the results at the end?

Describe:

Why?

6. If invited, would you accept the opportunity to plan a project with this group again?

Yes ____ No ____ Only if _____

Describe:

Why?

If you answered yes, to the last question, it was likely a favorable overall experience and the group might have used some of the recommended steps in a quality project management process. If you answered no, the prescription portion of this topic will reveal many good solutions for your next project. Projects fail because of the following reasons:

- Failure to plan
- Conflicting priorities
- Lack of vision
- Poor communication
- Lack of time
- Not enough resources
- No buy-in
- Changing priorities

Successful projects will do the following:

- Meet or exceed expectations
- Effectively use resources
- Build teams for future projects

The goal of the upcoming section is to get you to the end result, which is a successful project. If you have a project in which you are participating or directing, use it as a reference as you work through this chapter. These skills will help you course correct, regardless of how far you are into the project planning process.

PRESCRIPTION: HOW TO SUCCESSFULLY MANAGE A PROJECT

This is the last of five parts of a system that began in Chapter 8 with vision, mission, strategic planning, strategic goals, and now project management. In addition to the sequencing of skill sets just named, project management relies significantly on team-building skills (Cobb, 2012). As you are planning and executing the project, the workgroup is also growing into a team, which as we covered in Chapter 6, is the optimum of group interaction. As a leader, you are managing this development at two levels: the people on the team and the tasks of the project through six key steps.

Step 1: Successful Projects Begin With a Plan

The first step in project management is making a plan with the project team. But this part of the plan is not about due dates and who does what task; it is about determining how the scope of this project should look. This vision is influenced by the needs of the stakeholders. Stakeholders are not only the recipients of the project but also anyone impacted by the project, including people working on the tasks of the project and the project team. Therefore, identifying all the stakeholders of the project is Step 1 for the project team. There are two kinds of stakeholders:

1. Project Stakeholders – those who are actively involved or impacted by the project.

2. Key Project Stakeholders – those who judge whether the project meets expectations or not. Stakeholders making this determination can be clients, funders, or organization leadership.

Determine which stakeholders are involved and impacted by the project. Then determine which stakeholders will make the decisions regarding the success of the project. The second group is now elevated to a role comparable to a consultant. It is important to the project's success to regularly seek input from key stakeholders to learn their perspectives. Interviewing each key stakeholder will prevent major missteps and enlist their interest. The following is a list of questions for key stakeholder interviews.

- What does the stakeholder see as the purpose of this project?
- What would the stakeholder call a success for this project? Please share some details of that picture.
- Are there any particular restrictions or limitations related to this project that the stakeholders have concerns about or need to be made aware?

- How frequently would the stakeholder like to have updates regarding the progress of the project? What is the stakeholder's preferred method to receive this information?

Before each interview concludes, communicate a summary of the meeting with each stakeholder to confirm the accuracy of what you heard. After each stakeholder confirms or clarifies the information, schedule a meeting with your manager to relay the information you and your team have learned. (Include the person who delegated the project to you if this is not your manager.) The project group needs to review key stakeholder perspectives to determine and agree on a common definition of success. In addition, they also need to identify any red flags mentioned during the interview regarding restrictions or limitations (see below) that might cause you to not recommend proceeding with the proposed project. This important step is most often forgotten in our haste to push the "go" button on projects.

Determination of Restrictions and Limitations

Professionals in project management refer to determination of restrictions and limitations as constraints (Cobb, 2012). There are six constraints most commonly considered when analyzing a project.

- Scope – type of products, programs, and services being created by the project and their alignment with the organization's mission.
- Quality – the level at which the products, and so on meet specifications.
- Budget – amount of funds appropriated for the project.
- Resources – all other supplies, equipment, technology, as well as staff time and training required for the project.
- Risk – possible event or circumstance that could cause a problem with the project or have consequences for the organization.
- Time – intermediate target dates as well as due dates for all deliverables.

Budget constraints in a human services organization can come from a funding source such as a grant or donor. Other constraints can also arise from insurance coverage for health related services or the board of directors accepting the project as being under the umbrella of the organization's scope. They can also come from transportation sources, collaboration partners, and the economy if the organization's service is priced out of reach of the client. There is also an inverse relationship between three constraints: time, cost, and quality. It is difficult to produce a product or service at the highest quality if time and budget are in short supply. Likewise, if there is a time crunch, the quality of the program drops and the cost tends to increase. If there is a restriction on the budget, the quality is not at the level desired and the

Figure 9.1 Constraints of Quality, Time, and Budget

time to produce the program takes longer due to restricted funds. The triangle in Figure 9.1 demonstrates this tug-of-war between quality, time, and budget.

Once the analysis of key stakeholder interviews and constraints are complete, have the "go or no go" discussion with the project planning team and then your supervisor. Be certain that all are in agreement, critical details are identified, and negotiations for resources, time or other supports needed are secured to allow the project to move forward.

Step 2: Manage Risks

Following the identification of known constraints, the next step is for the planning group to specifically analyze the constraint called risks. Risks are situations that can stop a project in its tracks. They can include resignation of a planning team member, cutbacks in funding or other resources, a change in time or scope from key stakeholders, as well as weather issues or other natural disasters. Risk management is a function of the project planning team. This exercise enables the group to comprise a list of what could potentially go wrong. As each item on the list is discussed, the team determines if the probability of the risk is low, medium, or high. After the level of risk is determined, the group will then analyze the level of impact on the project if the risk occurred. The group can again assign a value of low, medium, or high based on how devastating the risk is believed to be to the project. Items that have a low probability and low impact can likely be monitored for the duration of the project. A medium score on one or both probability and impact should encourage the group to develop a back-up plan. If one or both scores is a rating of high, scheduling a meeting with your supervisor is recommended to discuss the risk assessment and determine if the risk is worth the investment of time and resources for the project. The risk assessment is the second opportunity to pause in project planning to consider the implications of pushing the "go or no go" button on the project.

Step 3: Develop a Project Schedule

When project management is described, people most often talk about the spreadsheets of tasks broken down into subtasks with names and due dates in columns. Completing this task might seem tedious to some of you, but the project schedule will guide you and your team through the completion of the project. To successfully complete the spreadsheet schedule, the team must create multiple lists of details and tasks related to each subset of the project. Many times it is easier to create the lists of tasks using another method. There is an exercise, especially appreciated by the nonlinear thinkers in the group, called mind mapping. Mind mapping provides a nonlinear way to list the major and minor tasks as well as create an ordering sequence for each task. It presents ideas in a networked form allowing the user to connect ideas without the restrictions of rows and columns.

An example of a mind-mapping diagram is depicted in Figure 9.2. Mind maps can look like a series of spiders. By creating a center shape (oval, circle, square) for each major component of the project, lines (or spider legs) are labeled to represent minor tasks of the map's components. The minor tasks do not have to be listed in any particular order. As tasks emerge in the dialogue of the project-planning group, they can be added to the diagram. Once the group believes they have identified all the subtasks, then the collaborative process of determining the order begins. Using this diagram, the sequencing evolves by numbering the lines/legs of the spider. Numbering can easily be adjusted as the dialogue progresses without recreating a

Figure 9.2   Mind Map

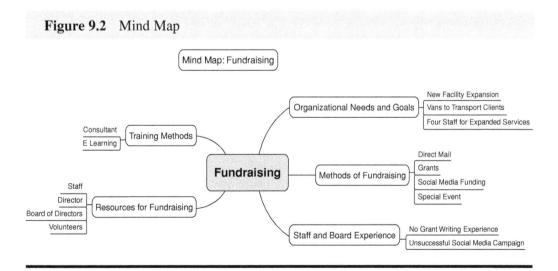

table of lines and columns. If color is a helpful identifier of project components, mind mapping can easily accommodate color codes. There are even software programs available to draw mind maps and spider diagrams. The diagram in Figure 9.2 is an example of a diagram used by a human service organization in a discussion about a fundraising project.

Once the project-planning group is in agreement with the layout and order of the mind map, it is translated to a spreadsheet and used as a daily guide for all to stay on schedule with the project. Table 9.2 is an example of a project schedule.

Completing a project schedule such as this does not ensure project task completion. It is a tool that must be used daily and updated regularly by the entire project-planning group, both individually and in meetings, to monitor the completion of the project parts, tasks, and subtasks.

Step 4: Communication Plan

Communication is the glue that holds the project-planning group together. It ensures all members of the group understand the project, the deadlines, the tasks, as well as who is assigned to each task. In fact, every step of the project planning process involves communication. It played a significant role during step 1 when you interviewed the key stakeholders. Every meeting with the project-planning group involves significant communication skills on everyone's part. As you and the team developed your mind map, you communicated as a group to ensure every task required for the project's success was covered. A communication plan is an intentional effort by the project leader to ensure that every key stakeholder receives the necessary project updates, organizational leadership meetings include project status reports, and the project-planning group members receive special attention and appreciation for adding this work to their load. Without a plan and spreadsheet for this important work, leaders often forget or downplay the importance of regular communication.

Table 9.2 Project Schedule

Status	% Complete	Activity/Task	Start Date	Completion Date	Person Responsible	Budget/ Resources

There are two major components to the communication plan. First is to schedule regular communication with the project-planning group. Having a dialogue about how and when you will communicate, the expectations you have for their communication with each other, as well as how best to respond to you is a critical agenda item for the group. Communication with the key stakeholders is the second important component to the communication plan. This group will judge your leadership ability by your follow-through on commitments after the stakeholder interviews. Based on their requests, you may be using several methods. Project status reports and any updates regarding the project scope are likely what you will submit. Keeping communication open and flowing will enable you to more easily resolve other challenges that might need input from the key stakeholders. When communicating about the project either in writing or in a presentation, be sure to give credit to the entire project-planning group. Be sure all names are listed on project documents, power point presentations, and so on. Part of your task is to help this group develop as a team. Sharing the credit is critical to their respect for you as a leader and their commitment to the project.

Step 5: Execution

Execution is the skill that breathes life into the project. It marries several skills discussed in this book: time management, managers, motivation, and change. It requires a leader to be vigilant about their self-management, ability to motivate and monitor for progress, and to communicate in a way that brings clarity and simplification to a complex initiative. It is easy for group members and even the project itself to become lost. Like the radar at an airport, leaders must be the beacons of light that cuts through the fog and lands the project squarely on the runway. The following first-aid kit for project execution is designed to prevent your project from becoming lost, unsuccessful, or forgotten.

A. Productivity

The day-to-day onslaught of activities in your life has been referred to by McChesney, Covey, and Huling (2012) as the whirlwind. It is the intense swirl of daily activities and the effort it takes for you to make those daily tasks happen in all the chaos. Finding the time and energy to add managing a new project can seem impossible, even if you believe in the idea.

Looking back at Chapter 5 and how you manage your time can provide insight here. If you live in the world of the urgent (day-to-day activities), you will be challenged to carve out time to live in the world of the important (planning and achieving new projects). Today's whirlwind has become a consistent weather pattern in the workplace. It impacts our attention, decisions, and energy. How do you move your attention at work from the urgent to the important? How do you tame the demands of electronic communication to carve out that block of time to think and be creative? It requires a clear sense of purpose and a predetermined commitment to the truly important work. It encourages negotiation between managers and leaders to delay, delegate, or prioritize work to allow time to focus on the important. A project leader role models the personal management skills that enable focus, which enables others to learn to manage their whirlwind.

B. Advocate for the Opportunity to Focus

Multitasking may be good in theory but not in practice. It leads to mediocre work and unfinished business. Strictly focusing on important tasks is the choice of good leaders. Jim Collins (2001) is fond of saying, "The good is the enemy of the great." There are many good jobs to do in a human services organization. Leaders identify the strategic tasks to do. As part of the discussion to lead the new project-planning group, let go of the less important tasks on your plate. Negotiate for release time, adjust deadlines for other responsibilities, or cross-train staff to share workload. Assist your team through the same negotiations. Human services organizations are not typically attentive to workload issues. Once the leader is focused on the great project, the group then becomes focused and the project is on track for completion.

C. The Right Data

During project implementation, setting up feedback signals that measure progress and maintain the project's course is vital to its success. Like landing a jet in the fog, many times you must rely on instruments to measure and communicate the signals. Those instruments must report immediately whether the flight path is off course. Organizations set up feedback signals by collecting data that describe clients served, funds dispersed and collected, programs delivered, and achievements for the year. Some measures in an organization give data so infrequently it is impossible to course correct. An annual report is such an example. Obviously jets flying in a fog need feedback data more often than annually. For a new project, measures that provide timely data as a picture of current standing for possible course correction are necessary for success. For some human services projects, especially those involving human subjects, measuring a concept or result can be challenging. In those situations leaders will use indicators of a project's progress. For example, if there is a program to teach children alternative choices to disruptive behaviors at school, it might be difficult to directly measure the behavior change in a child. However, a child exhibiting positive behaviors is present in school more often, spends more time on task, and is sent to the principal's office less frequently. Therefore, using daily school attendance records, time on task measures, and incident reports from the principal's office are examples of data that would indicate progress toward the goal. These indicators can be measured daily and communicated with frequency to allow for course corrections in the project if needed. There should be at least one member of the project-planning group whose talent is in measures and data.

D. Communicating Data

Although Chapter 10 will provide more details about this concept, establishing change is a process that requires time and much communication. Initial victories are not enough to convince stakeholders, foundations, and community leaders that the previous ways will not eventually prevail. Keeping a work group motivated and committed to the long road of a sustained change requires a leader to be knowledgeable about theories of motivation. Chapter 6 underscored that employees need to know they matter, that what they do on a daily basis makes a difference in their community. As a leader, you must communicate frequently the details of the progress being made. The data and associated feedback described in the previous paragraph must be communicated regularly to the project-planning group and other employees who are helping to move the project forward. Returning to our airplane metaphor, everyone on the plane needs to know how close he or she is to the runway and what he or she will do on a daily basis that keeps the plane in the air and on course. If you were collecting data on a school program teaching children positive behavior choices, charts or graphs posted in an employee lounge or staff meeting room with the measures showing increases in school attendance, time on task, and decreases in incident reports communicate everyone's efforts were making a difference. Keeping the data current is an additional leadership commitment to maintain motivation. Agree on how frequently data will be collected and be faithful in updating the graphs.

E. Syncopation of Follow-Up

Create a new rhythm to the project-planning group meetings. Initiating a project takes time and energy away from the project group members' other duties, which have not disappeared. As a leader, be both conscious of the workload as well as the time you request for meetings. Master the art of the 20-minute follow-up meeting. (However, meetings for the project stages prior to implementation will likely require more than 20 minutes.) During implementation, there are only a few things that need to be accomplished in a meeting.

a. Report what each person accomplished on his or her action item.

b. Request assistance on items where difficulties were encountered.

c. Update and review the progress data charts and graphs.

d. Make new or renew commitments for the next time period.

e. Celebrate successes! Express appreciation!

Step 6: Evaluation and Ending the Project

Evaluation of the project and its impact is essential to the organization and all the stakeholders. This is called program evaluation. Asking the recipients of the service to relate their satisfaction and instituting a series of effectiveness measures are what funders and donors expect. Measures will be expected at both the output and outcome levels. Outputs are easier to measure. They will tell you how many participants were at the program, how many canned goods were donated, or how many counseling appointments were made in an annual report. Outcomes measure transformation, change, and learning. Outcomes are the changes in behaviors human services professionals hope to influence through the programs and services offered. Sample project outcomes are written in formats as below:

- Program participants made healthier choices by purchasing 25% more fruits and vegetables in weekly grocery purchases over 6 months for families on food assistance programs.
- Eighty percent of city high school students spent 60 minutes each day reading for pleasure and decreased TV time by 60 minutes per day for 3 months.
- Program participants increased end-of-grade math assessment scores by a minimum of 7%.

Evaluation of the process of project planning is important as well. This information should be solicited from the project-planning group, project task teams, your supervisor, and organizational leadership. Questions must include the following:

- Analysis of each of the six phases of the project.
  - What worked well?
  - What did you learn?
  - What could be improved?
- Did the project meet your expectations? The expectations of the key stakeholders?
- Were resources used efficiently and effectively?
- Did the project meet quality expectations?
- Were constraints managed well?
- Did the planning group become a team? Are you willing to engage in another project with this group?

Successfully closing a project includes the following:

- Evaluate the task list.
- Confirm completion of the project goals and deliverables.
- Close all related budgets and other lines of funding.
- Submitting a final status report to key stakeholders and the project-planning group.
- Archive important documents.
- Celebrate, recognize, and thank all involved.

Evaluating, communicating, documenting, and thanking all concerned are the critical tasks at the end of a project. Plan to keep your energy level and excitement for the project through these last important steps, not just to deliver the final product. This is a common and significant leadership error, which causes long-term consequences such as the project team's dissatisfaction, budget and administrative angst, as well as future organization leaders and teams unable and unwilling to learn and progress beyond this initiative.

SUMMARY

Successfully leading a project-planning group is the integration of many of the skills in this text. There should be no surprise what a desirable skill set this is to an employer. Keeping the strategic planning session momentum and energy flowing happens best through a strategic goal analysis process. It also ensures only the best goals are resourced and implemented. Project management skills engage the leaders attention on the proposed new set of tasks, the development of a project group into a team, and the growth and strategic positioning of the organization. The six step process begins with planning, reviews contingencies, and makes a risk analysis plan. The project is reviewed to be sure implementation is appropriate. Then a project schedule is created, a communication plan is established, stages of the plan are executed, and effectiveness is measured. The team's hard work is recognized and celebrated. And finally the project is closed.

REFERENCES

Blanchard, K. (2013). Goal setting needs to be a partnership. *Ignite! Newsletter.* Retrieved from http://www.kenblanchard.com/Leading-Research/Ignite -Newsletter/January-2013

Cobb, A. T. (2012). *Leading project teams: The basics of project management and team leadership.* Thousand Oaks, CA: Sage.

Collins, J. (2001). *Good to great: Why some companies make the leap and others don't.* New York, NY: Harper Business.

Kerzner, H. (2009). Blog. Retrieved from http://www.drharoldkerzner.com/blog/

McChesney, C., Covey, S., & Huling, J. (2012). *The four disciplines of execution: Achieving your wildly important goals.* New York, NY: Free Press.

Neilson, G. L., Martin, K. L., & Powers, E. (2008). The secrets to successful strategy execution. *Harvard Business Review.* Retrieved from http://www.hbr .org/208/06/the-secrets-to-successful-strategy-execution/ar/pr

Organizational Management—Processes, Growth Measures, and Performance Excellence

LEARNING OBJECTIVES

The student will

- construct, examine, and evaluate the steps of an organizational process;
- describe the five categories that measure the growth of human services organizations;
- identify key customers, market segment, stakeholders, and competitors for a human services organization;
- explain a plan-do-check-act process;
- list and explain the seven systems evaluated in an organizational performance excellence initiative; and
- explain the eight steps to establish change in an organization.

PROCESSES

A process is an interrelated set of activities when combined produces an outcome (Melan, 1993). It is the way an organization works. Whether an organization produces goods or services, the role you hold in the workplace is responsible for interrelated sets of activities as well as some specialization surrounding the duties of your job.

Unless you are the sole employee, it is likely you do not produce the entire outcome of your organization's program or service. You are usually responsible for a portion of the processes.

REFLECTION: HOW DO PROCESSES IMPACT YOU?

Have you ever started a new job, attended a new school, or completed papers for a medical treatment and wondered the following:

- Do they know how many times they have asked for this information?
- I can't believe all these forms are necessary just to get this service!
- It's been an hour. I wonder if they know I am still in their waiting room?

As you work your way through their system, you see more duplication and delays, which leads you to question their overall competence. If they can't design a logical process to enter you as a client into their system of services, why would you trust their services and advice?

Now switch roles; instead of reflecting on a process from your perspective as a client, let's consider one in which you are the process owner. It is Monday morning, and you are preparing to leave for school or work. Your weekend socializing lasted a bit longer than you had planned on Sunday. You are hunting for your car keys and the papers you brought home on Friday with good intentions to complete. Victory! Keys in hand you begin your commute. Now you are really late, having already returned home twice to retrieve first your coffee and those errant papers, and then next your planning calendar. Exasperated, you slam the door and grumble again, "The Monday morning chaos has to stop!" You have a dysfunctional process for getting ready to go to school or work. Processes play an important part of our lives and routines. What kinds of work functions in a human services organization do processes handle?

- Client intake
- Case management
- Hiring
- Payroll
- Transporting clients to an off-site function
- Employee training
- Staff communication/meetings
- Purchases
- Fund raising campaigns
- Program evaluation

Organizations have developed processes for handling many functions. Individually, you have developed processes for how you do everything, from cleaning your home, to getting ready for bed, to celebrating a holiday. This chapter will demonstrate not only how processes inhabit our world but also how good leaders become masters of process design, which can unlock the door to a much more effective and efficient work environment.

DIAGNOSIS: IDENTIFYING THE ACTIVITIES IN A PROCESS

Designing successful and efficient processes is an important function of a leader. It is a skill set that is taught more often in the for-profit sectors but is integral to all work sectors. Designing a well thought-out process can make any job easier, less prone to errors, and the resulting outputs (programs and services) more appealing to the client/customer. In fact, most customers expect to receive products and services that are consistent and similar to the previous visit. Designing processes are not simply nice for clients; they are necessary.

Examining the need for good process design is best illustrated with a short case:

Sonia (from Chapter 8) is the director of a new after-school program called A+ Tutors that provides extensive academic tutoring for children in elementary school grades. When starting her center, she was lucky to find an empty storefront across the street from an elementary school. It provides a convenient location with good parking. Her program is currently a fee-for-service program without individual tuition rates based on economic need. She knows there is a community need for children to have access to her organization's services who cannot afford the current tuition. She has been in business for a year and is exploring applications for grants to support new program ideas, tutoring scholarships, staffing needs, as well as organizational growth. Her three part-time tutors are frequently lured away by competitors (other tutoring agencies) who can consistently offer 15 to 20 hours of higher paid employment a week.

Sonia designed a start-up marketing strategy to communicate with the parents at the school where her best friend teaches. Her current clients come from that elementary school across the street, which is located in a mostly middle-class neighborhood. Broadening her client base will enable her to keep her tutors employed, as well as increase her eligibility for grant funding to allocate toward tutoring materials and tuition assistance. Reviewing her current client list, she realizes she cannot answer some of the grant proposal's questions because her client application does not collect the proposal's required data. She had not given much thought to the application parents complete other than having enough information to track down a bad check or emergency contact information. There is not a formal process for how new students become a client of A+ Tutors.

Parents and teachers request Sonia's services for the children she tutors. However, she has not implemented a pretesting process to measure the student's current level of educational growth. The tutors are all elementary licensed teachers. Currently, Sonia measures organizational success by the positive feedback from parents stating their child received a high mark on a test or positive teacher's comments regarding the student's contributions in class. Sonia uses no posttest to demonstrate the effectiveness of the tutoring sessions.

Can you identify any processes Sonia needs to implement so her human services organization can grow and become more successful? Consider these ideas:

- An application process that includes the child's academic history
- A future application process that includes parent financial information to be used in an application for tuition assistance
- Preassessment and postassessment processes for measuring each tutoring content area and grade-level gain
- A retention process to retain high quality tutors
- Marketing, hiring, and training processes for filling open tutoring positions
- Marketing process that will build clientele by communicating with parents and teachers from other schools in the community

Continue your review as Sonia's business coach; evaluate the training process for new tutors. See if you can identify missing components as you think like an employer. This was Sonia's initial process for training tutors:

1. Welcome to the A+ Tutors: history and purpose of organization

2. Job description review

3. Work hours, scheduling, and time sheets

4. Content needs and goals of current clients

5. Client's daily progress report

6. Monthly staff meeting agendas

What other items can you think of that would be important to include in Sonia's process for training tutors? These items are called activities in "process language." In other words, the process of tutor training is made up of several activities. Identifying the activities in a process is what creates a logical, successful, efficient process. Over time, Sonia realized she had not answered even half of the questions her new tutors had asked regarding their jobs. To remedy this, she began keeping a list of all the tutor's questions, and even the mistakes made, to help her identify missing activities from her training list to improve her training process. Here are the additional items she added to her list:

- Sonia's role and job description
- Emergency information for the tutors and Sonia
- Confidentiality of clientele records
- Opening and closing (security) of facility
- Best practices in tutoring procedures
- How to handle various emergencies with children or parents
- Appropriate electronic communication with clients
- Expectations, policies, and procedures

At this point, you probably have several items to add to Sonia's list. Processes usually have a preferred order, but not all processes are linear, especially in human services organizations. As is true for all processes, there is a starting and ending point, but it is the in-between activities that may vary. Some activities in a process may happen sequentially, in tandem, or even in a circular, ongoing loop. Some of the activities are smaller processes inside a larger one. Training the tutors how to open and close the office is a small process in itself. From making keys, to knowing which lights to turn on or off or set on a timer, to locking back doors, and then setting or disarming an alarm—all of these activities are part of the process to open and close the facility, which is part of the tutor training process.

How do you create processes that are effective and efficient?

PRESCRIPTION: MONITORING THE IMPACT OF PROCESSES

Leaders who introduce process thinking to their organization create great value for their clients, employees, and communities. Even Sonia's short list of activities from her tutor training process will engage leaders by improving communication or crossover thinking. From the example in which you imagined yourself in Sonia's position, you learned that redoing the client application as part of an improved intake process will add value to the client. It will also provide more thorough documentation regarding client backgrounds to be used in future grant applications. Using process thinking helps you see the application as more than a few facts to start a payment file; instead, the application becomes part of an introduction of the client to the service provider and the service provider to the client. The purpose of a for-profit and nonprofit organization is meeting client, customer, or community needs. Therefore, the process of how an organization first interacts with and learns about client needs is important to the organization's success. In fact, looking through a process improvement lens and using process thinking is what caused Japanese products (especially automobiles and personal technology products) to have such a high demand in American markets due to their reliability and high quality over the last quarter of the 20th century. In today's Internet world, customers and clients are not forced to wait for foreign products and services to be imported. Today's consumer has access to most information, programs, and services online, an ability that has resulted in a global competition of service providers that will continue to expand while simultaneously become increasingly more competitive. Human service organizations are not exempt from having to compete in a global environment. In fact, organizations that are easily accessible and able to successfully and easily help the client make order out of the chaos of all that is available will be the client's chosen service provider. E. H. Melan's (1993) experience as a quality manager, consultant, and author established his expertise on organization processes. Using Melan's (1993, p. 24) four characteristics of a service process, use Table 10.1 to consider how clients are introduced to A+ Tutors and the client application.

Process thinking broadened and clarified the entire purpose of the organization and gave dimension to the application, marketing process, and the other activities that connect to intake.

As Sonia's organization grows, she may add tutoring services for middle school children. This expansion of services might require her to open another facility, one facility that specializes in services for elementary grade children and another that specializes in middle school grade children. Another facilities option would be to divide by subject areas such as reading and math. However she organizes the growing organization, she will likely create processes for each. Some processes may work at each facility, while some unique features will require unique activities or even whole processes. Sonia will enable herself to more efficiently manage similarly skilled tutors at each site. Regardless of how Sonia organizes her facilities expansion, clients may move children for services from one facility to another and therefore, expect a smooth transition. Sonia's ability to lead the whole organization will determine the client experience.

In midsized to large organizations, a process is usually developed by several employees. Although Sonia is not leading a midsized to large organization yet, she imagines the staff who might be in her organization's future. The future of A+ Tutors as a larger organization could have a client contact process including a receptionist who registers and checks in clients, a scholarship analyst who reviews academic records and gives a pretest assessment, a tutor who sees the client on a scheduled basis, and a billing agent who sends and receives the billing

Table 10.1 Four Characteristics of a Service Process: Focus on Intake at A+ Tutors

Service Process Characteristic	Current State	Desired State	Process Thinking
Define the service to provide.	Client purchases block of tutor time to fix children's education problems.	Customer is invited to partner with A+ Tutors to rebuild reading or math fundamentals for their children, relieve anxiety about child's academic challenges, and build an academic learning strategy for future success.	A+ Tutors sees itself as more than selling a block of tutor time. The organization sees itself as a problem solver, stress reliever, long-term partner, and learning professional.
Degree of Customer Contact	Customer is asked to come in to complete an application form and select service and payment option.	Customer is asked to communicate academic needs through application and interview questions. Invitation to become a client can be started in person or online and continues throughout each interaction.	A+ Tutors Organization knows that building a long-term customer/client relationship requires results-based services, convenient time and location, and ongoing parent communication.
Intangibility	Intake language is transactional, fee for service. Application is simple: name, contact information, emergency numbers, payment choice.	Intake language should be persuasive and invitational, reflect desire for long-term client relationship. Website with application should have links to prerecorded client testimonials of A+ Tutors. Application cover letter should express appreciation for opportunity to partner and examples of client results. Application should request access to school academic information and include optional application for scholarship opportunity.	A+ Tutors knows that decision makers use their hearts and heads to make choices. Making information available in an application packet and other marketing pieces and being deliberate in the tone of the language all enable clients to develop a sense about the organization and whether they want to do business there.

(continued)

Table 10.1 (Continued)

Service Process Characteristic	Current State	Desired State	Process Thinking
Immediacy	Units of tutoring are not made in advance and placed on a shelf. The tutoring requires blocks of time, mutually arranged, for interaction between the tutor and the child	Although tutoring is not premade, it requires preparation to meet unique learning needs of each child. Preassessment tests as part of the application will ensure such individualization.	A+ Tutors know children are not alike, thus the process of learning foundational reading and math concepts will be somewhat different for each child.
Nonaccumulation	Tutoring services do not accumulate or have an inventory number; they are consumed. Tutors are reserved and paid by the hour.	The tutoring hours required by each child varies. Although an hour is the unit by which tutors get paid, success is defined by the number of concepts learned. What if salaries were paid based on units learned as opposed to hours worked? Tutoring for more complex concepts would be priced higher. Other alternatives?	Success for A+ Tutors is defined by each child's success in school. Likewise, successful tutors must be recognized and rewarded for preparation, time spent, and the number of concepts learned by each child.

and payments. To understand the details of the more complex process, Sonia will include all employees who are assigned a part of the client contact process, seek their perspective, map the steps of the process, and with feedback, make improvements. She may even assign a member of that team to "own" the process for future monitoring and convening of the team. Sonia needs to ensure that when it comes time for her to expand, processes are identified, reviewed regularly, and have "owners" for ongoing monitoring.

The work of monitoring a process is called process control. Control should not be arbitrary and therefore, requires some agreed upon data points that, when implemented, could alert assigned monitors about a problem. For Sonia, establishing owners of each major process will ensure the data points are monitored. It also will elevate the importance of collecting data to the staff and ensure its collection. In a human services organization, collecting client data provides knowledge about the clients' needs and desires as well as an awareness on how well the organization is meeting those needs. Here are a few suggestions regarding basic data collection:

- Complaint/comment forms are good indicators of a problem's existence but not its cause or resolution.
- Clients' postservice evaluations of the organization through the lens of their expectations do not assume you know what the clients want. Be sure to ask.
- Client surveys during service delivery provide the following information:
  o A list of service options and their availability.
  o Client feelings about treatment during service delivery.
  o Client feelings and perspective on treatment providers.
  o Clients' rankings of the organization as compared to others performing the same services.

Effective and efficient processes are reflective of good process controls. If a process is not effective, this feedback can be found in customer complaints and there could be a lack of corrective action regarding the complaints. If the quality of the program or service diminishes or is inconsistent, it will lead to client/customer dissatisfaction. Lack of efficiency is the result of overutilizing resources compared to the value of the process.

SUMMARY

Processes are part of your work and personal life. They help to identify the organization's interrelated activities and potential opportunities to add value to its many component parts. Identifying, mapping, discussing, monitoring, and measuring processes provide methods to lead and manage the operations of an organization. Good process management results in a reduction of errors. Teams have enough to do without adding rework and putting out fires regularly. Increased client satisfaction is a goal most organizations both value and need in order to maintain community support, government budget allocations, and fundraising. High quality processes enable staff to provide consistent high quality programs and services.

GROWTH MEASURES

As human services professionals, the focus of your work is on the improved quality of life for your clients and their communities. An important part of your job is to measure indicators of those results, including studies of human behavior, behavior change, and learning. Now your role has grown from service provider to leader in the organization. Part of your new leadership role is learning how to measure the health and growth of the organization. As a leader, your focus must now include understanding organizational growth.

REFLECTION: COMPARING QUALITIES OF ORGANIZATIONS

Being a student of leadership you may soon be thinking about the organization for which you want to work. When describing the human services organization you want to work for, you might choose words like growing, forward-looking, innovative, respected, and successful. With those as your benchmarks, how will you identify these organizations? Will you ask your peers or faculty members? Are there professional journals and newsletters that evaluate, rate, and publish lists of human services organizations with these characteristics? What if you had to do your own rating, where would you start? What would you use to measure and evaluate each organization?

DIAGNOSIS: KEY GROWTH AREAS OF HUMAN SERVICES ORGANIZATIONS

It is common for leaders of human services organizations to think about quantifying the growth characteristics of organizations when reviewing budgets, numbers of programs, and numbers of clients served (Alexander, 2000). In fact, human services organizations measure growth in five different areas:

1. Financial resources: This area will be different depending on the economic model of the organization.
   a. For-profit resources come from investors (family or private investor-owned or publicly traded stock) and fees for products or services.
   b. Nonprofit resources come from donors, grants, and fees for service.
   c. Government organization resources come from taxes and grants.

2. Human resources are salaried and hourly employees who deliver products, programs, and services. Nonprofits also rely on a significant volunteer work force.

3. Products, programs, and services are the deliverables to clients and communities.

4. Customer satisfaction represents the likelihood of a client to recommend your organization's programs and services.

5. Partnerships are key relationships and commitments among organizations that provide value added products, programs, and services no one organization can provide alone.

Depending on the economic model of the organization, there may be more than five growth areas. In a for-profit organization, there is usually a sixth category called shareholder value. If you have invested money in an organization, this would be an important area of growth to you. In a nonprofit organization, the sixth category is the organization's ability to deliver on its mission. So what does this measure look like, and how is it applied? Using Sonia's A+ Tutors, we will evaluate how the five growth measures apply to her organization.

Over the past 3 years, Sonia has successfully grown her organization and operates two successful locations. One location services elementary-age students, the other middle school. Both locations focus on math and reading. The vision statement for A+ Tutors is "To Be The First Choice Tutoring Service in the Community." The mission statement is "To provide accurate learning assessment and quality instruction that enables every child to have academic success." Sonia has an opportunity to expand A+ Tutors again by opening a new location in a nearby community. To do this, she has advertised to hire an associate director. Is this an example of a growing organization? Table 10.2 is focused on financial growth. Note the questions about the organization's financial status.

Sonia's organization is in its 3rd year having successfully grown to two locations. Current revenue and expenses are able to pay the rent, utilities, materials, licenses, and salaries for Sonia and her part-time employees. There are no funds for health

Table 10.2   Measures of Organizational Growth: Financial

	Measures of Growth for A+ Tutors
Financial Growth	• What is the current revenue/expense balance?
	• What is the level of debt?
	• What is the nonprofit status and donor or grant total?
	• Is the current budget funded as it was projected?

Source: Adapted from Alexander, J. (2000). Adaptive strategies of nonprofit human service organizations in an era of devolution and new public management. *Nonprofit Management & Leadership, 10,* 287–303. doi: 10.1002/nml.10305

Table 10.3   Measures of Organizational Growth: Human Resources

Human Resources	• Are all tutor positions currently filled?
	• What is the turnover rate for tutors? What is the average length of employment for tutors?
	• Are all employees clear on the mission and vision? Can they describe how it applies to their day-to-day job?
	• Are tutors regularly provided training on current teaching approaches and learning disabilities, and so on?

Source: Adapted from Alexander, J. (2000). Adaptive strategies of nonprofit human service organizations in an era of devolution and new public management. *Nonprofit Management & Leadership, 10,* 287–303. doi: 10.1002/nml.10305

insurance (currently not in violation of federal law) or raises of any kind. Sonia has a $10,000 debt from a start-up loan; $8,000 is still owed with total due in 2 years. Sonia's 501c3 status was just approved so that donations and grants can be accessed. Current financial projections are not as originally planned. The nonprofit status was approved 6 months later than anticipated. Expansion to the second location happened in year two but not originally anticipated untill year four. Table 10.3 is focused on human resources. Note the questions about the status of human resources at A+ Tutors.

Tutor positions are currently filled at both sites. Tutors are staying for 12 months on average. Because they have teacher licenses, many are seeking positions in the school system and see this as a temporary step. All have seen the mission statement, but few can recite it from memory. Sonia holds a monthly in-service workshop on teaching methods and individualized learning strategies. Table 10.4 is focused on programs and services. Note the questions regarding programs and services at A+ Tutors.

Sonia has implemented a preassessment and a postassessment using instruments approved by the local schools. There have been no parent or student complaints regarding tutoring results. Not all clients report follow-up scores. Due to confidentiality, unless the parent shares, Sonia does not know the school reported academic

Table 10.4   Measures of Organizational Growth: Programs and Services

Programs and Services	• Are preassessments and postassessments in alignment with school curriculum and tutoring approaches?
	• Are current programs and services meeting the needs of the clients?
	• Are current programs and services fully described and communicated to potential clients?
	• Are client outcomes attributable to the organization's programs and services?

Source: Adapted from Alexander, J. (2000). Adaptive strategies of nonprofit human service organizations in an era of devolution and new public management. *Nonprofit Management & Leadership, 10,* 287–303. doi: 10.1002/nml.10305

Table 10.5   Measures of Organizational Growth: Customer Satisfaction

Customer Satisfaction	• How do clients rate the organization in their surveys?
	• At what confidence level will clients recommend the programs and services?
	• Using regional branding measures, is the organization considered the number one provider of such programs and services?

Source: Adapted from Alexander, J. (2000). Adaptive strategies of nonprofit human service organizations in an era of devolution and new public management. *Nonprofit Management & Leadership, 10,* 287–303. doi: 10.1002/nml.10305

improvement for each student. She does have her posttest data. Marketing has improved somewhat. The website is not up to date, and brochures are a year old. Table 10.5 is focused on customer satisfaction. Note the questions regarding customer satisfaction data at A+ Tutors.

Sonia has not taken a formal client satisfaction survey. She hopes to do that in the next year. She does collect referral information on the application and offers a one-session discount for a referral. She has logged 12 referrals, 8 at the first site and 4 at the second for this year. Sonia is not aware of regional branding services or consultants to have such a measure. She believes that to be an expense to explore and fund in the future. Table 10.6 is focused on partnerships. Note the questions about community outreach and partnerships.

Sonia believes from her postassessment data and her partial parent feedback that she is offering a valued and needed service. She is not engaged in any additional responsibilities or activities that would attach the term expert to her credentials. She is learning quickly how to lead, supervise, and launch a nonprofit organization. Although she is not involved in formal collaborations

Table 10.6 Measures of Organizational Growth: Partnerships

Partnerships	Are organization programs and services perceived to add value to the community?
	Are organization leaders considered experts in the profession?
	Are organization leaders engaged in community development efforts?
	Do organization leaders invite other community leaders and organizations to collaborate on programs and services?
	Does the organization empower employees to engage in community initiatives?

Source: Adapted from Alexander, J. (2000). Adaptive strategies of nonprofit human service organizations in an era of devolution and new public management. *Nonprofit Management & Leadership, 10,* 287–303. doi: 10.1002/nml.10305

yet, she is networked through her five-person board of directors consisting of a parent of a former client, two elementary teachers, a middle school teacher, and an elementary school principal. The tutors and Sonia are encouraged by the board to participate in programs at the two schools where the majority of their clients attend.

How might you rate A+ Tutors as a growth organization? Does it have potential? If you chose to work there, do you believe your leadership skills will positively impact the organization's growth and development? Are you starting to think of ideas to share with Sonia?

PRESCRIPTION: THE LEADERSHIP ROLE IN ORGANIZATIONAL GROWTH

As a leader of a human services organization, a large portion of your job is focused on the organization's growth. Your employees, clients, and community are counting on you to assess, monitor, and position the organization to succeed. This expectation requires attention to operational excellence. As an employee, your day was consumed by client contact and service delivery. Now as a leader, your day should be filled with the following types of activities:

- Regular staff communications
- Meetings with direct reports
- Monitoring progress toward organizational goals
- Monitoring organization processes
- Financial resources monitoring
- Review of program evaluations and measures of results

- Review of client satisfaction data
- Employee talent assessments and performance evaluations
- Community networking
- Fundraising (if nonprofit)
- Professional development for self and employees
- Mentoring future organization leaders
- Communicating organizational mission, vision, and values
- Researching future community service needs

Your role becomes one of a communicator, monitor, mentor, and future analyst, focused on the goals, results, and impact of the organization. You are linking the measures of organizational growth to strategy (Kaplan & Norton, 2011, p. 100) and asking key questions:

- What is my vision of the organization's future?
- If my vision succeeds, how will the organization be different?
- What are the critical success factors?
- What are the critical measures?

The last question in this set requires study and understanding, so much so that you may not identify them on the first try. Critical measures give you feedback on the progress of important goals (see Chapters 8 and 9) in a specific block of time so changes can be made if the progress is not positive. Think about the speedometer on your car. It reads instantly so you can increase your speed if you are below the posted limit or reduce your speed if you are above. Organizational measures will most likely not give instant results. However, waiting until the publication of the annual report for data is not going to help you change direction in time to improve. Other helpful criteria regarding key growth measures are to keep them simple. Everyone's workday is already busy. Finding an indicator that is easy to count and predictive of the goal is what keeps organizations from giving up on this important feedback. Pull together a small team to determine the growth indicators for your organization. There are likely more than one. In fact, there should be an indicator for each of the five areas just discussed. Once selected, assign an employee or a team of five to post weekly progress in each growth indicator. Post the data so employees can see frequently their progress in helping the organization achieve its goals.

Ask yourself, what is the strategic difference between your organization and what your service competitors provide? What makes your organization unique? This answer is found in the combination of operational excellence, attention to growth, and organizational distinction that leads to long-term success.

SUMMARY

Selecting and monitoring growth measures provides a stream of feedback data that functions like a dashboard for leaders to use when leading the organization to a successful future. Like driving a vehicle in unchartered territory without a GPS device, lack of feedback data forces leaders to make high-risk decisions. Though the selection of important data might vary by type of organization, there are five categories that measure the growth of human services organizations. Measuring organizational performance in financial resources, human resources, results of programs and services, client satisfaction, and partnerships make the difference in how the organization will be positioned for future success.

PERFORMANCE EXCELLENCE

Performance excellence is the overall improvement of an organization's capabilities and effectiveness. It is a process of analysis and learning that expands organizational value to clients and communities. The process of improvement seeks to align planning, measures, goals, processes, people, actions, and results in a way that maintains the focus on the organization's mission regarding delivery, superior client programs and services, community satisfaction, and loyalty.

REFLECTION: FROM INDIVIDUAL IMPROVEMENT TO ORGANIZATIONAL IMPROVEMENT

From magazines to websites to self-help books to personal coaches improving how we function, we are surrounded by messages to help us hone our inner strengths and abilities. As an individual, self-improvement encompasses four major functional areas:

- Physical
- Mental
- Social
- Spiritual

From Covey's "Sharpen the Saw" (Covey, 1998) to Loehr and Schwartz's (2003) "Four Cylinders," improvement models for individuals have been recommended based on the authors' researched success. To make improvements requires some self-assessment, commitment to changing behaviors, as well as the discipline to continually improve upon these skills. For example, if your focus is on physical functioning, your exercise and eating habits are examined. If your focus is on social functioning, relationships with family and friends are examined.

Self-improvement is tough enough. Improving an organization's performance is a major challenge for many leaders. How do you translate improving human systems to organization systems? What should be the leader's focus and what systems are key to organizational performance excellence?

DIAGNOSIS: CREATING A PROFILE OF KEY ORGANIZATION INFORMATION

Performance excellence begins with the organization's mission, vision, and values, which were covered in Chapter 8. After those are established, the organization must then define and focus on who are their key customers, their customers' requirements, the organization's key processes, and strategies to meet those needs. Research about industrial models of performance excellence and improvement processes were developed in Japan, the United States, and Europe. Malcolm Baldrige served as the United States Secretary of Commerce from 1981 until 1987. His interest and support led to the development of national criteria and a method for organizations to benchmark their success as well as opportunities for improvement. The Baldrige criteria and National Performance Excellence Award carries his name because of his efforts to establish federal government support for an improvement process for American companies. Using the Baldrige Organizational Profile (TNCPE, 2014–2015) leaders can assess and clarify their organization's systems in regard to their customers, processes, and strategies. The Baldrige profile is a collection of questions that when answered by the organization provide insight and understanding of the organization's basic picture as well as the key processes and strategies. Although originally developed for the for-profit sector, all types of organizations—for-profit, nonprofit, and government—use the criteria.

Answer as many of the following Baldrige Organizational Profile Questions as you are able for an organization where you are a member. (Question numbers correspond to *TNCPE Manual*.) This organization could be where you work or attend school or be a community organization. Interview one of the organization's leaders to help you answer questions you alone cannot.

I have answered the questions using Sonia's A+ Tutors organization (pre-expansion) as an example.

1a.   What are the programs and services your organization provides? What is the importance of each to your organization's success?

     A+ Tutors provide one-on-one reading and math tutoring to elementary and middle school children (Grades K–7). The organization communicates monthly with the teachers of the enrolled children. Selection of curricula is influenced by the curricula used by the local schools as well as the latest methods taught by the regional university's accredited college of education. Grant funds provide scholarship funds for economically at-risk students to enroll in tutoring services.

Math and reading are key skills for children to be successful in middle and high school grades. It is important to be current with curricula and methods to ensure children are provided the best support as well as allowing for a smooth transition to more independent learning in the classroom environment. Grant support allows all children to have access to tutoring services.

2a.   What are your stated mission, vision, and values? What are your organization's core competencies (greatest expertise), and how do these competencies relate to the mission?

Mission: To provide accurate learning assessment and quality instruction that enables every child to have academic success

Vision: To be the first choice tutoring service in the community

Values: Numbers 1, 2, 3, 8, 9, 10 of the InTASC Model Core Teaching Standards (Council of Chief State School Officers, 2011)

- *The teacher understands the central concepts, tools of inquiry, and structures of the discipline(s) he or she teaches and can create learning experiences that make these aspects of subject matter meaningful for students.*
- *The teacher understands how children learn and develop and can provide learning opportunities that support their intellectual, social, and personal needs.*
- *The teacher understands how students differ in their approaches to learning and creates instructional opportunities that are adapted to diverse learners.*
- *The teacher understands and uses formal and informal assessment strategies to evaluate and ensure the continuous intellectual, social, and physical development of the learner.*
- *The teacher is a reflective practitioner who continually evaluates the effects of his or her choices and actions on others (students, parents, and other professionals in the learning community) and who actively seeks opportunities to grow professionally.*
- *The teacher fosters relationships with school colleagues, parents, and agencies in the larger community to support students' learning and well-being.*

A+ Tutors core competencies are the expertise of its staff in the following areas:

- *Diagnosis of academic difficulties*
- *Knowledge of child development theory and well-being*

- *Teaching methods for literacy*
- *Teaching methods for mathematics*

These skills enable the staff to be successful with all children no matter their academic difficulty. The mission is to enable all children to have academic success.

3a. What are your employee groups/segments, volunteer groups/segments, education levels, and diversity demographics? What keeps employees and volunteers engaged in achieving the mission?

- *There are currently eight part-time tutors at the elementary level facility and six middle school tutors at the second facility. All have bachelor's degrees and current teacher certification in either English or mathematics. The director holds a bachelor's degree and a teaching certificate in elementary education and a master's degree in middle school teaching methods for STEM classes. The two receptionists are community college graduates. Each site has a part-time educational psychologist from the nearby university on contract for the initial pretests and posttests.*
- *All employees are female, three tutors are Caucasian, two tutors are Asian American, and one tutor is African American.*

Employee training includes discussion of the mission and goals and how the tutor's job helps the organization achieve the mission.

4a. Describe the organization's facility, major equipment, and technology.

- *Each tutor site has a business office for record keeping and storing confidential records. It has phone, Internet, a PC, copy/fax machine, desk, filing cabinets, and other office supplies. There are 12 small tutoring rooms that all have Internet access and PCs for student tutoring sessions and required testing. There is a reception/parent waiting area at each facility. The director's office is in the elementary tutoring site, equipped similarly as the receptionist's office. One receptionist and two tutors speak Spanish.*

5a. Describe regulatory requirements under which you operate. Include accreditation, certification, legal, ethical, or registration requirements.

- *The employees who tutor and the director meet all the standards and requirements to be a classroom teacher in the state. All state laws and ethical standards expected of a classroom teacher are expected of A+ Tutors. All business licenses are up-to-date, and the nonprofit charter is completed.*

1b.   Describe the organizational and governance structures as well as parent organizations.

- *City and county business licenses.*
- *State chartered nonprofit.*
- *This is a local nonprofit with two locations.*
- *There is a 12-person board of directors comprised of teachers, parents, and those interested in educational excellence.*

2b.   Who are your key customers and what are their requirements? What are your market segments? Who are your stakeholders?

- Key customers: *Children and their parents. Their requirements are safe, effective, convenient tutoring, reducing stress at home and school, and building academic skills and confidence of the child.*
- Market segments: *Elementary and middle school children having trouble with grade-level math and reading skills.*
- Stakeholders: *Local teachers and principals who make referrals and parents who have children from their classes enrolled in A+ Tutors. Key customers are stakeholders as well.*

3b.   Who are your partners and collaborators? What role do they play in delivering programs and services?

- *Local university college of education provides assistance with training tutors, curricula recommendations, part-time educational psychologists on contract, and teacher candidates who become tutors.*
- *Local school systems provide client referrals, curricula recommendations, and tutor training assistance.*

1c.   How many and what type of competitors do you have? (Competitors are organizations who provide similar programs, recruit the same clients, or request donations from the same funders.) What is your relative size as compared to most other organizations in your field?

- *50% of the competition is from private individuals who tutor in homes.*
- *10% of the market is the national organizations, such as Sylvan Learning Centers.*
- *20% of the market is in after-school childcare programs.*
- *20% of the market is in small nonprofits like A+ Tutors.*

2c.   What key changes, if any, are affecting your service area/marketplace?

- *There is a new volunteer tutor corps being organized at the local senior center.*
- *School system has received a federal grant to support five additional teachers' aids for 2 years to help with teaching reading in three elementary schools.*

3c. What comparative data is available from within your industry? How are you doing in comparison to other organizations providing similar programs and services?

- *According to the American Association of After-School Tutors, the year 2 start-up plan for A+ Tutors was in the top-10 list of new tutoring organizations based on the number of empty tutor time blocks over 12 months and measures of grade-level improvement in elementary grade reading scores.*

4c. What are your key strategic challenges and advantages in your service area/marketplace?

- Challenges: *Competing with convenience of individual private tutoring services traveling to homes.*
  - ○ *Retaining teacher certified, highly trained tutors.*
- Advantages: *Well-known and respected in school system.*
  - ○ *Received positive referrals from parents, former clients, and siblings of former clients.*

5c. What are the key elements of your performance improvement process?

- *Continuing to detail and develop A+ Tutors processes.*
- *Using plan-do-check-act when problem solving and before starting new services.*

Picture yourself as the organization leader having completed this organizational profile. Now you have a detailed picture and critical data at your fingertips. How do you move to the next step of improvement?

PRESCRIPTION: USING THE PROFILE TO ACHIEVE EXCELLENCE

A four-step iterative process created by Dr. Edwards Deming, modern father of quality control, best manages continuous improvement in organizations. Called plan-do-check-act, this method will provide a simple set of steps that when implemented will improve an organization's process.

- Plan – State what you are doing and how you will accomplish it.
- Do – Carry out the plan.
- Check – See if the desired results were achieved.
- Act – Analyze reason for achieving or not achieving results. If not achieved, make the necessary changes to achieve the desired results. Standardize the process after the desired results have been achieved.

Some organizational improvement is the result of the reduction or elimination of duplicative, unnecessary, or outdated tasks. It can also be the result of increasing a task's speed, capacity, results, or development. Therefore, the goal is to reduce or eliminate nonvalue adding activities. If work activities are not contributing to the mission, key requirements, or organizational goals, then why are you doing them? Examples include the following:

- Unneeded activities
- Unneeded inventory or supplies
- Underutilized people
- Duplication of services
- Rework
- Redundancies
- Delays
- Clutter
- Nonvalue-adding programs and services

Seeking opportunities to stop this type of waste will improve both efficiency and effectiveness. "Lean" is a popular business management approach for eliminating waste in the workplace. Other improvement efforts take the opposite approach by focusing on building capacity, increasing organizational strength, adding employee skill sets, and improving strategy. Examples of these include the following:

- Productivity
- Organizational agility and flexibility
- Employee abilities
- Employee learning
- Organizational learning
- Technological infrastructure
- Conceptual framework
- Acquiring resources

Expanding and growing organizational capacity in these areas will position your organization for strategic growth. Think of an organization as a living organism with systems that enable it to breathe, flex, and grow. Tyagi and Piccotti (2012) have developed a service quality framework appropriate for human services organizations. The quality management knowledge areas are as follows:

- Leadership
- Strategic planning
- Programs and services management systems

- Process management
- Client/customer focus
- Measurement, analysis, and knowledge management
- Workforce/volunteer focus
- Information management
- Environment and infrastructure
- Results/mission delivery

Globally, there are over 100 performance excellence models (TNCP, 2014–2015). Most are based on seven systems and use Baldrige criteria to determine effectiveness (EFQM, 2013–2014).

Your new knowledge in processes and measures will help you identify the relationships among the seven systems listed below and why they are so foundational. Each of the seven systems will be described in terms of criteria. Used as an assessment for the key management areas, the criteria will point to improvements and recommendations for an organization. The criteria for each of the seven systems are derived from the descriptions in the 2014–2015 Baldrige Criteria for Performance Excellence (TNCPE, 2014–2015).

1. Leadership: How does the organization's leadership set and commit to the vision, values, and mission? How do they promote and ensure legal and ethical behavior? How do leaders create a sustainable organization from the mission, to the culture of the workplace, to an innovative and rich learning environment? How do the leaders govern to ensure accountability, sound fiscal management, transparency, as well as the development of leaders ready for succession? Do senior leaders commit to responsibility for local communities, the environmental and social systems impacted by the organization?

2. Strategy: How does the organization engage key stakeholders in the planning process, assess risk and opportunities, as well as set a plan for innovation? What are the key processes of the organization and core competencies that support them? What are the organization's strategic objectives, and how will it be implemented with appropriate resources, action plans, and performance measures?

3. Customers: How does the organization listen to current and potential customers? What are the customers' level of satisfaction? Is the organization poised to build long-term relationships with customers and achieve high recommendation status? What are the market segments of the customers? How do you manage and rectify their complaints?

4. Measurement, Analysis, and Knowledge Management: How does the organization use data to measure performance, decision making, and improvements?

How does the organization communicate workforce knowledge and facilitate learning about the organization? How are data sets managed and information communicated? Are emergency procedures in place regarding data and technology?

5. Workforce: How do you build a capable and effective workforce? How do you attract, hire, and train new employees? How is work managed and organized? Are plans in place if there is opportunity for workplace growth or necessity for reductions? How do you create a work environment with appropriate rewards, benefits, and training to allow growth and increased capacity for the organization? Are factors to support employee engagement identified and monitored?

6. Operations: How do you design, monitor, control, and improve key processes in the organization? How do you control costs, prevent errors, and ensure quality? How do you select partners and collaboration opportunities? Is there a plan for emergency operation?

7. Results: What are the key results from the programs and services of the organization? Are there measures of effectiveness, efficiency, and innovation? What are the performance results in customer service, workforce engagement, strategy implementation, and budgetary performance?

Although you are not expected to be able to answer all of these questions now, having such answers provides a clear path to improvements. Typically an organization using these criteria will find their growth patterns clustered in stages (TNCPE, 2014–2015, p. 32):

- Stage 1: Operations are characterized by activities rather than processes and largely responsive to immediate needs. Example: Goals are poorly defined.
- Stage 2: The organization is beginning to carry out operations with repeatable processes, evaluation and improvement. Example: Strategy and goals are being defined.
- Stage 3: Operations are characterized by repeatable processes that are evaluated for improvement. Example: Learning is shared, and coordination is evident. Processes address strategies and goals.
- Stage 4: Operations are characterized by repeatable processes that are evaluated for improvement in collaboration with all units. Example: The organization seeks effectiveness and efficiency using analysis, innovation, and sharing of knowledge and ideas. Processes and measures track progress on key strategies and goals.

Returning to Sonia's A+ Tutors, you observed how the organization progressed along the continuum as it developed and grew. Using the guidelines above, the third year of operation of A+ Tutors is identified on the four-stage measure between the second and third stages.

The improvement steps of plan-do-check-act lead to the last stage of improvement: standardization. The key to following new standards is to put them in writing, train all people who need to use the process, and share them with the whole organization. Policies and procedures must be updated to incorporate the new standards as they are developed, verified, and approved. Employee training manuals as well as job descriptions must also reflect the new standards.

A full set of resources about Baldrige criteria are available on their website (http://www.nist.gov/baldrige). On the site, you will also find detailed application summaries from Baldrige award winning organizations representing all workplace sectors with role model practices.

You do not have to be an award applicant in order to use these criteria to improve. Work on one or two changes at a time. Start with the organizational profile. Realize that implementation of an organizational improvement process takes time and is in addition to the day-to-day tasks for you and the other employees in your organization. Be supportive of your team as they take on the extra load. Planning and implementing an improvement is both a science and an art. Encourage your team to be open to new ideas and to give balanced consideration between the data-driven decisions, the creativity, as well as the intuition and skills. Gang (2013) warns that organizations can suffer from "implementation fatigue," which can result from moving too slowly, improving too many processes at one time, or rolling out other new programs that require significant time and attention which in turn limits the amount of time employees can focus on a new process. As a leader, you must be mindful of the load you put on your employees (see Chapter 9 on execution). Gang (2013, p. 5) also makes an excellent point with this question: "Whose responsibility is it anyway?" When a leader speaks about quality and improvement as "everyone's job," it translates to employees as "not anyone's job" because ownership was not assigned. Ownership must be specific as well as supported by leadership communications and organizational recognition. These lessons in perceptions of people in the workplace provide an important transition to a discussion of change and what helps a new initiative become a standard operating procedure.

All change initiatives risk falling into the excitement of wanting change and improvement, only to face the reality you may actually have to permanently do something a different way. Like a rubber band, most people in a change process have trouble resisting the strength of the rubber band snapping back to its original shape. How do you lead a group to not only make a change in the organization but also maintain the change by integrating it into the fabric of the organization? We will rely on the wisdom of John Kotter, the Konosuke Matsushita Professor of Leadership at the Harvard Business School who has written many books and articles on the subject of change. Kotter (1995) defines eight critical steps in a change process that must be implemented for the change process to be successful.

1. Establish a sense of urgency: An organizational transformation requires the commitment of many people. Tapping into their motivation requires touching both the emotional and logical side of their commitment (Heath and Heath, 2010). The leader must make the current state feel more risky as a state of being rather than the new way. Kotter (1995) believes 75% of the organization's leadership must believe change is urgently needed for the process to succeed.

2. Form a powerful guiding coalition: Organizations require a critical mass of key leaders, including the executive director/CEO, to actively support the change initiative. This group must be well informed, connected (see social network in Chapter 12), have expertise, key organization positions, and solid reputations. The actual head count of this group varies according to the size of the organization. What is important is the person who leads this group. She must be both a quality leader as well as an integral line manager—that is a person from the main economic engine of the organization. A staff executive from human resources or technology support is not going to carry the political weight required.

3. Create the vision: Creating a vision takes time. The guiding coalition must spend its first few months visioning, polishing, considering, and polishing again. This vision helps establish the sense of urgency in step 1. It must be crystal clear and communicate a picture that captures interest, understanding, and positive emotions. It must also be simple enough to communicate in 5 minutes or less.

4. Commnicate the vision: Frequently communicating the new vision sets the rhythm and pace of the transformation. Transformation is about changing hearts and minds. Think about this as if it was a theme song. Has it been played every day? Did the guiding coalition sing along? Did they lead others to join in the chorus? An announcement at a quarterly meeting or a weekly update at a staff meeting is not enough. Transformation is difficult and the rubber band is powerful. As a leader ask yourself, are you singing in tune

(walking your talk)? Is there an item on your daily productivity list for the vision every day? Is the transformation part of the employee performance appraisal? "Communication comes in both words and deeds," said Kotter, (1995, p. 64), "and the latter are often the most powerful form."

5. Empower others to act on the vision: Change impacts more than leaders anticipate. Even as we say to others, "Come join the new effort," we must be prepared to embrace employees who respond in different ways: acting outside of their job descriptions or quell jealous behaviors of colleagues who think others' interest and extra effort makes them look bad. Leaders must remove obstacles and organizational processes that impede employees from fully participating to move the vision forward. Leaders may be forced to confront a manager who feels threatened and tries to block the forward progress of the initiative because they feel their position and authority are threatened.

6. Plan for, create, and celebrate short-term wins: No one can sustain the effort for a marathon race without training for shorter distances first. A change initiative works in the same fashion. Usually a new runner first trains for a 5K race. What are the planned 5K goals in the change initiative? Leaders must identify them, plan for them, create them, and measure their success. Then when they have succeeded, big announcements, celebrations, and recognition are shared with all involved. It is those moments that keep employee motivation soaring and pressing toward the marathon goal.

7. Consolidate improvements and do not declare victory too soon: Because change takes years, leadership may change, outside influences may evolve, client needs may shift, and employees become tired and bored. As a leader it is tempting to declare victory as soon as the first improvement measure is noted. After all, everyone has worked so hard. It would be nice to declare victory and move on to something new and different. However, you must know that over the ridgeline is an army of resisters waiting to snap the rubber band back to its original, comfortable position. Pause, be happy, share the good news, but do not declare it to be more than what it is. Running one marathon does not make you a marathon runner. It takes a series of races to create the habits of preparation, training, and execution to successfully complete a multitude of races. When there are several years of improvement victories, then the leadership can evaluate for step 8, and possibly declare a victory.

8. Institutionalize change: Anchoring change is like establishing a new habit. Time, practice, feedback, measurement, and commitment are all key to the process. Establishing a new habit becomes a "normal" habit when it is a behavior

that does not require intention and thought. Kotter (1995, p. 67) calls it "the way we do things around here." When the change initiative has been integrated into the organizational culture it becomes institutionalized. For its longevity, it still needs to be protected by sharing the journey of change and improvement with boards of directors and other stakeholders who can influence changes in leadership who may not see the value of the change. Internal performance reviews and criteria for promotion must also reflect the new behaviors. The value of change is enormous in today's world. The environment where organizations live is not stagnant. Organizations that are not continually adapting to new conditions and creating new processes lose touch with client and customer needs. Therefore, for organizations to survive and stay relevant, successful change is required.

SUMMARY

The word excellence can be intimidating. Yet it is a level the best leaders wish to reach. Having the knowledge and skills to assess the key components of your organization, understand the importance of organizational processes, believe in the value of growth measures and data driven decision making, and nurturing a process for leading organizational change will give you the ability to reach for excellence. It is excellence that sustains organizations and allows them to grow with the changes of society.

REFERENCES

Alexander, J. (2000). Adaptive strategies of nonprofit human service organizations in an era of devolution and new public management. *Nonprofit Management & Leadership, 10*, 287–303. doi: 10.1002/nml.10305

Council of Chief State School Officers. (2011). *InTASC model core teaching standards: A resource for state dialogue.* Retrieved from http://www.CCSSO.org/documents/2011/intasc_model_core_teaching_standards_2011.pdf

Covey, S. R. (1989). *The seven habits of highly effective people: Powerful lessons in personal change.* New York, NY: Simon and Schuster.

EFQM. (2013-2014). *European foundation for quality management.* Brussels, Belgium. Retrieved from http://www.efqm.org

Gang, Y. (2013). The quest for quality in China. *The Quality Management Forum, 39*(1), 1, 3–5.

Heath, C. & Heath, D. (2010). *Switch: How to change things when change is hard.* New York: Broadway Books.

Kaplan, R. S. & Norton, D. P. (2011). Putting the balanced scorecard to work. In *HBR's ten must reads: The essentials* (pp. 85–112). Boston, MA: Harvard Business Review Press.

Kotter, J. (1995). Leading change: Why transformation efforts fail. *Harvard Business Review, 73*(3/4), 59–67.

Loehr, J., & Schwartz, T. (2003). *The power of full engagement: Managing energy, not time, is the key to high performance and personal renewal.* New York, NY: The Free Press.

Melan, E. H. (1993). *Process management: Methods for improving products and service.* New York, NY: McGraw-Hill.

TNCPE. (2014-2015). *Criteria for performance excellence.* Gaithersburg, MD: U.S. Department of Commerce, National Institutes of Standards and Technology.

Tyagi, R., & Piccotti, J. (2012). A service framework: An inside look at a specialized resource for quality professionals in the service sector. *Quality Progress, 45*(10), 40–45.

Chapter 11

Self-Management—Communications as Listening: Presentation, Electronic and Web-Based, and Performance Feedback

LEARNING OBJECTIVES

The student will

- describe the four styles of listening;
- role-play an example of empathic listening;
- compare and contrast the audience impact of a lecture given as a report, a presentation, and a story;
- explain and practice proper etiquette in professional electronic communication; and
- explain the eight steps of a learning conversation.

LISTENING

Communication is to leadership what the cardio vascular system is to the human body. Like the blood stream that carries life supporting oxygen and protective antibodies, communication carries team supporting "oxygen" that enables team members to successfully work together and achieve a common goal. A leader's communication not only provides instruction, motivation and support but also ensures a listening ear for feedback that will allow the team to communicate concerns and in turn, course-correct as well as problem solve. Communication is more than just the confidence that your policy or memo was understood by members of your team or the enthusiasm created by the memorable words delivered in your last presentation. Communication is about the many messages "sent" and "received" daily, formally and informally, through spoken words and body language, with positive and negative emotions, and through a variety of mediums, media, and technologies. The depth of this subject is covered in a multitude of courses, books, and seminars. An entire college degree program is accredited and dedicated to the understanding and practice of communication. This chapter will provide a focus on selected skill sets that are critical to effective leadership communication. I hope your interest will be sparked, and you will choose to continue your learning in the broader topic of communication and leadership.

Specifically, this chapter will cover skill sets regarding listening, presentations, electronic communication, negotiation, and feedback. Although many communication efforts begin with a focus on the message "sending" portion of the process, this chapter will begin with a look at "receiving" the message.

REFLECTION: THE IMPORTANCE OF FEELING HEARD

Generally, "hearing" is defined as the detection of sounds or words. However, to truly be heard means the recipient must also understand. Therefore, to say "I heard you" is a matter of interpretation, and herein lays the essence of the leadership problem. A leader must learn to hear in a way that assures the person communicating that he or she understands. This is what is known as listening. The fact that our ear can detect sound coming from a device or person should not be construed as listening. The art of listening begins with the knowledge that words and sentences were transmitted, but listening is so much more. The International Listening Association (http://www.listen.org) defines listening as the process of receiving, constructing meaning from, and responding to spoken and/or nonverbal messages. In fact, Hawkins and Fillion (1999) and Covey (1989) consider it the most important communication skill needed by leaders and team members alike. For example, think about a time you wanted to share some news (good or bad) with an important person in your life. You share your news but come away from that communication feeling unfulfilled. In a situation like that, the complaint most commonly shared is "I didn't *feel* heard." I am sure you could say with certainty that the person who heard your news detected your sounds and the majority of your words, but you needed to "feel heard" at the end of the conversation.

The world we live in today doesn't teach us how to actively listen. Distractions surround us. Everything moves at lightning speed. We have been trained to hear only the surface topic so we can move quickly from one subject to the next. Even as you are reading this, you are probably thinking about the time until lunch, a conversation with a friend, or what you have to do at work today. Whether they are important or unimportant distractions, they prevent us from being attentive, active listeners.

The technologies by which we surround ourselves encourage rapid response and multitasking. We text, watch TV, and respond to emails all while we work on writing a report or eating dinner with our family. In a world in which 24-hour communication technologies surround us, everything has become NOW, NOW, NOW, and we're afraid if we delay, we'll miss something. So we engage in everything simultaneously.

In addition to the chaotic culture of distractions we live in, many other things can get in the way of our focus on listening. Many times our mind races to create a response while the other person is talking. Unfortunately, many years in the classroom have conditioned us to prioritize our potential response for a teacher over listening. Other times we just listen partially because we have other things we deem more important to do. Cell phones allow us to do many things while we supposedly listen to the person on the other end of the conversation. For some, listening is really about interrupting the conversation to "fix" the other person's problem. We forget that many times the value of telling our story is not in receiving a "fix" but in receiving empathy. Then there are those who interrupt to tell a similar story about themselves and turn the focus away from the person initially sharing to the listeners' "more interesting" problems and experiences. And for others, listening to someone's experience can cause a reaction and mental judgment that communicates disagreement or even condemnation for what the speaker is sharing. Partial listening, fixing another's problem, autobiographic responses, and judgments are responses that lead to an unsatisfactory feeling of "nobody is listening," which then translates into "nobody cares." The person who shares a concern is not always seeking a fix, to know how another might handle a similar problem, approval, or to know the next step after achieving a goal. That person sharing a concern is seeking an emotional connection through the story, just to know the selected listener cares.

Have you ever experienced or done the following:

- Shared a heartfelt concern with a parent or spouse only to have the listener's unsolicited solution thrust upon you.
- Listened to a friend's story of difficulty and responded by trumping that story with "You think that's bad, last year this is what happened to me!"
- Enthusiastically shared an achievement with a parent or supervisor yet found yourself in a "goal setting" lecture outlining the next items on your agenda rather than celebrating your success.

As a leader, you can find yourself in similar situations with the members of your team. It is easy to become a nonlistener when deadlines loom, you believe your ideas are clearly superior to the team's, or celebrating small victories for others is not as important as the ever-growing to do list. Make the choice, take the time, and learn to listen.

DIAGNOSIS: WHAT TYPE OF LISTENER ARE YOU?

According to Ripley and Watson (2014), there are four styles of listening: people oriented, action oriented, content oriented, and time oriented. Bodie, Villaume, and Imhof provide descriptions of the four types.

- **People-Oriented** listeners are responsive, seek areas of common ground between themselves and the speaker, and are concerned about other people's feelings and emotions. They demonstrate empathetic and caring characteristics (Bodie & Villaume, 2003).
- **Action-Oriented** listeners like organized, efficient, and error-free messages. They can become impatient with a speaker and are likely to miss the emotional-relational dimension of a message (Imhof, 2004)
- **Content-Oriented** listeners enjoy learning by listening to complex information and engaging in a dialogue of questions, followed by an analysis of all sides of an issue before determining an opinion (Bodie & Villaume, 2003).
- **Time-Oriented** listeners begin the process by determining an allocation of time to be given to the speaker. They have a low tolerance for lengthy discussions and may even dismiss a speaker if the exchange has exceeded the time allotted (Bodie & Villaume, 2003).

Similar to behavior styles in Chapter 3, it is common for individuals to have primary and secondary listening preferences. The purpose for determining listening styles is to enable the presenter to make choices about the presentation to increase the attention time for the recipients. Should the presentation focus on facts and data or on human-interest stories? It also serves to remind presenters to employ focus points for all four styles, especially if presenting to a large group. The result is better communication and learning and increased productivity.

What is your listening style? There are assessments that will help you determine your listening style; the International Listening Association (http://www.listen.org) also hosts conferences and publishes research on the subject of listening. The questions in Table 11.1 will help you determine the preferences you have in how you listen.

Just like there is value in having different behavior and personality styles on a team (Chapter 3), there is also value in having different listening styles. And there

Table 11.1 Listening Preferences

Listening Preferences
Indicate how true each statement is for you by using the following scale.
If the statement is always true, write a 5 in the blank.
If the statement is frequently true, write a 4 in the blank.
If the statement is sometimes true, write a 3 in the blank.
If the statement is infrequently true, write a 2 in the blank.
If the statement is never true, write a 1 in the blank.

____ 1. My behavior style (Chapter 3) is below the line (persuader or stabilizer), and I am most interested in human-interest stories.

____ 2. When attending or giving a presentation, I quickly notice if others are interested or bored.

____ 3. When I hear stories of those who struggle, my heart goes out to them, and I look for ways to help.

____ 4. I am comfortable making eye contact to show interest in others' points of view.

____ 5. I am frustrated in presentations that are not logical and thoughtful.

____ 6. I am persuaded by facts and data; therefore, I focus on those items almost to the exclusion of other discussion items shared.

____ 7. Impatience and my broad knowledge of so many topics cause me to imagine giving the presentation myself.

____ 8. "Just get to the point" is on the tip of my tongue in most meetings.

____ 9. I want to know and share all the details in the fine print.

____ 10. I need to analyze the data myself after it is presented.

____ 11. I am motivated and challenged by sorting out the complexities in a discussion.

____ 12. Questions are the most effective way to get the information I want.

____ 13. I live in a world of precise time allocations and expect others to share information in the time allotted.

____ 14. I feel robbed when others can't make their point in a given amount of time.

____ 15. I interrupt others when I feel time pressure.

____ 16. I don't go anywhere without a watch or other visible timekeeping device.

Scoring
People-oriented listening score: Add your scores for items 1, 2, 3, and 4.
Action-oriented listening score: Add your scores for items 7, 8, 11, and 12.
Content-oriented listening score: Add your scores for items 5, 6, 9, and 10.
Time-oriented listening score: Add your scores for items 13, 14, 15, and 16.

are connections between listening styles and behavior styles. There are times when understanding content must prevail or situations of complexity are in need of exacting analysis. As a leader, you must be aware of your "listening style preference" and work to enhance your listening abilities in all situations since not every style works best in every situation. Leaders find they use empathic skills most often, therefore developing and improving your people-oriented, empathic listening skills will make you a better leader.

Now that you have shed some light on your listening tendencies, take a moment to think about the barriers to staying focused in a listening situation. On a scale of 1 to 5 with 5 high and 1 low, give yourself a score for each distraction's ability to detour you from your "listening course."

1 2 3 4 5   Boredom

1 2 3 4 5   Distracted by the history shared with the speaker

1 2 3 4 5   No desire to consider a different opinion

1 2 3 4 5   Allow emotions to overrule logic

1 2 3 4 5   Allow logic to overrule emotions

1 2 3 4 5   Focus on speaker's appearance, verbal characteristics, and so on instead of his or her message

1 2 3 4 5   Planning your response to the dialogue

1 2 3 4 5   Daydreaming

1 2 3 4 5   Distracted by disturbances in the room or with other participants

1 2 3 4 5   Texting, emailing, or other technology distractions

1 2 3 4 5   Concentrating on a personal memory of similar circumstances triggered by the speaker's story (autobiographical response)

Sources: Covey, S. R. (1989). *The seven habits of highly effective people: Powerful lessons in personal change.* New York, NY: Simon and Schuster. Golen, S. (1990). A factor analysis of barriers to effective listening. *Journal of Business Communication, 27,* 25–36.

Distractions play a large role in your inability to listen more than superficially. Find the discipline to give your attention to the speaker. As a leader, you are responsible for all information that is shared. You cannot always judge or make assumptions about information shared based on the person who shares it or whether it captures your attention immediately.

PRESCRIPTION: INCREASING EMPATHIC LISTENING SKILLS

Now that you know the universal importance of "feeling heard," what behaviors can help you make that happen? As the speaker, you want the listener to both hear your words and connect with the feelings you expressed when you spoke them. For those in human services professions, you will recognize that skill as empathic listening. Many human services professionals will be focused on their clients' stories that expect them to not only hear but also empathize with their experiences. Empathic listening is listening to understand another, to allow oneself to be influenced by the uniqueness of the other person. Next to physical survival, psychological survival (feeling understood, affirmed, validated, and appreciated) is an influential motivating force in humanity (Covey, 1989).

The Chinese symbol for listening (Figure 11.1) encompasses three senses in the empathic listening process: to hear, to see, and to feel with your heart.

To engage all three senses requires the message receivers to be very focused and give their undivided attention to the message senders. Operating the three listening senses simultaneously is a high-energy activity.

Communications experts identified sources of communication by type: 10% of communication is through words, 30% by sounds, and 60% by body language. Human services professionals, counselors, health care professionals, reporters, sales persons, attorneys, as well as other professionals engaged in a high percentage of human contact activities pay attention to these details to further understand and help their clients.

Figure 11.1   Chinese Symbol for Listening

Ear   Eyes   Undivided Attention   Heart

Source: U.S. Department of State. (n.d.). Active listening. Retrieved http://www.state.gov/m/a/os/65759.htm

A leader's role is enabling team members to sustain their motivation and work at the highest level. To accomplish high-level work, a leader must be willing and able to listen for understanding ideas, feedback, and concerns that are transmitted regularly from the team. This level of understanding is only achieved through active, empathic listening.

Here are some steps to improve your empathic listening skills.

1. First, determine if this is an empathic listening situation. Is there potential stress, short deadlines, excitement, or conflict in the work team? Are current or potential long-term relationships being built or at risk? What signs do you see?

2. Focus on the three senses (eyes, ears, heart) as you listen to the team members. What does each of the three senses tell you? Think of yourself as a physician who must diagnose before you can prescribe. This type of role-play will force you to focus on what you are seeing, hearing, and feeling before you respond with a prescription/solution.

3. Listen for both content and emotion as the team discusses the decision, potential new process, change in personnel, and so on. Ask them a nonspecific follow-up question such as "Tell me more" or "Can you clarify?" Share the feelings you heard expressed: "I see you are __ (insert a feelings word as described in number 4)." Do not judge the members' responses. Refrain from sharing your own personal anecdotes regarding the situation. Stay focused on the individual or team with whom you are communicating.

4. Spend some time enhancing your feelings vocabulary. Play a "Scattegories-like" game with yourself, listing as many feelings adjectives (positive and negative) as you can. Do this with friends. Include your friends' lists of adjectives with yours. Learn to use these new words as you listen to others describe what they are experiencing. What someone might have previously described as "upset" with a bigger vocabulary becomes "frustration," "fear," or "confusion." As a leader, you can more easily connect by expressing specific emotions. When an emotion is more specifically described by the listener, the team or individual feels heard and will more easily engage in a process to resolve the issue of concern.

5. Practice understanding the speaker's feelings before understanding the content of his or her message. Years of schooling taught us how to listen for content by delivering the majority of our education through lectures and question-answer sessions on many topics. Retool your listening focus with practice sessions. To develop an understanding of the speaker's feelings, listen to conversations around you, on television, or film for cues to identify emotions. Role-play dialogue in literature and analyze for emotion. Use some of the new vocabulary you developed from step number 4.

6. Make good eye contact. Inquiry, paraphrasing, and acknowledgement are good techniques in listening. Repeat a phrase or two in your own words representing how the speaker feels. Reflection of feelings does not mean you are in agreement with his or her decisions. You are simply showing you understand what he or she is feeling. Resist the temptation to give advice or fix the problem. The individual/team may ask for your help. If so, you may respond to the request. Without the speaker's request, you might say, "If you want my assistance later sorting this out, I am always willing to help." This process does not give the listener license to solve the problem. Be careful that an inquiry doesn't sound like sarcasm or an attack. Keep in mind that less is more; after all, your job as the listener is to focus on the speaker. Use phrases that indicate you are listening and want to hear more.

7. Although empathic listening works to resolve issues relatively quickly, there is a tendency to rush or cut off the critical initial sharing of the concern from the speaker. To prevent this from happening, use the Native American Talking Stick approach to guide the flow of the dialogue. The speaker holds the talking stick until he or she believes the listener has heard both the feeling and content of his or her point of view. Then the stick is passed to the other party to share and achieve understanding in the same manner. The stick prevents the speaker from feeling rushed or cut off as listeners in this process may only ask clarifying questions. The goal of this exercise is for participants to understand rather than judge or give advice.

SUMMARY

Consider how respected and affirmed you felt when a supervisor, colleague, or family member really listened to you. The listener tuned in to both the content as well as the feelings you shared. The listener did not judge you or tell you what to do. In your eyes, the credibility of the listener increased such that you believed this person had your best interest at heart. As a leader, the rewards of building that kind of relationship in your work group simply by being a skilled listener will create a culture of strong working relationships anchored in trust and respect.

PRESENTATIONS

Addressing a group of people is a great opportunity for a leader to share original ideas and new information, secure additional funding, and connect with untapped champions for his or her organization. Developing successful presentations will play an important role in the future of your organization and your career. Although it is not typically something a leader does on a daily or weekly basis, it can lead to greater productivity and innovation.

Nancy Duarte (2010, p. xix) frames the importance of this skill set. "It is the dawn of the information age, and we are all overwhelmed with too many messages bombarding us and trying to lure us to acquire and consume information.... Technology has given us many ways to communicate, but only one is truly human: in-person presentations."

When done correctly, presentations can bring a large return on your investment. This section will discuss the common mistakes presenters make and will teach you proven methods for you to be successful. Strategies will be shared to help speakers become stage ready.

REFLECTION: POTENTIAL OF PRESENTATION IMPACT

Consider the impact of Dr. King's speech "I Have a Dream." You studied his influence, felt moved and hopeful from his passionate delivery, and were captured by the vision of the future he painted. This same level of passion was seen in the early Earth Day campaigns when school-aged youth and environmentalists teamed to promote recycling programs. Their slogan was "It's Good to be Green," and it changed the habits of governments, businesses, and communities. Citizens heard scientific facts about the future livability of the planet from earnest faces of future generations and were moved to change. Another presentation that might have moved you would have been from a professor who shaped the direction of your career. You attribute this to his or her passion and zeal at the front of the classroom. As you can see, successful presenters find a way to connect with and inspire their audience.

Conversely, have you ever been victim of a boring presentation? Or possibly worse, have you ever realized you were boring the audience during your presentation? You may have even questioned an invitation to speak to a group wondering what value you could bring to an audience. Have you experienced anxiety about an upcoming presentation and considered any excuse to be relieved of your responsibility? Consider for a moment that it may not be a matter of nerves and fears but instead a desire to feel more confident and connected with the audience. Therefore, the question is how can you better communicate the passion of your ideas?

Presenters have a responsibility to their audience to engage and inspire them. Those in human services and nonprofit sectors have important messages to share regarding social change initiatives that require coalitions of support. How do you convince others to change their minds, be open to new information, and become an advocate for your organization? George Bernard Shaw said it best: "Progress is impossible without change; and those who cannot change their minds cannot change anything."

DIAGNOSIS: RATING THE IMPACT OF YOUR PRESENTATIONS

Preparing an impactful presentation is more than a few PowerPoint slides with data. A good presentation is a cross between a report (factual) and a story (taps emotions) (Duarte, 2010). Analysis might excite the mind, but it hardly offers a route to the heart, says Stephen Denning (2013, p. 117). The truth of influence is to understand the emotional nature of humans. Marketing experts know that emotions rule. And what better way to incorporate the power of emotion into a presentation than through stories. A report given in a presentation usually consists of an endless set of slides with tables and charts of data, goal measures, program assessments, and surveys of client needs all communicated in a precise linear format.

A story in a presentation has a beginning, middle, and end with characters you can relate to and view as heroines and heroes. They face the same problems as we do, struggle to overcome situations, and achieve victories just as we want to see ourselves win. The heroines and heroes learn lessons to guide their future choices as well as others in the struggle (Denning, 2013). Whether *Star Wars*, *Harry Potter*, or *The Hunger Games*, the story formula works every time.

Using the key elements of a story, can you find the four elements (plot, struggle, heroines and heroes, lessons learned) in a recent presentation (slides and notes) you delivered? Was your presentation more like a report or a story?

Feedback from a trusted colleague is critical to determine if you made a connection with the audience. Morgan (2013) refers to this connection as an authentic connection, one that communicates through body language before our words are even heard. Feelings and emotions are sensed by the presenter first, resulting in appropriate gestures, facial expressions, and finally, words. Better rehearsals start with getting in touch with presenter emotions, not just practicing words. When the presenter feels the appropriate emotion, there is authenticity the audience feels before the words are ever translated. A presenter wants the audience to sense openness, connection, and passion. Once the presenter is tuned into his or her own feelings, he or she can tune into the audience's emotions during the presentation. Morgan (2013) calls this listening to the audience. Good presenters can "hear" when the pace needs to quicken, the language needs to come alive, or when the presentation might need to end early because of a need to clarify.

Ask a good friend, colleague, or faculty member to rate you on a scale of 1 to 5 (1 low, 5 high) using the rubric in Table 11.2 for a presentation you will give.

Table 11.2   Presentation Feedback

Question/Reflection/Observation	Rating Scale Low High				
1. Did the presenter display mannerisms of openness? Describe.	1	2	3	4	5
2. Did the presenter connect/engage with the audience? Describe.	1	2	3	4	5
3. Did the presenter deliver with passion; touch the audience emotions? Describe.	1	2	3	4	5
4. Did the presenter deliver with a story: plot, heroine/hero, struggle, lessons learned? Describe.	1	2	3	4	5
5. Did the presenter listen to the audience? Describe.	1	2	3	4	5

Improvement is only possible when you are open to feedback. Make these feedback arrangements as often as you can. Have a friend record you. Most smart phones and tablets have video recording capability. There is nothing like being able to view the actual presentation. You want to know patterns about your stage presence, body language, as well as speech patterns. It is much better to hear feedback this way than if it was for a grade, job, or other high stakes situation. This feedback guide provides specific questions for a guided coaching.

Detailed Presentation Assessment Rubric

1. Describe the presenter's facial expression at the beginning, middle, and end of the presentation.
   - Beginning: _____
   - Middle: _____
   - End: _____
   - Eye contact with audience was
     ___Limited?   ___Focused left?   ___Focused right?   ___Focused front?
   - Facial expression denoted
     ___Passion?   ___Commitment?   ___Happiness?   ___Anxiety?
     ___Little expression?

2. Describe the tone of voice:
   - ___Upbeat, high energy, passionate?
   - ___Low energy, monotone?
   - ___Inconsistent energy level?

3. Speaker's introduction:
   - ___Added credibility.
   - ___Added enthusiasm.
   - ___Connected with audience.
   - ___Added no value.

4. Content:
   - ___Key points were clear, distinctive, memorable.
   - ___Key points were ___ were not ___ overwhelming in number.
   - ___Key points were given ___ adequate ___ too much ___ too little time.
   - ___Key points were supported ___ not supported ___by facts/research.
   - ___Key points made ___ did not make ___ an emotional connection
   - ___Key points made ___ did not make ___ an emotional connection through story.

5. What did the presenter ask the audience to do at the end of the presentation?
   - ___Learn
   - ___Purchase
   - ___Donate
   - ___Change a behavior
   - ___Volunteer
   - ___Support a cause/organization
   - ___Nothing

6. Audience seemed engaged:
   - ___Attentive with few distractions, some taking notes?
   - Presentation elicited an audience response: ___ attention, ___ smile, ___nodding, ___ laughter, ___ tears, ___ applause, ___ silence, ___ debate, ___ sleep, ___quick departure.
   - ___Asked questions publicly or stayed after to discuss?
   - ___Distracted, disengaged, bored, sleeping, texting, otherwise occupied?

Review the results of the assessments. What is the information telling you about the various parts of your presentation? Like all skills, this is one that will improve through intentional design influenced by this chapter and through practice.

PRESCRIPTION: HOW TO BE MEMORABLE

Having a presentation plan is a tool most leaders use to ensure the content of the presentation is factual and the facility is appropriate. Here are important items to include in making a presentation plan worksheet:

- Date and start/end time of presentation.
- Purpose of presentation.
- Time facility opens. (Best to allow an hour for set-up of technical equipment.)
- Address and directions to facility.
- Seating capacity, arrangement of table and chairs. (Best to see the room for yourself if you can.)
- Equipment provided: microphone (lapel or platform); ability to play video with sound; computer; projector; remote; ability to darken room; ability to move from the podium, or will you be tethered by technology?
- Dates and times of communication/confirmation with host. (Record email and phone number.)
- Date and times of communication with facility staff. (Record email and phone number.)
- Number, description, needs of participants. (Number of handouts if any.)
- Date to make copies or order materials.
- Alternate contact information if a Monday, evening, or weekend presentation.

Designing a presentation is more comprehensive than compiling a set of PowerPoint slides. You are making this presentation for a purpose. What is the purpose? Is it to educate? Persuade? Share results? If your purpose is to share results, then a memo will suffice. Next, what do you want the audience to do with the material in the presentation? Do you want the audience to learn it? Apply it? Change their attitudes regarding it? Join your cause? Sell it? Buy it? Tell others about it? Most presenters fail because they were unable to clearly define for the audience what they wanted them to do. A presenter must intentionally plan to enable the audience to use the material.

Duarte (2012) describes an audience as a temporary assembly of individuals who, for a block of time, share one thing in common, your presentation. Just because they are in the same room hearing the same words does not mean they are processing your message in the same way. As the presenter, you must find a way to connect with each of them. To successfully connect with your audience, you must first find out who they are? Your audience could be work colleagues or students you taught in other classes. They could also be total strangers or a roster of names on a registration list. Even as a roster of unknown names, you can likely determine where they work, their education level, and possibly their lifestyle, values, and needs. Did they sign up because it was required or because it was their choice? The person or organization hosting the event at which you are speaking can answer some of these questions. Once you have a few basic answers, you will likely unlock a few more answers as you prepare. And it is not inappropriate to ask your audience a few questions individually as they take their seats or even from the stage in polling-type process.

Connecting with your audience is similar to connecting with an individual. As the presenter, you begin looking for common ground. The presenter shares content-related experiences, needs, and emotions that the audience has experienced, too. I used this technique in this book, particularly in the reflection sections of each chapter. In each reflection section, I describe what I believe to be common actions or beliefs about leadership and group experiences; I hope you will nod and say, "Yes, that happened to me, too." Common experiences enable me to connect with your mind and heart; when presenting, it is important to connect at both levels. Without connection to the audience members' emotional side, your message will not resonate in a memorable way. Emotion creates personal conviction. When two products have the same features, the one that appeals to an emotional need will be chosen. Understanding the emotional side to human nature is a more recent focus of research. Until 1987, expressing emotions publicly was considered inappropriate. Products and solutions were created based on need, not desire. Today, a presenter must appeal to the desire of the audience as well as to their needs. To do this, the presenter must search for common goals and work to find the overlap of common ground. Not only must you find common ground, you want to help the participant feel like he or she is a part of your presentation. You must learn to tell a story.

The power of story, according to Duarte (2010), causes a presentation to do the following:

- Become dynamic.
- Link one heart to another.
- Intertwine values, beliefs, and norms among listeners.
- Bring life to ideas.
- Show vulnerability of presenter, and expose humanity and flaws.
- Help audience cheer and connect with heroes who overcome.

Duarte (2012) provides additional tips in crafting a story. Build tension by toggling back and forth between what is and what could be, finally arriving at true bliss. The action of toggling back and forth makes the middle of the story interesting and compelling as the heroine or hero struggles. Personal stories, if you have one, have the most impact. Help the audience laugh or feel fear. This is where the audience becomes convinced of the better way. Build a powerful ending with more than just a few goals to achieve. Instead say how these new achievements will benefit the audience, clients, organization, and the community.

Stories help us feel and connect with the facts of the presentation. Stories are easier to remember. Whenever you can convey a story about your organization, the staff, or the recipients of your organization's services, it is much more powerful and memorable than columns of data depicting how much food was distributed, the demographics of families who were counseled, or the amount of money raised. Stories amuse us and make us think, dream, empathize, cry, and laugh. The emotional connections from stories inspire us and commit us to a cause, idea, person, team, or family.

To create a story arc within your presentation, consider laying out the parts like sections of a storyboard. If you have never crafted a story, it follows a pattern. In each case, there are three basic acts in which the heroine or hero travels a journey (Duarte, 2010, p. 30-31):

- Act 1
  - Plot Situation
    - Plot point 1 – captures audience attention
    - A turning point
- Act 2
  - Plot Complication
    - Midpoint
    - Plot point 2
- Act 3
  - Plot Resolution

A good storyteller compels the audience to feel like the hero of the tale. This is what creates the emotional connection and audience buy-in. The hero's journey through a presentation/story will to the following:

- Describe the Setting: Show the audience the current realities of the world. (Create a picture.)
- Call to Action: Describe the gap between what is and what could be in the world. (Presents imbalance for the audience.)
- Show this contrast not just with facts but with emotion. Take them from familiar to unfamiliar and back again. This keeps their attention and creates forward motion in the presentation/story.
- Turning Point: Resolve the imbalance. Share wisdom and tools.
- Teach the audience how to use wisdom and tools.

- Practice.
- Create a memorable conclusion. The conclusion is just as important as the rest of the story arc.

Keep the audience engaged all the way until your last words are shared. Describe the new choice, idea, product, service, and so on. Use descriptive words that enable the audience to hear, see, smell, taste, and feel it. Be clear about what you want the audience members to do when they leave. This is a common mistake presenters make. Do you want the audience to vote for something, advocate for it, take action with you, join your cause, or purchase the product? Duarte (2012, p. 41) describes four types of audience members.

1. Doers – instigate activities, follow through, and recruit others.

2. Suppliers – get resources: people, funding, supplies.

3. Influencers – change perceptions, persuade others to support.

4. Innovators – generate ideas, create and build on ideas, create new programs and services.

Plan for and design an action each type of audience member can take post presentation. Be clear and be memorable.

SUMMARY

Having the opportunity to present should be considered a gift. People's time and attention is precious. A presentation is an opportunity to influence a group of people; if done well and effectively, it could lead to a follow-up invitation. Plan the presentation from the opening hook through the final ask. It is all about telling your story in a way that you are credible, memorable, and persuasive. Don't be afraid to invite the audience to do what you ask. That is why you are there. Rehearse until it is natural. Adopting this new perspective on presentations will make your organization and team more committed to the mission and influential in community.

ELECTRONIC AND WEB-BASED COMMUNICATION

This section on electronic communication may be obsolete before the book is even published, yet this chapter's overarching principles will remain constant. Our ability to send and receive electronic messages in real time is both a blessing and a curse. Smart phone features have reduced the multiple rounds of daily phone tag played, and the speed of email reduces delays caused by what we now call snail mail. The price we pay for modern technology is the nonstop deluge of messages, which create expectations and make demands on us. Handling this information overload requires new skills and a refresher on basic personal management principles.

REFLECTION: THE GIFT AND THE CURSE OF TECHNOLOGY

Imagine living in the pre-1990s world where communication was tethered to your home or office through a device called a telephone and answering machine. Just prior to the turn of the century, telephones evolved into cell phones, and since the millennium, the cell phone has become a smart phone. In addition to calling, you can email; text; tweet; surf the Internet; and record photos, music, and video as well as use a variety of apps. The device serves as a camera, alarm clock, television, movie theatre, GPS, newspaper, and video recorder. And when it seems it has reached its peak, 6 months later a new device with even more features will be released. This tool has become as important as our reliance on automobiles. Individuals feel lost and disoriented without their smart phone.

Facebook, Twitter, and Foursquare are just a few of the websites and web-based applications that have evolved in tandem with the smart phone. We are mayors of the supermarket and tweet the details of an accident we encounter during our commute. No longer are we required to know who we are interacting with online. In 2011, Twitter posts alerted people in New York City that an earthquake was traveling up the east coast giving them an 11 second warning before the first tremor was felt. Instant communication has further perpetuated the 24-hour news cycle. Bloggers out scoop reporters. Passersby are capturing heroes, heroines, and villains in action. Newscasters rely on tweets to better and more quickly understand breaking stories. As the viewer, we expect to learn everything we can from a news source because if we are not satisfied, we will change the channel or app news source.

All sectors of the workplace strive to keep up with changes in technology. They have Facebook pages, hold meetings in Second Life, and videoconference with clients over Skype. However, there are potential access barriers. Employers must provide access to most of this technology through relaxed firewalls and software to enable employees to use these communications tools. Keeping up with the constant changes in software and equipment can be expensive, especially for resource-strapped employers. If upper management in human services organizations is resistant or unfamiliar with these tools, then the organization might also be left behind and lose opportunities for funding, collaborations, branding, as well as volunteer recruitment.

G-chat, Skype, Facebook Messenger, and Face Time have replaced AOL (American Online) Instant Messanger and Yahoo Messenger. Soon technology will morph again. Currently, the Smart Watch and fitness bands have captured the fancy of early adopters on new technology. We can text and video chat from almost any device with Internet access or a cellular data plan. If that wasn't enough, texting with our smart phones has evolved to include notifications that the message has been delivered, read, and when the reader is responding. This certainly makes for a more transparent work environment as well as personal relationships. As such, we are able to know almost everything about each other as it is happening, eliminating the typical dinnertime question, "How was your day?"

Our need for information has become a race to see who knows about a press release or other bit of information first. It's not enough to know how your children's school day was by dinnertime, you feel entitled to know this as it unfolds during the day through texting. Have we stopped to ask ourselves why we really need to know immediately? And what is the cost to our concentration at work or in class? Efficiency experts at organizations such as FranklinCovey report in their *5 Choices* productivity training program that it takes 15 to 20 minutes for the human brain to get refocused again once interrupted. (Kogan, Merrill, & Rinne, 2014) Now if you can, count the number of text messages you received today. Facebook or Twitter notifications? News notifications? Think about the amount of time that was lost every time you had to refocus your attention back to your task after checking these messages.

As great as this new technology is, making us that much more connected and up-to-date with what's happening around the world, it comes with a new set of unstandardized rules. For example, though your company might have a Facebook page, your coworkers might not want to be tagged in the posted photo. Do you friend your boss? Your coworker? Your students? Your clients? Do you create separate personal and professional accounts? How much should you post? It is unnecessary to tweet your every move, thought, or action. Further, the need to reduce the number of characters used to communicate has created a new language. Yet as acceptable as "BTW" or "LOL" is in a tweet or text, they are unacceptable for all forms of professional communication. An email to your boss is not restricted to 140 characters; therefore, to maintain your professional credibility, spell out all words and phrases.

At this point, you are either reading this section with enthusiasm or utter confusion. Your positive or negative response to the ever-changing technical modes of communication is called the generational digital divide. Some of us are fully swimming with the digital currents, embracing each new gadget, app, software update, and new generation of smart phone and tablet. Then there are others who use some of it, are weary of each new iteration, and who rely heavily on the swimmers to bridge them forward in this new world. The multigenerational workforce of today does not use or understand the impact or capacity of the technology revolution.

This lack of understanding creates difficulties in the workplace regarding how, when, and where employees work, competitiveness in frequency of communication, expectations for employee work–life balance, determination of valid sources of research, managing virtual meetings, standards for professionalism in electronic communication, and many other workplace choices made different by electronic and web-based communication. Leaders must step up to become educated and comfortable with new communication methods and tools. Leaders must not let the standards and expectations of the organization become either sacrificed or the barrier to this new world. It will take dialogue, some risk, and flexibility to allow the key principles of leadership, quality, and innovation to play well together.

DIAGNOSIS: MEASURING THE NEGATIVE IMPACT OF TECHNOLOGY

Is texting or other electronic communication's shorthand creeping into your documents? Has your use of standard English become sloppy? Look at the most recent paragraph, letter, or report (nonschool related) you wrote. Check it for the following:

- Abbreviated and nonabbreviated words
- Workplace or other jargon
- Use of capital letters
- Use of emoticons
- Use of commas and periods
- Correct spelling
- Correct grammar – subject, verb, tense agreement
- Introduction and closing sentences or paragraphs

If you write a potential client using the organization's email, you represent the organization. Therefore, proofreading it for correct grammar and spelling and omitting all shorthand is imperative. Email etiquette has become a new needed skill set for most all employees in today's world. Do you find email used inappropriately to convey an immediate rather than thoughtful response? Because of the ability to fire off an immediate response, too many inappropriate emotion-laden emails are sent. Unlike losing your cool in a passing hallway conversation (inappropriate as well), the email can be saved, printed, forwarded, and shared beyond anything you intended.

A McKinsey Global Institute study found that the average worker spends 28% of the workweek writing, reading, or responding to e-mails (Komando, 2012). How many emails a day do you receive? When you return from out of town, is your inbox over the limit?

Are all of your emails read and responded to every day? How many emails are sitting in your inbox right now? What is the date of the oldest email in your inbox? Keep a 7-day record:

- How often do you check your smart phone for personal messages during the work or school day?
- How many personal texts do you send during work or school hours each business day?
- How many other personal Internet use minutes are you logging each work or school day? (Facebook, Twitter, Pinterest, blogs, news, shopping, etc.)

Translate these numbers into number of interruptions to your "thinking" day. For each electronic/web-based interruption of a personal nature, add 15 minutes to your interruption total. Now add each 15-minute block of interruption time in that work/school week. This answer represents the number of minutes you lost time by having to refocus your attention. Researchers call this time to refocus a reduction in thinking time—being "out of the zone" of high productivity.

Do you find that email, texting, and other forms of electronic communication are the main tools you use to communicate? Have you ever had a misunderstanding with a friend or coworker due to an electronic message having been misrepresented? As useful as all forms of electronic communication are, it is important to not omit all of the other forms of communication, such as face-to-face or voice communication.

PRESCRIPTION: THE SOCIAL AND SAFETY RULES OF EMAIL AND ELECTRONIC DEVICES

Smart phone and tablet devices bring such amazing capability to our fingertips. They also bring a vast array of distractions. If you are using your smart phone and tablet for both work and personal use, it will become helpful to separate app icons so that those you use at work are in one folder and those that are for personal and entertainment use are in another. Separating provides a small but helpful extra step to keep you from being sucked into the distractions on the device. Some devices provide more flexibility for this separation than others. Instead of folders, you can drag and drop them into different pages. You might even cluster some of the games, photos, and other entertaining aspects of the device into folders. The less visible the distractions are, the less likely you are to be tempted to spend work time there.

How many interruptions from texts and emails did you calculate during your 7-day analysis? Did you notice that the blocks of 15 minutes for refocus add up fast? The first step to get back some of that time is to be more intentional about when you check your messages. Silence your phone and check your messages only when it is convenient, for example, only during lunch and at breaks. Communicate this schedule to family, friends, and colleagues to further reduce the number of distractions. Discussing expectations and setting boundaries will create a structure everyone can follow as well as set the foundation for you to be successful. Several Fortune 500 companies as well as other organizations have empowered employees to not respond to email immediately. Employers have designated email free hours of the workday so that employee productivity increases when all are allowed to focus time and attention on the important and not the urgent. Recent research on the brain's ability to create and study complex issues shows that frequent interruptions from technology and other sources prevent the deep level of thinking required.

Kim Komando (2012), radio and newspaper syndicated columnist and provider of technology help, makes these suggestions to take back control of your email:

1. Send less email. Use other forms of communication. Things that need decisions, debate, dialogue, or could have an emotional reaction should not be discussed over email. Face-to-face communication is best in those situations. After a face-to-face conversation, a follow-up email is appropriate to confirm the decision or new direction.

2. Send better email. Always use the subject line to direct the recipient to what you want them to do (approve, reply, file, etc.). Be intentional and concise in the body of the email. Use outlines, bullets, and bold key phrases. Because people scan emails, keep it short.

3. Create and save templates for announcements or messages you frequently send.

4. Unsubscribe from list serves or send unwanted email to junk mail. Use tools in your email program (Outlook, Entourage, Google, etc.) to sort or screen messages. Disabling the notifications received from social networking sites will also reduce the volume of email received and your temptations for distraction.

5. Utilize a free email service with a different email address to sign up for freebies or sales ads, and so on. Using a different email leaves your work or personal email free from distractions and if this inbox becomes unmanageable, close the account.

6. Automate the sorting of your inbox. Filters, rules, and color-coding messages will help you route emails to read-later folders or to urgent folders. Assigning a color to your spouse or supervisor's email can help you spot these in a hurry. However, color-coding everything will make your inbox look like a bowl of Fruit Loops and will not let you identify urgent action items.

7. Designate a time or set of times in your daily calendar when you will attend to email. Then deal with it. Similar to snail mail, your actions with email are

either respond, file, or delete. Now do just that. If you set aside the email or attachment to read later, be certain you create a scheduled time to read and act on the read-later file.

8. Your inbox is not a storage system; it is a delivery system. Get the tasks and calendar items out of the inbox and into your to do list and calendar. Again, your email program's tools can help facilitate this process.

Janis Fisher Chan (2008, p. 8) compiled a list of questions to determine if email is the best method of communication.

- Why am I writing this email? What is my purpose?
- Who is my audience, and what is my reader's point of view?
- What is the main point?
- What does my reader need to know?
- How should I organize the email so the main point is easily discernible?

Even if the email you are composing is in response to an email you received, it does not mean email is the best way to continue the conversation. Be careful not to fall into that trap. Most of these rules apply to personal email too, but work email should never be used to convey the following:

- Confidential or private (personal) information
  - Health
  - Employment status
  - Legal concerns
  - Performance issues
  - Illegal or unethical information
- Sensitive topics, especially those that can elicit an emotional response
  - Politics
  - Religion
  - Personal relationships
  - Work relationships
  - Opinions
  - Humor (forwarding jokes)
  - Inappropriate abbreviations such as would be used in a text or tweet
- Urgent Information
  - Client needs
  - Change orders when traceable to clients, personnel, or specific individuals
  - "All hands on deck" messages
  - Messages when your emotions are not in control

- Complex information
  - New or updated policies
  - Heavily formatted or long reports (this information is better received as an attachment)

Email should never take the place of a face-to-face meeting or phone call. Leaders must learn how to handle difficult dialogue and not hide behind an impersonal email. Emails have no privacy and can be printed and forwarded to anyone, anywhere. Requesting and honoring privacy within an email cannot be guaranteed. Who might be offended if others saw this email? Does your organization have rules about certain types of communication or does your professional association have a code of ethics, which prohibits certain forms of electronic communication? Hacking into supposedly secure web systems makes confidential data storage and email ripe for picking by pranksters or those who would do your organization harm. Use complex passwords and change them regularly. Invest in the most secure systems possible. Keep your professional accounts separate from your personal accounts. Save your email jokes and YouTube videos for sharing through your personal account. Do not use text language in emails or offensive text abbreviations in texts to professional associates. And even that electronic communication pipeline can still cause an unintended consequence. The real message here is that your reputation as a leader is affected by everything you do and say, even if it is a forwarded message. A message you forward implies you concur with the content. Remember, once you hit send, you cannot take it back. Everything you post online including pictures, status messages, and tweets are permanently added to the information on the Internet.

Electronic communication is swift to send both information and mistakes. Most email programs can be set up to automatically spell-check your email, but always proofread before you send your message. Be careful in what you forward and thoughtful if you need to reply or reply to all. Create a signature block that includes all ways the reader can communicate with you, including your phone number and email address so that your reader has the option to choose another communication method. If the email is forwarded in the response process, the second recipient is also able to communicate with all options as well. Use care in what you send. Create a draft of your email or text and reread before you click send.

Email messages are best when they are clear, concise, and convey one or two ideas. Use the subject line to let the reader know what you want him or her to do. For practice, retrieve three emails you recently sent in which you were communicating an idea or instruction. Using Chan's (2008) five questions for evaluating emails, determine if your emails were (1) clear and (2) well constructed. Based on Chan's (2008) three other factors, determine if your emails were

- formal or friendly,
- casual or professional, and
- abrupt or polite.

Take your time composing emails. Having a specific time to do this will give you thoughtful time instead of high-speed reaction time. Although email can arrive and be sent as quickly as a text, don't confuse the two. Professional emails should address the recipient and be signed by the sender. Too frequently, mystery emails arrive from a sender who forgets he or she is not texting. Carefully consider whether your email message should be formal or casual as well as what type of tone to use. Adding afterthoughts or corrections to email responses only clogs everyone's inbox.

SUMMARY

Electronic and web-based communication are tools that have enhanced our personal and professional ability to communicate, send data, network, and reach current as well as future clients. And the communication devices that continue to flood the marketplace continue to improve their flexibility, reach, and volume in the types of communication available to us. These new methods of communication also present their own risks, such as miscommunication and disconnectedness. Theft of private information over secure sites is a risk for consumers as well as all individuals with health records and organization records dependent on cloud storage. Scrutiny of employment candidates, political candidates, security background checks, and other decision-making situations about a person's future now includes review of social media. Be very aware of the risks of electronic communication for yourself, your organization, and for the clients you serve. Never underestimate the value of a face-to-face communication or a handwritten note, especially as a leader.

PERFORMANCE FEEDBACK

Leaders are responsible for maintaining the course as the team works to achieve a shared goal. Similar to navigating a vehicle, where the driver relies on experience and training, as well as knowledge of current road conditions to successfully reach the destination, a leader must also rely on experience, skills, and training to guide the team. Communicated data that leads to course correction on this journey to the goal is more commonly known as feedback. Feedback can be information shared about the goal, competitors, key stakeholders, internal organization conditions, or external organizational conditions. It can pertain to needs of the team members or even the leader. Leaders who create an open environment for the communication of feedback will foster the trust of the team. A leader with skills to share feedback with members of the team is more likely to have a high performing team. It can make the difference between a team thriving in an organizational learning environment seeking quality improvement and an environment of hidden agendas, status seeking, manipulation, and distrust.

REFLECTION: YOUR EXPERIENCES GIVING AND RECEIVING FEEDBACK

At one time or another, you have probably been the beneficiary or victim of feedback. Parents are frequent delivery systems of communicated feedback throughout our lives. As children and adults, we are most accepting of parental feedback. Yet as teens and 20-something adults, parental feedback was disregarded because it was presumed to be dated, irrelevant, and unwelcome to an age group striving for independence.

Likewise, we have all given advice, opinions, and directives sometimes without benefit of data to back it up. From politicians to sports referees, we have subjected many individuals to what we believe is divine knowledge. But as organization leaders, influence and decisions that impact others without the benefit of feedback is dangerous, and in some leadership roles, such as a supervisor, can be unethical and possibly illegal.

Think about situations where you provided feedback, then reflect on these questions:

- Have you communicated feedback to friends or family members that was intended to alter their behavior? Was it well received? Did you base your feedback on data? Was your feedback good news? Did the listener find you to be credible? Did you feel confident as you delivered the information? Did you provide data to support your feedback? Did you offer suggestions and support? Did you feel you had influence with this person?

Were you able to answer yes to all of these questions? Now think about a situation in which you were the recipient of feedback and then reflect on these questions:

- When you received feedback from a friend, spouse, or supervisor, did you think it was delivered fairly, with dignity and respect? Was it based on data?

Was it positive reinforcement or direction regarding how you could improve? Did the words seem credible? Did you receive suggestions and support for change? Is this person influential in your life?

Were you able to answer yes to all of these questions?

Giving and receiving feedback is an uncomfortable situation for most people, especially if you are requesting another to change. To avoid conflict, many opt to put up with the issue rather than engage in a difficult conversation. This section will give you the leadership tools needed to successfully conduct difficult conversations as well as to create an environment that fosters openness.

DIAGNOSIS: GIVING PERFORMANCE FEEDBACK TO YOURSELF

Providing negative feedback to employees is a process many supervisors are reluctant to deliver. Providing positive feedback is a process many supervisors consider unnecessary. Feedback that is both positive and change producing is critical to help employees build on their strengths and overcome their weaknesses (Buron & McDonald-Mann, 1999). Changing career-limiting behaviors can be crucial to an employee's success. VitalSmarts, a national consulting firm, found that 97% of employees have a career-limiting behavior (Grenny, 2015). Yet too many supervisors are uncomfortable or untrained in how to have this conversation.

Before we analyze how to provide or receive feedback from others, first assess how you provide it to yourself. Throughout the day, the person you receive the most feedback from is yourself. The comparative scientist in you notices you are treated differently in some aspects of your job. You first attribute it to something you did or said, then assess your skill sets and reflect on personality preferences; and then later, you get down on yourself for falling short of your goal. You give up on your efforts or conclude that life and this organization have it in for you. Did you notice the slippery slope and how the feedback you provided yourself did not offer you anything positive to build from or support for altering behavior? Feedback you provide yourself should be saturated with data and positive reinforcement. Let's try a new strategy.

First, seek data from several sources to determine why you perceive your supervisor treats you differently than your coworkers. Seek feedback from colleagues, supervisors, friends, or those who work in a similar environment. Probe for specifics and do not be afraid to ask for feedback frequently. Analyze the data you collected for patterns. Get outside perspectives on your analysis. Create a plan to modify a behavior you have identified as troubling. If the behavior is complex, break it into parts, working to change the behavior one step at a time. Determine standards for the new behaviors you want to achieve. Ask a colleague to be your accountability partner. With your accountability partner, describe your goals and standards and ask to be observed for the specific changes you are working to achieve. Track these behavior changes for several weeks. Celebrate (but keep monitoring) when you start to see desired behaviors repeated.

PRESCRIPTION: THE FEEDBACK-CHANGE PROCESS

You could clearly see the difference in your attitude before you began collecting data and seeking outside sources for your own feedback. Once you began the process, you were in a "learning mode." You were open to both feedback and exploring how to change. Now that you know how the change process works with you as your own coach, consider how you can influence someone else to make a positive change, especially when this person is unaware the problem exists. We will approach this skill set in two parts.

Part 1: Stone, Patton, and Heen (1999, pp. 131–162) of the Harvard Negotiation Project use an eight-step process enabling leaders and supervisors to initiate conversations regarding the feedback-change process with an employee. Their recommended process is called the Learning Conversation. The eight steps are described below:

1. Determine if you should initiate the conversation at all. This might feel as if you have taken two steps back, but all situations have two or more perspectives. Consider how much of the conflict is within you? Is there some history in the situation or relationship you own that may be the real trigger? Can you address the issue in another way? Sometimes looking for a root cause can reveal answers to these questions and possibly help you identify that the issue is not with the employee, but an internal adjustment you need to make instead.

2. Is your purpose for having the conversation clear? Before you start the conversation, be sure you can answer what you want the desired outcome to be.

   a. You cannot change other people. Such changes come only when the other party wants to change. If you can set up a conversation that allows both parties to learn, there is a greater likelihood of buy-in toward change for the other party. This person also has to feel there is an option not to change. If it is forced, there is a higher likelihood the person's response will be resistance to change.

   b. Venting about a situation has a time and place. Don't let your need for a short-term emotional release cost a long-term gain. Yes, your buttons have been pushed, intentionally or not, but venting now will only set your effort back or even bring it to a grinding halt. Return to your purpose statement. Instead, find a friend or family member you can vent to who isn't involved in the situation.

c. Don't hit and run. Timing is everything. Be selective about your choice of topics and be prepared to spend adequate time engaged in discussion. Again, return to your purpose. A 10-second sarcastic remark (hit-and-run) will usually result in a defensive response.

d. Sometimes it is best not to have the conversation at all. This can be a difficult call. Some would say, "You have to choose your battles." It is possible to let go of the injustice you feel through assistance with a counselor or even limiting the time you spend with this individual. However, if you are unable to move on emotionally, a conversation is in order.

3. Starting the conversation so both parties don't become hurt or angry can be challenging, but there is a formula mediators use to engage both parties without adding to the uneasiness. Mediators draw from a perspective called the Third Story. This is a neutral perspective that doesn't take a side. It simply states there is a difference in perspectives. To draft the Third Story, reflect on yours by removing the blame, judgments, and perspective that your way is the right way.

4. The next step is to invite each party to have a conversation with a common purpose of mutual understanding and problem solving. After the invitation has been accepted and the conversation has begun, each person shares his or her story one at a time. The other party does not share the story until they can successfully restate the other person's feelings and perspective in the story. It is important to note that retelling the feelings of the other person's perspective conveys understanding, not agreement; and most importantly, acknowledging feelings must always happen before problem solving can begin. As stories are shared, you may not agree on the "what happened" part of the story, but you cannot deny that their feelings are important. Skipping this step will leave the other person feeling unsatisfied and make it more difficult to resolve the issue at hand. Here is an example used by Stone et al. (1999, p. 183).

A: I have worked so hard for you and now you are transferring me. It's just not fair. What's going to happen to me?

B: I can see you feel very hurt and betrayed. I can see why that would be upsetting.

A: So you agree with me that this is unfair?

B: What I am saying is that I can see how upset you are feeling, and it hurts me to see you so upset. I also understand why you think this is unfair and why you think I have betrayed your loyalty. Those factors made the decision to transfer you very difficult for me. I fought hard to make this work. I feel badly for how it has turned out, but I do think it is the right decision, and overall I don't think it is unfair. We should talk about why I think it is the right decision.

Here B acknowledges the power of A's feelings, yet disagrees with the essence of what is said. Acknowledging feelings does not convey agreement to the facts.

5. When sharing your story, be sure to cover the following:

   a. Where the story comes from

   b. The impact of the situation on you

   c. Share your responsibility in the situation

   d. Describe your feelings

   e. Reflect on the identity issues (personal values and experiences) in the situation

   These questions will enable the other party to understand your feelings and their origins.

6. Practice the listening skills you learned earlier in this chapter. Ask the other person for help so you can understand his or her story. Be genuine in your desire to understand. Faking concern will hurt your credibility in the eyes of the other party. If you are unable to turn off the distracting, judgmental, or emotional voices in your head and focus on the other person, it is best to state that this is a bad time and schedule another time to have the conversation. Emphasize to the other person how you want to take a deep breath so you can return with a clearer head. It is important to come back together as soon as possible. After the meeting has been rescheduled, go for a walk, vent to an uninvolved friend, meditate, and so on—whatever it takes to clear your head.

7. Empathy is one journey where you will never fully reach your destination. We are a diverse set of individuals with unique experiences that have brought us to see the world as we do. This is our lens on life. For this reason, we will never truly be able to walk in another's shoes, but we can give the gift of curiosity by wanting to know more about the other person's story. When someone works hard to understand us, we feel respected and valued. This a treasured gift, especially during a difficult conversation.

8. Problem solving is the next step. Similar to the portion of the self-coaching section of this chapter, you have uncovered patterns in the data and determined there needs to be a change in behavior. However, just like you had to buy in to the change for yourself, you must help the other person see the pattern, clarify the situation, and help them discover they have a role in making it better. Remember, though you are leading the dialogue, you cannot force the other person's decision. (You can force consequences, but that is another chapter.) Too many supervisors believe this is the first step. If you skip steps 1 through 7, you will be unsuccessful influencing the other person to buy in to the change.

Table 11.3 Reframing Language

Destructive Language of Person A	Reframed Helpful Language of Person B
I am absolutely right!	I want to understand your perspective, especially since you feel so strongly about it. I'd like to share my perspective too.
You hurt me on purpose!	I can see you feel really angry about what I did. It wasn't my intention. Tell me more about how you feel.
This is your fault!	I'm sure I've contributed to the problem; we both have. Rather than focus on fault, let's explore how we got here and how we each contributed to the problem.
I am not a bad employee!	Goodness, I don't think you are either. I certainly hope you don't think I am a lousy colleague. I do see we disagree on how to handle this situation. The question is, can we work together to solve it and address both of our concerns.

Source: "Problem Solving: Take the Lead" from *Difficult Conversations: How to Discuss What Matters Most* by Douglas Stone, Bruce Patton, and Sheila Heen, copyright © 1999 by Douglas Stone, Bruce Patton, and Sheila Heen. Used by permission of Viking Books, an imprint of Penguin Publishing Group, a division of Penguin Random House LLC.

Leading this conversation requires skills in reframing comments and questions. Reframing is defined as translating from destructive language to helpful language. Again, the Harvard authors Stone et al. (1999, p. 204–205) share good examples in Table 11.3.

Here are the authors' suggestions for reframing:

- Trying to establish truth => Return to the different stories
- Accusations => Discuss intentions and impact
- Blame => Discuss contributions of each to situation
- Judgments => Reaffirm feelings
- Choose you *or* me => Discuss we, you, *and* me
- Roadblocks to discussion => Describe the blockage as a way of removing/preventing it

Part 2: Now we all see the same situation and its related patterns and impacts. The solution steps are similar to that above:

a. Agree with all parties on the proposed solution.

b. Create a test to see if the problem is what you thought.

c. Share what might persuade each other in viewing the situation and potential solutions.

d. Seek advice from each other.

e. Create solution options, prototypes, and countertypes.

f. Determine standards for the solution.

g. Test solutions and determine the best path forward.

h. Work to sustain the change and establish accountability.

SUMMARY

Good communication skills are derived from practice as well as observing successful leaders. As you've learned, communication is a key component of leadership. Today's work environment requires everyone to be proficient at this skill, yet this is an area in which we can all improve. Find a learning partner who wants to improve and meet for coffee to review your week. Ask them for feedback regarding their observations of your communications skills. This data will enable you to grow as a communicator. Keep in mind; a learning partner is different from a mentor, though both are important for personal and professional growth. A learning partner has set similar goals as you and through feedback is working to achieve them. A learning partnership allows for each party in the partnership to be student and teacher, a role sharing that brings greater depth of learning to each participant. Polishing your communication skills will be an ongoing process. Mastering face-to-face communication as well as technology-supported communication skills in listening, presenting, information sharing, feedback, and negotiation will give you a leadership edge and a strong future.

REFERENCES

Bodie, G. D., & Villaume, W. A. (2003). Aspects of receiving information: The relationship between listening preferences, communication apprehension, receiver apprehension, and communicator style. *International Journal of Listening, 17*, 47–67.

Buron, R., & McDonald-Mann, D. (1999). *Giving feedback to subordinates: For the practicing manager.* Greensboro, NC: Center for Creative Leadership.

Chan, J. F. (2008). *E-mail: A write it well guide: How to write and manage email in the workplace.* Oakland, CA: Write It Well.

Covey, S. R. (1989). *The seven habits of highly effective people: Powerful lessons in personal change.* New York, NY: Simon and Schuster.

Denning, S. (2013). Telling tales. In *HBR's 10 must reads on communication* (pp. 115–130). Boston, MA: Harvard Business Review Press.

Duarte, N. (2010). *Resonate: Present visual stories that transform audiences*. Hoboken, NJ: John Wiley and Sons.

Duarte, N. (2012). *HBR guide to persuasive presentations*. Boston, MA: Harvard Business Review Press.

Golen, S. (1990). A factor analysis of barriers to effective listening. *Journal of Business Communication, 27*, 25–36.

Grenny, J. (2015). You might be the reason your employees aren't changing. *Harvard Business Review*. Retrieved from https://hbr.org/2015/02/you-might -be-the-reason-your-employees-arent-changing

Hawkins, K.W., & Fillion, B. P. (1999). Perceived communication skill needs for work groups. *Communication Research Reports, 16*, 167–174.

Imhof, M. (2004). Who are we as we listen? Individual listening profiles in varying contexts. *International Journal of Listening, 18*, 36–45.

Kogan, K., Merrill, A., & Rinne, L. (2014). *The 5 choices: The path to extraordinary productivity*. New York, NY: Simon and Schuster.

Komando, K. (2012). Nine simple steps to get your email under control. *USA Today*. Retrieved from http://usatoday30.usatoday.com/tech/columnist/kimkomando/ story/2012-09-07/manage-email-inbox/57673010/1

Morgan, N. (2013). How to become an authentic speaker. In *HBR's 10 must reads on communication* (pp. 105–113). Boston, MA: Harvard Business Review Press.

Ripley, R., & Watson, K. (2014). We're learning — Are you listening? *Chief Learning Officer*, 34–37. Retrieved from www.CLOmedia.com

Stone, D., Patton, B., & Heen, S. (1999). *Difficult conversations: How to discuss what matters most*. New York, NY: Penguin Press.

US Department of State. (n.d.). *Active listening*. Retrieved from http://www.state .gov/m/a/os/65759.htm

Part IV

Influence

Chapter 12

Multicultural Leadership, Politics and Influence, Collaboration, and Social Entrepreneurship

LEARNING OBJECTIVES

The student will

- compare and contrast the terms *assimilation* and *acculturation*,
- examine four strategies for leading multicultural teams,
- describe politically smart behaviors,
- draw an influence diagram of his or her professional network,
- list and describe six principles of influence,
- list, describe, and apply the six factors that enable successful collaboration,
- create examples of a leader's sunshine and shadow power,
- describe six concerns to investigate before agreeing to collaborate, and
- apply the eight variables that contribute to a successful social venture.

MULTICULTURAL LEADERSHIP

Multicultural leadership brings a commitment to advance people who reflect the vitality, values, and voices of our diversity to all levels of organizations and society (Bordas, 2007, p. 8). In the United States, you can find a diverse selection of ethnic foods in grocery stores, hear many genres of music on satellite radio, purchase a multitude of items from every corner of the world in your local shopping mall, and attend school with students from many nations, ethnicities, and religions. However, in spite of our cultural diversity, leadership in our government, businesses, and organizations is practiced from an ethnocentric orientation—a universal standard built on one cultural orientation.

REFLECTION: THE IMPACT OF EXCLUSION AND THE CALL TO BECOME INCLUSIVE

Have you ever felt excluded from the favored and popular group at work or school? Maybe you felt rejected because all you could afford to wear were off-brand jeans, the office technology updates were prioritized for upper-management (all males) and their technology "hand-me-downs" were redistributed to their support staff (all females), or you had to miss office happy hours because they were always scheduled on Fridays when you and your family were headed to the synagogue for Shabbat. Take a moment to remember times when you felt excluded. When was it? What were the circumstances?

Have you or someone close to you ever felt excluded because of your race, ethnicity, faith, gender, sexual orientation, disability, height, or weight? How did you respond? Did that experience shape your choices and how you behave today?

Exclusion experiences evolve in new and obstructive ways, negatively affecting how you interact with the world. The perceived patterns in which work is organized seem to contradict workplace responses to diversity initiatives, and the result is complacency about perceived progress in eliminating discrimination (Ryan, 2006). Exclusion is a problem if people are physically prevented from participating; if there are barriers, physical or emotional, to an activity; or if they risk negative consequences by their participation. Multicultural leadership's mission is to be inclusive, value multiple perspectives, as well as engage and empower people.

As a future leader of a human services organization, becoming an inclusive, multicultural leader is part of the calling to commit to a profession of social justice and civic responsibility. Bordas (2007) used the Latino concept *destino* and the Native American tradition of *vision quest* to invite those who have accepted the calling to lead on a journey of learning, listening, and reflecting. Destino requires thinking about your life, family, significant events, talents, and attributes to develop a deeper understanding of the possibilities for your future. Vision quest reveals the meaning and purpose of one's life. This view is quite different from the American one of self-determination. Bordas (pp. 183, 185) calls the quest a "dance between individual efforts and the lessons, gifts, and experiences life brings … being in sync with the pulse of the times." You have already done much of the same type of reflective work for vision quest in previous chapters throughout this text. The focus of destino is on the journey of life rather than on the destination. The question changes from "What will I be when I graduate?" to "What challenges will I face and how will I continue to grow as I take each step on this exciting journey?" Destino is more than your life's journey; it is also the commitment you make to the journey to act with determination and heart for purposes greater than yourself.

DIAGNOSIS: ASSIMILATION AND ACCULTURATION

To become a multicultural leader, there are two words, assimilation and acculturation, which require understanding and analysis of their impact on current social outcomes. To assimilate means to remove the cultural, national, and ethnic differences of one's previous habits of daily life in order to become part of a new culture. The American melting pot created cultural uniformity by requiring immigrants to blend into their new surroundings with as few distinguishing characteristics as possible. Assimilation fed ethnocentricity, which bred cultural insensitivity and a predisposition to impose our values on others (Bordas, 2007, p. 186). Acculturation, on the other hand, embraces cultures of the previous time and the new location, while supporting a flexible adaptation that allows immigrants to "cross-over" by retaining their cultural pride and heritage. Having the anchor of familiarity along with valued previous experiences creates a type of confidence that enables someone to find a home in a new and unfamiliar life. The range of behaviors between assimilation and acculturation is a continuum. Understanding the difference in behaviors along the continuum allows people to be more intentional when learning and expanding their multicultural capacity. The assessment in Table 12.1 will give you a snapshot of your multicultural capacity on the continuum of assimilation and acculturation. Do a quick analysis of where you are now in your learning and experience by rating yourself on this scale: What did you learn from this exercise? Did you discover you have certain assimilation or acculturation expectations? Did this exercise help you generate ideas as to how you could increase your acculturation experience?

Assimilation and acculturation are not just behaviors for building multicultural leadership in regard to nationality, race, and ethnicity; this continuum of behaviors relates directly to the issue of gender and leadership. Over the last century, women have worked to assimilate into the workforce by seeking advanced education, taking assertiveness seminars, and dressing for success. Yet the result was limited opportunities, disapproval of "unlady-like" behaviors, and a clustering of employment in "pink ghetto" jobs, including many career fields in human services. Disproportionately, women comprise a larger part of the human services field's population, yet the top leaders are more often than not men. One study published

Table 12.1 Assimilation and Acculturation

Associations center on white culture					Many diverse cultural associations					
	Assimilation					Acculturation				
−5	−4	−3	−2	−1	0	1	2	3	4	5
Minimal experiences with other cultures					Seeks out diverse cultural experiences					
	Assimilation					Acculturation				
−5	−4	−3	−2	−1	0	1	2	3	4	5
Desire to fit in, conform					Has learning how to "fit it"					
	Assimilation					Acculturation				
−5	−4	−3	−2	−1	0	1	2	3	4	5
Belief that the white way is superior					Cultural flexibility—many ways					
	Assimilation					Acculturation				
−5	−4	−3	−2	−1	0	1	2	3	4	5
English only					Supports language and other cultural exposure					
	Assimilation					Acculturation				
−5	−4	−3	−2	−1	0	1	2	3	4	5

Source: Bordas, J. (2007). *Salsa, soul, and spirit, leadership for a multicultural age: New approaches to leadership from latino, black, and American Indian communities.* San Francisco, CA: Berrett-Koehler Publishers.

in *Social Work Today* (NASW Center for Workforce Studies, 2007) found that a disproportionate number of men served as managers in the social service arena, and in addition, women were promoted at a slower rate than men. Salary differences in the social work profession were also inequitable based on gender, with men on average earning 14% more than women (Whitaker et al., 2006). Women social workers made up 89% of the lower wage earners and 57% of higher wage earners. Men social workers made up 11% of lower wage earners, but 43% of higher wage earners were men. Sheryl Sandberg (2013), chief operating officer of Facebook and author of *Lean In*, stated, "Although thirty years ago women began earning fifty percent of college degrees in America, they are still holding only fourteen percent of C-suite jobs in corporate America and seventeen percent of board seats." Stephen Rush (2004) summarized the research of Stella Nkomo and Ella Edmonson Bell regarding black and white professional women. Women did not acculturate; instead, it was an environment of survival and perseverance. Black families warned their women of sex discrimination while white families did not. Women need someone who is willing to mentor and champion them, but many male executives are reluctant to mentor women.

A global research study, Empowering the Third Billion: Women and the World of Work in 2012 (Booz & Co., 2013), published The Equality Matrix, which measures the economic success for women (degree of inclusion and equality of pay) and measures the support for women (policies guaranteeing access to education, credit, and employment). Angel Gurria, secretary-general of the Organisation for Economic Co-operation and Development said, "Women are the most underutilized economic asset in the world's economy." Researchers of the study estimate 1 billion women could enter the global economy in the next decade. The study revealed additional critical facts:

- If women in the United States, Japan, and Egypt were employed at the same rates as men, the GDP's of those countries would be higher by 5 percent, 9 percent, and 34 percent, respectively.
- Tanzania has an estimated 1 million female entrepreneurs; but because tribal laws dictate that only sons inherit land, women lack the most common collateral for securing loans.
- In India, 5.5 million women enter the workforce each year, however, more than 50 percent of women report safety (robbery, assault, rape) as concerns related to commuting.
- In Saudi Arabia, women constitute 57 percent of university graduates but comprise only 12 percent of women participating in the workforce.
- Despite anti-discrimination laws, only 43 percent of women who try to rejoin the workforce after childbirth find jobs in Japan.
- Italian women spend five hours a day on housework while men spend less than 90 minutes. Italy has the second-lowest female labor participation rate in Europe.
- The United States is the only country in the Organisation for Economic Cooperation and Development that does not provide income support during parental leave.
- Half the world's self-made female billionaires are in China.
- In Argentina, women make up 24 percent of the national parliament, the highest proportion in the world.
- South Africa mandates a minimum of four months maternity leave for women who have worked at a company for at least two years.
- 73 percent of German companies offer flextime.

Source: Reprinted by permission of *Harvard Business Review*. Booz & Co. (2013). Women and the economics of equality. *Harvard Business Review*, *91*(4), 30-31. Copyright © 2013 by the Harvard Business School Publishing Corporation; all rights reserved.

Table 12.2 contains a similar set of questions as those in Table 12.1, but here the focus is on gender.

Table 12.2   Assimilation and Acculturation: Focus on Gender

Associations center on male hierarchical structure					More flat-structure governance associations					
Assimilation					Acculturation					
−5	−4	−3	−2	−1	0	1	2	3	4	5
Fewer professional experiences with other gender					Seeks out diverse professional experiences					
Assimilation					Acculturation					
−5	−4	−3	−2	−1	0	1	2	3	4	5
Desire to fit in, conform					Gives coaching on how to "fit it"					
Assimilation					Acculturation					
−5	−4	−3	−2	−1	0	1	2	3	4	5
Belief that the male perspective is superior					Cultural flexibility—many ways					
Assimilation					Acculturation					
−5	−4	−3	−2	−1	0	1	2	3	4	5
"If it ain't broke, don't fix it."					Supports expanding decision-making bodies to include outside perspectives.					
Assimilation					Acculturation					
−5	−4	−3	−2	−1	0	1	2	3	4	5

Source: Author created.

Again, what did you learn about your assimilation and acculturation experience? Did you identify ideas about actions you can take to increase your ability to acculturate? Which ones?

PRESCRIPTION: LEADING A MULTICULTURAL TEAM

Acculturation increases your cultural repertoire, creativity, and promises cross-cultural competency, helping you thrive in different cultural environments (Bordas, 2007, p. 188). The first step is to dismantle the dominance of the white middle-class perspective—hierarchical pluralism. The dominant culture's message is to "fit in," "read the instructions," and "walk, talk, and act like the rest of us." The cultures of most social institutions are built around white middle-class norms. In the same way, the leadership culture is built around white upper-class norms as well. In each case, this elusive set of rules and expectations is difficult to grasp for those whose families and neighborhoods are outside of the dominant culture. This is referred to as tacit knowledge, the lessons that come from our informal learning experiences as well as from the stories of families and friends (White, 1998). Hierarchical pluralism creates in-groups and out-groups (Chapter 2) with out-groups frequently made up of employees who have become isolated and estranged in the workplace. The alternative is egalitarian pluralism, which is a workplace culture of openness, welcoming to diverse leaders in both style and inclusion to the decision-making table.

As a leader of a multicultural team, one main challenge is to recognize cultural causes of conflict, to intervene in ways that get the team back on track, and to empower group members to deal with future cultural challenges (Brett et al., 2011). Multicultural teams bring richness to the organization because of their potential to innovate, knowledge of diverse communities and related markets, as well as an attention to culturally sensitive client services. Cultural challenges in teams are manageable if managers and team members focus on the right strategy and avoid imposing a hierarchical pluralistic style. Unfortunately, too many leaders assume the problem stems from issues with communication. According to Brett et al. (2011), that is only one of the four possible causes of friction at work:

1. Direct versus indirect communication – Direct and explicit is the communication style in Western cultures. A listener is not forced to interpret meaning; the intent is front and center. Many non-Western cultures use indirect communication where the meaning is hidden in the style of the message. It may even be framed in the style of a question instead of a direct statement. This style places the burden of interpretation on the listener. Non-Westerners therefore have to shift communication styles to accommodate non-Western team members. Awareness of communication styles is necessary to human services professions, especially when advice or communications involves families or other non-Western professionals. Sensitivity to styles of direct and indirect communication is important in helping professions.

2. Middle-class formal English, accents and fluency – Perceptions of status, education, and competence are filtered through spoken and written language. Much international business communication is done in English. Dominant culture team members become frustrated with nonnative speakers' accents and lack of dominant culture fluency. The nonnative speakers become reluctant to contribute due to the language difficulty, resulting in a lack of respect and assumptions of incompetence toward nonnative speakers. "The American

and I were at the same level, but he always led the team meetings. I had good questions, but it became apparent I was not perceived as one who could add value to the team," shared a member of an international human services organization (Brett et al., 2011, p. 111).

3. Evolving attitudes toward hierarchy and authority – One of the positive changes in organizational leadership structures in Western cultures is the reduction of workplace hierarchy structures. Organizations are getting flatter both for economic and inclusive reasons. However, many non-Western cultures have not made this shift. The historical male design of the workplace cultures also places high value on status and hierarchy. In many professions such as teaching and nursing, higher salaries and job titles only come with administrative duties. To be an outstanding caregiver or teacher is not rewarded in the current system. The value placed on title and rank impacts communication styles (direct and indirect) as well as with whom it is appropriate to communicate (status and level). It can signify a message of great disrespect and cause a major rift between team members and organizations if this respect is not honored.

4. Conflicting norms for decision making – Speed and level of detail for research and analysis are different by culture and impact the nature of decision making. Americans are notorious for wanting to move quickly with relatively little analysis. Negotiating how decisions will be made is imperative to successful partnering with non-American organizations.

Brett et al. (2011, pp. 116–122) recommend four strategies for leading multicultural teams through these cultural challenges. But first, assessing the situation and conditions must inform the choice that will be made. Does the project timeline allow for flexibility? Are there additional resources available? Is the team a permanent or temporary work group? Does the team leader have the authority to make changes?

1. Adaptation works (acculturation) when team members are willing to acknowledge and name their cultural differences and to assume responsibility for figuring out how to coexist with them.

2. Structural intervention is a deliberate reorganization to remove a source of conflict. This might involve breaking the larger team into several smaller ones or hiring a temporary team leader to enable members to better communicate if there is perceived conflict with the existing leader. This solution is usually temporary. It enables the team to develop and become internally strong.

In each case there is a process to reassemble the team with the original leader or reengage the subgroups into the larger team.

3. Managerial intervention works through an arbitration process with the team. It is useful for sorting out problems when efforts for the team to self-correct have reached a stalemate. This intervention can be useful in the early stages of the multicultural team development for setting norms and expectations. Establishing norms and expectations is a good practice for all teams because it prevents many problems that can arise later and derail the team from achieving their established goals.

4. Exiting a team is a strategy of last resort. It is used more often in permanent than temporary teams. In these cases, a team member may request to leave or the leader may ask the person to leave. In either case, it is usually because the situation is at a stalemate, the individual has lost the trust of the others, or he or she feels disrespected.

SUMMARY

Leadership in a multicultural world, where many cultures intersect and interact, creates questions and adaptations that have resulted in a slow reduction of Euro-American dominance that has shaped the previous five centuries (Bordas, 2007, p. 199). Bordas counsels leaders to look backward and forward like the West African bird Sankofa. It looks backward reminding us to learn from the past as its feet face forward inspiring us to take deliberate action for a more inspiring future. Multicultural leadership reflects humanistic values that promote justice, equality, and integrates spiritual responsibility with social accountability (Bordas, 2007, p. 200).

"All that we do now must be done to a sacred manner and in celebration. We are the ones we have been waiting for."—The Hopi Elders, Oraibi, Arizona.

POLITICS AND INFLUENCE

Politics and influence work hand in hand developing relationships between leaders and followers. Influence is the power and ability to personally affect others' actions, decisions, opinions, or thinking (Scharlatt & Smith, 2011, p. 7). Politics can be seen as a negative "game" built on bullying, favoritism, self-interest, and sabotage (Gentry & Leslie, 2012). Politics exists in all organizations and is essentially the art of coalition building in order to positively influence personal and organizational objectives.

REFLECTION: INFLUENTIAL LEADERS IN OUR LIVES

As you consider your desire to have influence and to be included in a network of respected leaders, consider who has had a positive influence in your life? Who is a leadership role model in your life? Kouzes and Posner (2012, pp. 330–331, 373), international leadership experts and authors, have asked that question to thousands of adults in the United States for over ten years. Make a list of three leaders who have had the most positive influence in your daily life. After each name, list three words that best describes what this person contributed to your life. After you have completed this exercise, we will compare your answers with the research of Kouzes and Posner.

1. _____

   3 words: _____   _____   _____

2. _____

   3 words: _____   _____   _____

3. _____

   3 words: _____   _____   _____

Kouzes and Posner (2012) found that leaders of influence in our lives come from those around us. They were our family members, friends, colleagues, supervisors, coaches, and teachers. They were also people we have known for at least 3 years (90%). The most common duration was 10 years. Granting someone the opportunity to have influence in our lives depends on the trust in the relationship; we know that building trust takes time. When asked what these leaders brought to the respondents' lives, these four themes and commonly cited terms were used:

- Trust – honesty, integrity, respect
- Compassion – caring, friendship, happiness, love
- Stability – security, strength, support, peace
- Hope – direction, faith, guidance

Now ask yourself the following:

- How did your names and their contributions compare to the Kouzes and Posner study?

- How long have you known these individuals?
- What were the themes of their contributions to your life?

What you have discovered are the types of leadership characteristics important to you in working with others. These are the leaders from whom you will welcome efforts to influence. As a developing leader, what kind of characteristics do others perceive about you? Will your efforts to influence be welcomed?

Part of positive influence involves being politically smart. How politically savvy are you? Gentry and Leslie (2012) describe four types of politically smart behaviors. Consider these skills as you reflect on your behaviors and strategies in the workplace or academia.

1. Mingle strategically – You have developed a network of faculty and professionals in your field who have power and influence and are in a position to connect you with opportunities for growth and development. Then follow up by sending a "happy to meet you" note, invite them to coffee, or continue a conversation you may have begun. Use the business cards stuffed in your wallet or cluttered on your desk. Add them to your contacts list in your database being sure to note where and when you met the person and what they do. This is the critical next step, call or email and set up a time to meet, have coffee, and explain how you think they could help you. Continue to grow your network.

2. Read the situation – You have taken the time to understand your style, strengths, and weaknesses. You are able to listen and interpret how others are feeling. You are a student of motivation and the importance of meeting people's needs.

3. Determine the appropriate action before acting – You have found and use your "pause button" regularly to prevent acting in haste. You maintain a positive attitude and apologize when you make an error. You try to anticipate other responses to ideas and think carefully about what and how you approach a situation.

4. Leave them with a good impression – Be open, honest, and credible. Show that you are adaptable to the situation and the needs of the people. Demonstrate dependability, go the "extra mile," and prioritize the needs of your team, boss, and organization. Seek to understand other's viewpoints, work to negotiate so as not to create adversarial relationships, and do not panic at the possibility of conflict.

Understanding workplace politics through these four skill sets may seem less threatening now that you are able to analyze the positive outcomes that will result from their mastery. Determine where you can start to grow politically and in your overall influence.

DIAGNOSIS: MAPPING YOUR INFLUENCE

Influence tactics can produce three different outcomes: resistance, compliance, and commitment (Yukl, 2010). Resistance is the effort to block influence by using excuses or delay tactics, putting up roadblocks, or pretending to agree but not following through. Compliance is the response that returns only enough effort to complete a small task or to strictly complete the minimum requirements. Commitment, the highest level of response to influence, is demonstrated by tasks endorsed by sustained effort, focus, and creativity.

There is no one set of rules for influencing others. It is dependent on individual personalities, values, goals, as well as organizational roles. It does, however, begin with the relationships you build. Like a wave that rolls across the beach, your influence rolls across people who also touch others in their paths. Influence, like the water, ebbs and flows through your initiatives, crashing onto the shore and then rolling back to the sea. It may help to take a snapshot of your current professional network (Gentrie & Leslie, 2012). To do this, find an 8 1/2 x 11 sheet of paper. Start in the center by drawing a small oval and writing your name in it. Around this center oval, draw six to eight additional small ovals; then repeat with another layer of small ovals around this near the edge of the paper (see below). In the inner circle of ovals, list those individuals in your network with whom you have close connections. In the outer circle of ovals, list those who you would like to get to know because of their influence, reputation, or power.

Your Influence Map

Look for patterns in your connections and determine if an inner circle connection can help you get to know an outer circle connection.

Your network may include colleagues, faculty members, professionals from other organizations, your boss, authors and presenters from professional associations, as well as community leaders. Your goal is to increase your political coalition by increasing the number of influential leaders in your inner circle. Remember, this is positive influence as long as the purpose is to increase the success of the team and the organization. Gentry and Leslie (2012) offer additional suggestions for building political savvy. Notice the networks of those you consider to be politically savvy for positive purposes. Who is part of their network? Seek an influential mentor to help you build your network. Become an observer of body language. Reading nonverbal cues can help you determine group

Figure 12.1   Your Influence Map

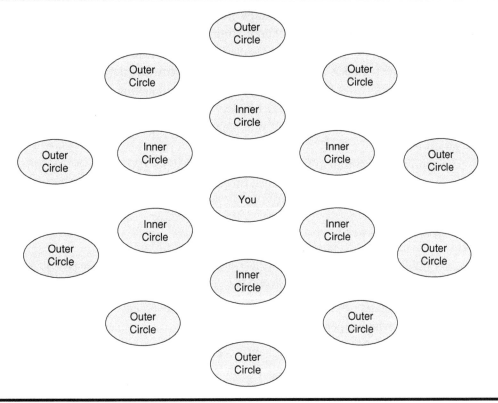

members' true feelings. Ask a coworker you trust to give you feedback regarding how group members perceive your actions. Does your tone match your facial expressions and body language? Learn to control impulses to share too much or to be one of the "gang," sharing gossip and others' poor attitudes. Know your hot buttons. Know how to handle conflict constructively. Always consider what the last impression you leave with a group will be because this is how they will remember you for the next assigned team project. Therefore, this is an important set of data to collect about yourself and your skills. If becoming politically savvy is your goal, this is the place to start.

PRESCRIPTION: INFLUENCE TACTICS

Leaders ask many things of their employees and organization members. They may request the completion a simple or complex task. It could also be to agree to support and carry out a change in direction for the organization. Each of these requests adds a higher level of complexity and commitment to the task. The first request is likely to receive minimal resistance, especially if the task is relevant to the group member's work and something they know how to do. The second and third request types will likely require more than a simple ask. Daniel Pink (2012) refers to it as "non-sales selling" in his book *To Sell Is Human: The Surprising Truth About Moving Others.* Pink's research revealed that across a variety of professions, 24 minutes of each work hour is spent persuading, influencing, and convincing others to support a request or idea. Leaders sell ideas and visions as opposed to products and services. What is it that captures our attention and motivates us to get on board?

Scharlatt and Smith (2011, p. 14) explain Yukl's (2010) work on influence tactics as effective ways to influence others. There are four core tactics and seven supplementary tactics that are used in conjunction with the four cores.

Four Core Tactics

1. Rational persuasion – Use logical arguments and factual evidence to show a request or proposal is feasible and relevant for attaining important task objectives.

2. Consultation – Ask the person to suggest improvements or help plan an activity for which a person's support is desired.

3. Inspirational appeals – Appeal to the person's values and ideals, or seek to arouse the person's emotions to gain commitment.

4. Collaboration – Offer to provide assistance or necessary resources for a project of common interest while inviting the person to work together.

Seven Supplementary Influence Tactics

1. Apprising – Explaining how the request will benefit a project.

2. Ingratiation – Use of praise and flattery in an attempt to influence the target person to support a request.

3. Exchange – Offer something the person wants or a reciprocal arrangement for another time in exchange for your request.

4. Personal appeals – Ask the person to carry out a request based on friendship.

5. Legitimating – Establish the legitimacy or verify the authority of a request.

6. Pressure – Use of demands, threats, or persistent reminders to fulfill a request.

7. Coalition – Enlist the support or endorsement of others to influence others to fulfill a request.

Consider the two major types of relationships in your life—work and personal. Which of the four major tactics are you more likely to use with family and friends? At work? Which of the seven supplementary tactics do you use? Although there are no absolute rules about which tactics to use with which individuals, the two most successful tactics are typically rational persuasion and consultation (Scharlatt & Smith, 2011).

Other important principles of influence involve the research of Robert B. Cialdini (2007). His book *Influence: The Psychology of Persuasion* explores six principles: consistency, reciprocation, social proof, authority, liking, and scarcity. Cialdini (2007) explained the complexity and rapidly moving nature of the 21st century and the need for shortcuts (rules of thumb to classify things) so people can respond more quickly in today's multistimulous environment, without lengthy analysis. In effect, our brain's need to create shortcuts causes humans to seek more efficient, automatic behaviors. His research explores the human response to another six psychological principles of influence and persuasion that guide us through the behavior shortcuts. As leaders you will see these principles at work in your organizations, teams, as well as yourself. [Note: Brief quotations detailing each of the six principles of influence from *Influence: The Psychology of Persuasion* by Robert Cialdini. Copyright © 1984, 1993 by Robert Cialdini. Reprinted by permission of Harper Collins Publishers.]

1. Consistency – People seek consistency in their environments as well as in their own decisions. People will choose to stay with first decisions "fooling themselves from time to time in order to keep thoughts and beliefs consistent with what is already done or decided" (Cialdini, 2007, p. 59). People are especially loyal to decisions if they are in writing and have been shared with others. If people have struggled to achieve this position or understanding, their loyalty to this position is very strong. In addition, if the person believes the choice was her own personal responsibility, the commitment to the position will be long-standing. "The drive to be and look consistent constitutes a highly potent weapon of social influence, often causing us to act in ways that are clearly contrary to our own best interests," says Cialdini (2007, p. 59).

2. Reciprocation – People from most global cultures feel an obligation to return a favor. It is a feeling of indebtedness and obligation to repay a kindness. Influence can also be extracted by offering a favor with the expectation of the reciprocal response. Cialdini (2007) reported, "The impressive aspect of the rule for reciprocation and the sense of obligation that goes with it is its pervasiveness in human culture. It is so widespread, that after intensive study, sociologists report that there is not a human society that does not subscribe to the rule" (p. 18).

3. Social Proof – Cialdini's (2007) principle of social proof states, "One means we use to determine what is correct is to find out what other people think is correct. The principle applies especially to the way we decide what constitutes correct behavior. We view a behavior as more correct in a given situation to the degree that we see others performing it" (p. 116). People are persuaded by the actions of others. They look to others, especially those like themselves, for direction when they are uncertain. Consider a recent invitation to a social event, did you ask your friends what they were wearing to the event?

4. Authority – "We are trained from birth that obedience to proper authority is right and disobedience is wrong," states Cialdini (2007, p. 216). Persons of authority are perceived to have superior information and power. People with such authority are pervasive in the systems and organizations of society: government, military, religious organizations, as well as the many profit-making organizations in communities today. Unfortunately, symbols of authority can elicit the same authority influence with the use of fake titles, uniforms, and other trappings.

5. Liking – According to Cialdini (2007), "We most prefer to say yes to the requests of someone we know and like" (p. 167). People are more open to influence if they believe you like them as well as to those they consider good looking. "In fact the response to those who represent the attractive members of the group is so strong, we automatically assign positive traits such as honesty, kindness, intelligent, and talented to good-looking individuals" (Cialdini, 2007, p. 171). Disharmony in groups can be reduced by collaborative efforts toward a common goal. Surrounding yourself with people who reflect success and glory causes your perceived superiority to rise. People associate bad news with the person delivering the news.

6. Scarcity – "The idea of potential loss plays a large role in human decision-making," reports Cialdini (2007). "In fact, people seem to be more motivated by the thought of losing something than by the thought of gaining something of equal value" (p. 238). People value opportunities more when they are limited. As the opportunities become less available, people lose the freedom to have something. If that lost opportunity was something they owned previously, people will react to regain what they have lost, possibly even resorting to violence. This is also true for access to information, which may become censored or banned, as it is in countries such as China or Russia. If there is an element of competition involved, people want the scarce item most of all.

You can see how each of these principles might exhibit themselves in an individual, team, or organizational situation. Team competitions, scarce organizational resources, instituting changes in policies or creating new programs, incorporating new members into a team, abuse of authority, consulting with peers when unclear about a new policy, and many other situations can be predicted by understanding these six principles.

What steps will you take to apply your new knowledge of influence and influence tactics? To become an effective leader in a world of influence and politics, it becomes important to develop a strategy for each situation. Because there are few universal rules in this skill set, the analysis of the situation is key. Scharlatt and Smith (2011) offer several suggestions to prepare for an influence session.

- Who are we attempting to influence and what position does that person or group occupy in relation to you? What are the power differences?
- What is the situation and why are you looking to gain influence? What do you hope the outcome will be?
- What benefits will come to you and the recipients of your influence?
- Is there influence directed toward you related to this situation? Who is it from and what is the outcome?
- What influence tactics do you see being used by others? What is the recipients' response?
- What tactics will you choose? Why? What response do you anticipate? What conversation points will you make? For what goals will you enlist support? What are the benefits you will communicate?
- When will be a good time to begin the process? What setting will enhance this dialogue?
- Create a counter argument and develop a response, should you need it.
- How will you close the dialogue? Prepare two positive closings, one for a positive and a negative response.

Most often politics is talked about with a reticence that makes you almost apologize for discussing the topic. The politics of the workplace concerns influence and your awareness about your ability to influence others. As a human services leader your influence must also reach out into the community. Developing strategies and measures for determining your network reach are important to the future success of human services organizations.

SUMMARY

Politics and influence are positive skill sets for leaders when used for positive purposes. In today's world of information overload combined with the need to work across organizations with individuals and groups who do not report to you or your organization, having skills in politics and influence are a necessity. Understand your own power base and political network. Observe how others utilize influence tactics. Practice, seek feedback, and practice again.

COLLABORATION

Collaboration is a mutually beneficial and well-defined relationship entered into by two or more organizations to achieve results they are more likely to achieve together than alone (Winer & Ray, 1994). The relationship includes a commitment to mutual relationships and goals, a jointly developed structure and shared responsibility, mutual authority and accountability for success, and shared resources and rewards.

REFLECTION: THE PROCESS OF REVEALING QUALITIES OF A COLLABORATION PARTNER

Consider the goal of finding a life partner. Some would refer to this person as a husband, wife, or soul mate. It is a process of getting to know and evaluating individuals who bring positive qualities into your life. You are seeking someone who has a history of positive regard, talents to share, can contribute to the economic viability of the relationship, is trustworthy, holds high standards and values, makes decisions for the good of others as well as self, is able to compromise, engages in goal achievement, is flexible, communicates well, shares a common passion for the future, willing to share in the leadership of the relationship, and has a passion for the love of the relationship. You work to identify these characteristics through meetings and dialogue as well as sharing enjoyable experiences. You include friends and family in some stages of the evaluation process. When a mutual regard for each party is established, a commitment is made and the process continues through additional stages of setting traditions, rituals, and short and long-term goals. Although this description of the stages of a relationship—friendship, dating, courtship, and marriage—might seem a bit sterile in the choice of words, my purpose is to compare it to the process of organizations coming together in a commitment for a long-term collaboration. The steps of the process and desirable qualities of the collaborative parties are similar.

DIAGNOSIS: SUCCESS FACTORS OF A COLLABORATION

The Fieldstone Alliance has engaged in over 8 years of research regarding the success factors of collaboration (Mattessich, Murray-Close, & Monsey, 2001). They identified 20 success factors, which are placed in six categories in Table 12.3.

Table 12.3   Factors Influencing the Success of Collaboration

Environment	Process and Structure
• A history of collaboration or cooperation in the community. • Collaborative group seen as a legitimate leader in the community. • Favorable political and social climate.	• Members share a stake in both process and outcome. • Multiple layers of participation. • Flexibility. • Development of clear goals and policy guidelines. • Adaptability. • Appropriate pace of development.
Membership Characteristics	**Communication**
• Mutual respect, understanding, and trust. • Appropriate cross section of members. • Members see collaboration as in their self-interest. • Ability to compromise.	• Open and frequent communication. • Established informal relationships and communication links.
Purpose	**Resources**
• Concrete attainable goals and objectives. • Shared vision. • Unique purpose.	• Sufficient funds, staff, materials, and time. • Skilled leadership.

Source: Adapted from Mattessich, P. W., Murray-Close, M., & Monsey, B. R. (2001). *Collaboration: What makes it work* (2nd ed.). Saint Paul, MN: Fieldstone Alliance.

The Fieldstone Alliance's Wilder Collaboration Factors Inventory is an excellent tool to evaluate your group's strengths and readiness for successful collaboration. As students, is it likely you are not part of an organization engaged in a collaboration? I have translated the intent of this inventory so it focuses on individual readiness and engages members or leaders of a collaborative. This will help you reflect and consider your readiness and strengths for participating or leading a collaborative project. Instructions for the inventory are as follows:

• Circle the word that indicates how much you agree or disagree with each item.
• Do not skip any questions.
• If you do not know or have an opinion, circle the neutral response.
• If you feel your response lies between two words, select the least strong description of the two.

Individual Collaboration Factors Inventory (Based on the Wilder Collaboration Factors Inventory)

1. I am aware of agencies in my community working together.

   Strongly Disagree   Disagree   Neutral   Agree   Strongly Agree

2. Trying to solve problems through collaboration has been common in my experience. It's been done many times in my family, faith organization, school, or work.

   Strongly Disagree   Disagree   Neutral   Agree   Strongly Agree

3. I see better results when true collaboration is achieved.

   Strongly Disagree   Disagree   Neutral   Agree   Strongly Agree

4. My colleagues or classmates would generally agree that my skills and demeanor would be desirable to work on a collaborative project.

   Strongly Disagree   Disagree   Neutral   Agree   Strongly Agree

5. I am able to evaluate the political and social climate in organizations.

   Strongly Disagree   Disagree   Neutral   Agree   Strongly Agree

6. I am considered by others to be a trustworthy person.

   Strongly Disagree   Disagree   Neutral   Agree   Strongly Agree

7. I think win-win and seek out opportunities for collaboration.

   Strongly Disagree   Disagree   Neutral   Agree   Strongly Agree

8. If I were to select people for a collaborative project, I would seek to select across a diverse representation of members, employees, and clients from all stakeholders of the project.

   Strongly Disagree   Disagree   Neutral   Agree   Strongly Agree

9. If I were to select people from several organizations for a collaborative project, I would know how to influence those organizations to nominate a cross section of members, employees, and clients (those who have a stake in the results) to serve on the project.

   Strongly Disagree   Disagree   Neutral   Agree   Strongly Agree

10. My perspective on collaboration will benefit my organization as I work with others.

    Strongly Disagree   Disagree   Neutral   Agree   Strongly Agree

11. I am comfortable with the effort it requires in reaching a win-win solution on important aspects of a project.

Strongly Disagree   Disagree   Neutral   Agree   Strongly Agree

12. I realize working in collaborative efforts is a longer process, and I am willing to invest the time.

Strongly Disagree   Disagree   Neutral   Agree   Strongly Agree

13. I always keep my focus on the results the organization seeks.

Strongly Disagree   Disagree   Neutral   Agree   Strongly Agree

14. I am always open and seek to value other's approaches to methods of working on assignments.

Strongly Disagree   Disagree   Neutral   Agree   Strongly Agree

15. When major decisions are made, I frequently seek input from others on a course of action.

Strongly Disagree   Disagree   Neutral   Agree   Strongly Agree

16. I believe collaborative groups must explore several options when making decisions.

Strongly Disagree   Disagree   Neutral   Agree   Strongly Agree

17. I have a clear process for making decisions in my life.

Strongly Disagree   Disagree   Neutral   Agree   Strongly Agree

18. In my employment or student status, I have a clear sense of my roles and responsibilities.

Strongly Disagree   Disagree   Neutral   Agree   Strongly Agree

19. I am able to adapt easily to changing conditions, such as reduction in resources, changes in policies, changing technology, or changes in relationships and family dynamics.

Strongly Disagree   Disagree   Neutral   Agree   Strongly Agree

20. I can handle making major changes in plans or overcoming new obstacles in order to reach my goals.

Strongly Disagree   Disagree   Neutral   Agree   Strongly Agree

21. I am careful to not overcommit my time, pace myself, and to take on the right amount of work to achieve my goals and maintain personal balance.

Strongly Disagree   Disagree   Neutral   Agree   Strongly Agree

22. Given my current leadership abilities, I am able to manage the work necessary to coordinate all the people, organizations, resources, and activities related to a collaborative project.

    Strongly Disagree   Disagree   Neutral   Agree   Strongly Agree

23. I am skilled in written, oral, and distance communication with others to maintain a transparent work environment.

    Strongly Disagree   Disagree   Neutral   Agree   Strongly Agree

24. I value information and seek to stay informed at the international, national, state, and local levels as often as I should.

    Strongly Disagree   Disagree   Neutral   Agree   Strongly Agree

25. I keep current with electronic communication (email, snail mail, current events, social media).

    Strongly Disagree   Disagree   Neutral   Agree   Strongly Agree

26. I have informal conversations through my network of friends and colleagues about important issues at work, school, home, my community, and my country.

    Strongly Disagree   Disagree   Neutral   Agree   Strongly Agree

27. I have established clear, attainable goals for myself each year as well as long-term goals for my future.

    Strongly Disagree   Disagree   Neutral   Agree   Strongly Agree

28. I am passionate about achieving my goals.

    Strongly Disagree   Disagree   Neutral   Agree   Strongly Agree

29. I have shared my goals with others.

    Strongly Disagree   Disagree   Neutral   Agree   Strongly Agree

30. I realize I have unique talents and gifts and that my mission in life is important and unique.

    Strongly Disagree   Disagree   Neutral   Agree   Strongly Agree

31. I have adequate resources to accomplish my mission and goals.

    Strongly Disagree   Disagree   Neutral   Agree   Strongly Agree

32. I have developed a strong network of "people power" to support and cheer me on to victory.

    Strongly Disagree   Disagree   Neutral   Agree   Strongly Agree

33. As a leader, I have confidence in with other people and organizations.

Strongly Disagree   Disagree   Neutral   Agree   Strongly Agree

If you were to take the Wilder Collaboration Factors Inventory (available online at http://www.fieldstonealliance.org under free resources, then assessment tools), the program would generate a summary score for each factor of success for collaboration among organizations. These questions assess your readiness to be an active participant in a collaboration. I suggest you review your answers with a classmate, mentor, colleague, or faculty member, especially those responses you scored as a neutral, disagree, or strongly disagree. Consider your plan for your leadership development journey, and seek to focus some attention on these areas. As you reflect on what you have learned so far in the context of leading a collaboration, you will recognize the skills, knowledge, and abilities to be developed.

PRESCRIPTION: FROM ALLIANCE TO COLLABORATION

Hoskins and Angelica (2005) describe four levels of how organizations work with others and capture the word alliance to refer to this working relationship, "An alliance is a relationship between partners that is strategically formed to accomplish goals that benefit the community while strengthening the partners."

As an alliance becomes more complex and intense the working relationships grow from cooperation to coordination to collaboration to a merger. Cooperation is a very short-term, informal relationship while coordination is a longer-term connection requiring an understanding of missions. Collaboration is a longer, stronger relationship where separate organizations come together to create a common mission. A merger is a lifetime commitment to join two organizations as one.

Sharon Kagan (1991) created a specific scale based on intensity for determining if organizations were truly collaborating or merely cooperating. The more intensity invested in the relationship, the higher the level of involvement and commitment, and the more likely the relationship is collaborative. In the example detailed in Table 12.4, please reference A+ Tutors (from Chapter 10) to demonstrate the details of intensity.

When leading a collaborative effort, the previous instincts of charging forward on a new idea or making a decision to revise a policy take on a new way of thinking and acting. You are no longer working for the goals of just your department or organization; you are working for a more complex and dynamic group. Although

Table 12.4   Relationships and Intensity

Descriptor	A+ Tutors
Cooperation: Shorter-term, informal relationships that exist without any clearly defined mission, structure, or planning effort. Information is shared about the subject at hand. Each organization retains authority and keeps resources separate so virtually no risk exists.	A+ Tutors cooperates with the local schools by exchanging information about its mutual clients' grades, attendance, and test scores (with client permission).
Coordination: More formal relationships with focus on a longer-term interaction around a specific program. Requires some planning, communication channels, and division of roles. Authority still stays with individual organizations; everyone's risk increases. Resources are made available to participants and rewards are shared. Power can be an issue.	In addition to above, A+ Tutors coordinates with the local schools by using curricula selected by the schools. Management of A+ Tutors hosts semi-annual meetings with curriculum planners in each school district. Schools invite A+ Tutors to share tutoring techniques at the annual teacher training conference.
Collaboration: A long-term and pervasive relationship exists with full commitment to a common mission. There are well-defined communication channels operating on all levels. There is a mutual determination of authority and risk is even greater due to the contributed resources and reputation. Partners share results and rewards. Power is likely unequal and can be an issue.	In addition to above, A+ Tutors is located in a portable classroom at each elementary school. Teachers collaborate with A+ Tutor management to train tutors and select materials. Tutors actively consult with teachers on mutual client progress. Measures of success are included in reports for schools' annual academic measures.

Source: Adapted from Kagan, S. L. (1991). *United we stand: Collaboration for child care and early education services.* New York, NY: Teachers College Press.

collaboration is considered to be a high level of operating and achieving results, it may not always be a marriage made in heaven. The following concerns should be reviewed before an organizational commitment is made (Winer & Ray, 1994).

- Ideology – Values and beliefs may not align well or allow the flexibility needed for collaboration.
- Leadership – Group collaborations often fail because the leader may not have the power to bring all parties together or cannot run an effective meeting with the added complexities.
- Power – Power is rarely equal among members of a collaborative effort. However, the group must achieve a melding of powers and balance the inequities. Equity is the goal, not equality.

- History – If there is historical "baggage" between organizations of the collaboration or individual members, preparation, dialogue, and new understanding must be achieved for the collaboration to be successful.
- Competition – Is there really a joint effort or a "marriage of convenience" because the funder will only consider collaboration? If funding is the only reason to be together, there is no collaboration.
- Resources – Collaborations require resources contributed by all members. Employees who are assigned to participate must be given time to engage in the work of the collaboration. Other difficulties include leadership time commitments, information technology is not adequate, or skills of the organization are not at the level required. Organizations must assess the needs of the partnership before commitment.

Potential threats to a collaboration are possible at several stages of the process. In fact, one of the major threats is to ignore the key stages of the process of forming the collaboration, and proceed as if it is similar to a typical project plan. In the human services sector, the need to collaborate among organizations is high. Community problems are numerous and complex while resources are scarce. If solutions are to be sustainable, all stakeholders must be involved. Stephen R. Covey (2011) identified a successful collaborative process called synergy: seeking a third alternative. A third alternative is not my idea or your idea. It is a new idea that resolves everyone's concerns. The steps to achieve such an idea are foundational to a successful collaboration.

- Invite the stakeholders to the table
- Identify a clear "end in mind," describe and agree on the results the collaborative has in mind.
- Listen to the needs and voices of each represented group, and affirm the value of the talents and ideas represented there.
- Encourage each stakeholder to restate the needs and ideas of the other stakeholders there.
- Explore many ideas for resolving the needs and concerns at hand.
- Determine a solution (third alternative) to which all will commit and enroll in its success.

Other success factors include involving leaders who can see and think beyond their own needs as well as collaborating with organizations that are financially healthy and not seeking this opportunity to fix an organizational problem.

Getting started is very important. It is possible that the initiator of the collaboration is not the best choice of convener for the meetings. Initiators had the energy, persuasion, and passion to invite and bring people to the table. Now a convener is needed to help the group find its center. What will be its purpose, mission, and vision? How will the group bring this to life? And how will this happen so all can say with pride, "We made a significant contribution to this success!"

In addition to the previous discussion of power of the groups in the partnership, there are additional descriptions of power as it relates to individuals that can be helpful for the convener. Individuals can wield power in a helpful or harmful manner. Winer and Ray (1994, p. 34) describe helpful power as "sunshine power" and power that is destructive as "shadow power."

Sunshine Power – visible influence

- Charisma, enthusiasm, confidence
- Making connections to others with power
- Applying knowledge, skills, experience
- Demonstrating consistency
- Contributing so others can learn
- Having clear boundaries, ability to go through channels
- Choosing to reward others

Shadow Power – hidden influence

- Seize power by making people afraid
- Having clear boundaries, knowing how to go through channels
- Withholding knowledge, skills, experience
- Acting inconsistently, creating confusion
- Making excuses for not contributing
- Bullying others
- Remaining isolated, demanding
- Withholding needed resources

Power is an important commodity for members of an alliance. Like any skill, it can be used well or used to abuse. It is helpful to see both sides of each type of power described as you might see it when convening a group on the path to collaboration.

The stages of a group of organizations building a collaboration follows the same Tuckman (1965) stages of group development all teams and groups face when learning to work together. You can refer to Chapter 6 about teams to refresh your understanding of those details. Here is a summary of those stages:

1. Forming – The group establishes individual roles within the new collaboration. They seek to establish trust, affirm their vision, and define the desired results of the project. The project work assignments begin as individuals.

2. Storming – In this stage they are unsure of the authority vested in them by their organizations, and are unsure of their roles in the collaboration.

The group tests their authority, argues about purpose, and becomes bogged down. They are caught in conflict trying to get organized.

3. Norming – Over a period of several months, members found ways for the collaboration to interact. They built joint systems and policies, managing the work, evaluating results, and renewing efforts. The work shifts from individual to organization.

4. Performing – After many months the projects of the partnership are humming along, it has grown to involve more organizations, and the baton has been passed to a new leader. There is increased community recognition and resources. The collaboration has community recognition, involvement, and established change. The work encompasses the community.

Collaboration is like creating a piece of art. It may not be as we first thought, but it is better because we allowed ourselves to be influenced by the voices of others. It creates a unique alternative no one in the collaborative came to the table ready to propose. Covey (2011) called this a "third alternative." Reaching a third alternative requires the establishment of trust among all the members. Trust builds through the investment of time as well as the ability to set agendas aside and listen. Commitment to the process is vital to successfully finding an alternative all believe in. Once each member knows the collaborative understands each person's story and values the person and organization represented, new ideas will flow like water from a faucet. No one will hold back, shared ownership will emerge, and transformation will define the outcomes of the initiative. This process of coming together is most helpful when the group must become a high functioning team, when there has been a history of distrust, when emotions are high, and when a significant change must be created, planned, executed, and sustained.

In addition to the synergy of a collaboration, there are other structured, formal leadership options to consider when choosing how to work together with other organizations. Decisions must be made considering how long the partnership will be joined, how important teamwork is to the goals of the initiative, and how closely the partners will work together. Utilizing the concept of the three types of an alliance (Hoskins & Angelica, 2005), note the arrangements for administration, communication, and service delivery for each type:

Cooperation

- Board and staff development of all organizations in alliance
- Data sharing of program assessments
- Shared program expenses
- Shared customer information
- Shared program level leadership, informal structure, low level authority

Coordination

- Shared central staff, offices, and equipment with supported organizations nearby (mall approach)
- Joint intake and information system
- Program cosponsorships
- Joint advocacy
- Shared mid-level leadership, informal structure, moderate level authority, one organization is seen as the coordinator

Collaboration

- On-site, joint administrative staff
- Shared sponsor, funding requests, and funds received
- Seamless, innovative service delivery
- Shared top level leadership, formal structures, high level authority

The needs and purpose of the alliance, and the level of trust among organizations will determine the type of alliance chosen. Spelling out the expectations and operations of the alliance should be put in writing. Verbal agreements hold no weight in matters of disagreements of resources, staffing and needed client services. Most often alliances utilize a memorandum of understanding signed by all parties. It can be written so that there are specific paragraphs for each of the partner's responsibilities and common paragraphs appropriate to all. Typical topics include the following:

- Mission
- Goals
- Strategic plans
- Resources
- Staffing
- Partners
- Stakeholders
- Timeframe
- Structure
- Authority, decision making
- Communication
- Conflict of interest
- Public relations
- Legal and contract requirements (grants, rental of space, etc.)

This leads to the final point about collaborations. Unlike marriages, collaborations are supposed to end. Different community needs emerge, organizations grow, relationships evolve, and people change. The new program may become institutionalized to its own organization with legal standing, its own staff and a board of directors, or become part of a different existing agency. It is important to end the original partnership with a ritual that includes appreciation for everyone's efforts, celebration for shared accomplishments, and recollections of the journey.

SUMMARY

Leading an alliance of organizations is a culminating experience for many. It brings a special set of challenges, and likewise, a special feeling of accomplishment. The successful alliance requires leadership skills and abilities applied to a complex set of relationships among organizations. Will it become a cooperative effort, a coordination of programs and services, or a high level collaboration with shared leadership, resources, and a synergy that transforms communities. Leadership must match the needs of the purpose for the alliance and the trust level of the participating partners with the appropriate structure in order to deliver expected outcomes.

SOCIAL ENTREPRENEURSHIP

Whether a human services professional, a board member of a human services organization, or a corporate partner who is committed to the needs of the people of the community, it is frequent that such individuals experience new ideas for programs or services through the spark of that classic "Ah ha" moment: Wouldn't it be great if …? Social entrepreneurs answer the call to "what if" and create new programs, services, products, organizations, and collaborations. Who are these individuals and what does it take to bring a new social idea to life? How can you answer your call to "what if?"

REFLECTION: THE TEAR IN YOUR EYE, LUMP IN YOUR THROAT...LOOK WHAT THEY DID!

Some were mentioned in the introduction to this book. Others you have read about in the history of the human services profession. A few have even received the Nobel Peace Prize. You see them highlighted on news programs (NBC Evening News: Making a Difference) and various talk shows. George H. W. Bush, 41st president of the United States, started a national program in 1989 to recognize those who volunteer and start new programs with a Point of Light Award. This national recognition for community service and leadership recognizes many unsung heroes and heroines across the country. Adults of all ages, teens, and children in this country and around the world have all contributed to the improvement of the human condition. It is not impossible to become a social entrepreneur. It does require leadership skills and some additional knowledge and skills.

What ideas have you considered regarding new programs or services. Is there a new nonprofit idea you have been pondering? Social entrepreneurism is a relatively new area of study. Most of the literature is about twenty years old. Entrepreneurism is not much older as a course of study. And some of the literature of the former helps inform the latter. Even the definition of a social entrepreneur is not tidy and concise. Peredo and McLean (2006, p. 63) conducted a review of the literature and compiled these characteristics of a social entrepreneur:

- Exercised whether as an individual or a group
- Aims to create social value
- Has capacity to recognize opportunity to create the social value
- Employs innovation in the creation or distribution of the social value
- Willing to accept above-average risk in the creation process
- Is resourceful and undaunted by scarce resources in the beginning of the process

The most important characteristic is the purpose to create social value. It is also important to note that the process is not the purview of just an individual, but groups and organizations can assume the title of social entrepreneur.

DIAGNOSIS: INDIVIDUAL OR GROUP: WHAT ARE THE SKILLS AND NEEDED TALENTS?

Gallup research is working on the identification of entrepreneurial characteristics and key talents. Clifton and Badal (2014) determined the importance of entrepreneurism to the future of the world's economic growth and identified specific strengths of successful entrepreneurs. Building on the years of research in the area of individual strengths, Gallup has developed an assessment to determine the level of each of the 10 essential talents of entrepreneurs. Reading Gallup's full report, the researchers have certainly not surveyed the full range of human characteristics and talents, but they have a beginning look at important talents of entrepreneurs. This work translates well to the world of social entrepreneurism. The top 10 talents are detailed in Table 12.5.

Determining the talents you possess in relation to the tasks of a start-up organization demands honesty and even an outside perspective. Consult with a mentor or work colleague for an unbiased perspective. It's not a test you have to pass but rather an incentive to bring partners into the process. Multiple talents are exponentially better than limited talents.

Table 12.5   The Top 10 Essential Talents of Entrepreneurs

Top 10 Talent	Description of Talent	Connection to Social Entrepreneur (SE)
Confidence	Know Yourself Influence Others Action-Oriented	Due to limited resources in a SE project, confidence and influence are a must.
Creative Thinker	See Beyond Boundaries Mind Fires With New Ideas Curious and Quick Learner	It is the creativity that brings an SE to the "what if " idea.
Delegator	Proactively Collaborate Recognize Other's Talents Promote Team Members	Many SE projects involve collaborative groups. Promoting the team and their talents is necessary to succeed with groups.
Determination	Tremendous Work Ethic Overcome Obstacles Undeterred by Failures	SEs are driven, both by the passion for the project, but also for the need to find necessary start-up resources.
Independent	Strong Sense of Responsibility Handle Multiple Tasks High Level of Competence	SEs have a keen sense of responsibility to humanity. They are used to leading teams and are skilled in multiple tasks.
Knowledge Seeker	Use Knowledge as a Competitive Advantage Anticipate Knowledge Needs	SEs are quick learners and use this to their flexible advantage.
Promoter	Make Your Case Effectively Communicate Your Vision Clear Growth Strategy	SEs can tell their story with passion. They can make the listener become the hero by joining the cause.
Relationship Builder	Open Demeanor High Social Awareness Relationships Go Beyond Work	SEs have large networks of good friends. They support each other and have for years.
Risk Taker	Highly Optimistic Make Complex Decisions Easily	SEs are bold regarding risk, but do mitigate some risk through the likely collaboration.
Business Focus	Clear Goals Invest in Planning Judge Value by Impact	SEs have a dual focus: both business and social value. Innovative revenue is what fuels many SE projects.

Source: Adapted from Clifton, J., & Badal, S. B. (2014). *Entrepreneurial strengths finder*. New York, NY: Gallup Press. pp. 60–140.

PRESCRIPTION: A MODEL AND SUCCESS VARIABLES IMPACT SOCIAL ENTREPRENEURSHIP

Unlike a business entrepreneur who might obtain investors for an innovative product or service, a social entrepreneur does not usually have a product to sell. The programs and services are typically targeted to the at-risk population whose income is usually stretched already. Affording another expense is not likely, no matter how needed. Resource identification and development are the biggest challenges for the social entrepreneur. In their multidimensional model of social entrepreneurship, Weerawardena and Mort (2006, pp. 31–32) suggest that social entrepreneurship behavior is influenced by the concurrent requirements of the environment, the need to establish a sustainable organization, and the need to achieve social mission. These three constraints provide the turbulence as social entrepreneurs seek to manage risks, innovate to support the new social enterprise, and act proactively in the process of building the new program or organization. Visualize the three sides of a triangle (environment, sustainability, and social mission) framing the interaction of proactivity, risk management, and innovation.

What is it that social entrepreneurs do to create the most likely chance for the success of their "what if" idea. Sharir and Lerner (2006) studied 33 Israeli new social ventures (human services organizations) across 15 different variables with the potential to influence the agencies' success. Eight of the variables demonstrated a positive impact on the recently formed organizations. Successful organizations were defined as reaching their goals, attaining resources to sustain the organization, and supporting further growth. The eight variables (Sharir & Lerner, 2006, pp. 11–15) in order of influence are the following:

1. Social Network – The actions of the focal people in the social network within which the entrepreneur operates are likely to be decisive in determining if the effort is supported or blocked.

2. Total Dedication – They create opportunities and make them work. There is focus on the vision, not the difficulties.

3. Capital Base – Social venturing lacks a venture capital infrastructure for the initiation and establishment stages. Finding capital to pay salaries of a core group of employees is significant.

4. Acceptance of the Venture in the Public Discourse – If the prevailing cultural and societal norms accept the venture, it will likely succeed.

5. Previous Managerial Experience – Having supervisory, as well as financial management experience was a large boost to the success of the new ventures.

6. The Venture's Team – Building an actual team with friendly relationships and a variety of talents brought excellence to the organization and operational sustainability.

7. Standing the Market Test – This determines if the clientele will support the organization. The community must see the venture organization as the agency of choice.

8. Follow-Up Results – When the venture organization reaches the institutionalization stage, it is truly sustained both financially and culturally.

The study of and support for social entreprencurs and venture organizations is increasing rapidly. Universities such as George Mason, Stanford, and the University of Maryland are hosting centers to teach and provide experiences in social value creation. In Minnesota, the governor recently (2014) signed into law a new category of business called the Public Benefit Corporation It provides more flexibility in how profits are distributed allowing for more support to social value programs. Such communities and institutions are leading the way to provide support for community leaders to create new social/service sector organizations.

SUMMARY

Much of the work to create a new social venture is similar to a business venture. Key differences lie in the lack of venture capital infrastructure and the emphasis on the social value of the new program. This leads to the importance of finding sustainable financial resources and the passion for the social issue and needs being met.

Becoming a social entrepreneur is a dedicated journey of sustained hope and vision. As others are drawn to your cause, the journey becomes one of leadership and entrepreneurism. There are so many needs to be met in this country as well as globally. But you will not find a legacy purpose more fulfilling and exciting than this. You can do it! What if you don't?

REFERENCES

Bordas, J. (2007). *Salsa, soul, and spirit, leadership for a multicultural age: New approaches to leadership from latino, black, and American Indian communities.* San Francisco, CA: Berrett-Koehler Publishers.

Booz & Co. (2013). Women and the economics of equality. *Harvard Business Review, 91*(4), 30–31.

Brett, J., Behfar, K., & Kern, M. C. (2011). Managing multicultural teams. In *Harvard Business Review: Building better teams* (pp. 103–124). Boston, MA: Harvard Business Review Press.

Cialdini, R. B. (2007). *Influence: The psychology of persuasion.* New York, NY: Collins Business.

Clifton, J., & Badal, S. B. (2014). *Entrepreneurial strengths finder.* New York, NY: Gallup Press.

Covey, S. R. (2011). *The 3rd alternative: Solving life's most difficult problems.* New York, NY: Free Press.

Gentry, W. A., & Leslie, J. B. (2012). *Developing political savvy.* Greensboro, NC: Center for Creative Leadership.

Hoskins, L., & Angelica, E. (2005). *Forming alliances: Working together to achieve mutual goals.* St. Paul, MN: Fieldstone Alliance.

Kagan, S. L. (1991). *United we stand: Collaboration for child care and early education services.* New York, NY: Teachers College Press.

Kouzes, J., & Posner, B. (2012). *The leadership challenge: How to make extraordinary things happen in organizations* (5th ed.). San Francisco, CA: Jossey-Bass.

Mattessich, P. W., Murray-Close, M., & Monsey, B. R. (2001). *Collaboration: What makes it work* (2nd ed.). Saint Paul, MN: Fieldstone Alliance.

Minnesota Public Benefit Corporation: http://www.bizjournals.com/twincities/news/2015/01/06/minnesotas-first-public-benefit-corporations.html

NASW Center for Workplace Studies. (2007). *More money—less money: Factors associated with the highest and lowest social work salaries.* Retrieved from http://workforce.socialworkers.org/whatsnew/salaryreport.pdf

NBC News. (n.d.). Making a difference. Retrieved from http://www.nbcnews.com/feature/making-a-difference

Peredo, A. M., & McLean, M. (2006). Social entrepreneurship: A critical review of the concept. *Journal of World Business, 41*(1), 56–65.

Pink, D. (2012). *To sell is human: The surprising truth about moving others.* New York, NY: Riverhead Books.

Points of Light Award: http://www.pointsoflight.org/?gclid=CjwKEAiAxNilBRD8 8r2azcqB2zsSJABy2B960YiOamTmgMvFeccdAnxYGYS0NjQxdWdN giA0gV8BChoCOH7w_wcB

Ryan, J. (2006). *Inclusive leadership.* San Francisco, CA: Jossey-Bass.

Rush, S. (2004). Telling the untold story: A conversation with Stella M. Nkomo. In *The CCL guide to leadership in action: How managers and organizations can improve the practice of leadership* (pp. 205–233). San Francisco, CA: Jossey-Bass.

Sandberg, S. (2013). Interview: Now is our time. *Harvard Business Review, 91*(4), 84–88.

Scharlatt, H., & Smith, R. (2011). *Influence: Gaining commitment, getting results* (2nd ed.). Greensboro, NC: Center for Creative Leadership.

Sharir, M., & Lerner, M. (2006). Gauging the success of social ventures initiated by individual social entrepreneurs. *Journal of World Business, 41*(1), 6–20.

Tuckman, B. (1965). Developmental sequence in small groups. *Psychological Bulletin, 63*, 384–399.

Weerawardena, J., & Mort, G. S. (2006). Investigating social entrepreneurship: A multidimensional model. *World Business Journal, 41*(1), 21–35.

Whitaker, T., Weismiller, T., & Clark, E. (2006). *Assuring the sufficiency of a frontline workforce: A national study of licensed social workers. Executive Summary.* Washington DC: National Association of Social Workers.

Winer, M., & Ray, K. (1994). *Collaboration handbook: Creating, sustaining, and enjoying the journey.* Saint Paul, MN: Fieldstone Alliance.

White, Deborah H. (1998). *The impact of cocurricular experience on leadership development.* (Unpublished doctorate dissertation.) Department of Educational Leadership and Policy Analysis, East Tennessee State University, Johnson City, TN.

Yukl, G. (2010). *Leadership in organizations.* Upper Saddle River, NJ: Pearson Education.

Chapter 13

Prognosis—Your Future Leadership Growth

LEARNING OBJECTIVES

The student will

- describe how to use a plan-do-check-act process when changing a personal behavior,
- describe the strategies of success for a behavior change plan,
- explain the overuse of willpower in behavior change, and
- create a plan for a personal behavior change.

PROGNOSIS

It's appropriate to close this book with a chapter that reveals your prognosis as a future leader and gives you tried and true methods for the practice of new leadership behaviors. Other texts will ask you to learn many facts to either hold in memory as background information, to problem solve, or to apply in a lab setting. I ask you not only to learn new facts but also more importantly, to change, adopt, and practice new leadership behaviors. When you are engaged with real teams in real organizations on a day-to-day basis, it is the adoption of successful leadership actions and new thought processes that will determine your success as a leader. Leadership is not a one-time lesson. The best leaders spend most of their careers polishing their skills. Your success lies with your ability to change behaviors and to apply a plan-do-check-act process to achieve and monitor the changes you want and keep them polished.

REFLECTION: THE TYPICAL RESOLUTION FOR PERSONAL CHANGE

If you have ever watched friends attempt to alter a behavior in their life such as adopting a regular exercise schedule or choosing to get 8 hours sleep a night, you know this process usually tracks along the following cycle:

- New goal announcement.
- Week 1, effort of pride, excitement, and some success.
- Week 2, effort of similar success.
- Weeks 3 through 5 of progressively less effort, fewer attempts, and very little mention of the goal.
- Week 6, an admission to self of failure, and no more comments about the effort to others.

The time frame may vary some; however, this cycle is the most common experience for those who are not aware of our human tendencies and how to achieve a behavior change through effective management of these tendencies.

DIAGNOSIS: WILL YOU AND WILLPOWER BE ABLE TO SAVE THE DAY?

Unfortunately, it appears that those who profit most from less effective personal choices have become astute students of human behavior. To fill the knowledge gap of the profiteers in what they don't know, human behavior experts are hired to guide their strategy. Consider the following questions:

1. Do you blame yourself for the inability to sustain the will to change a behavior?

    ___yes   ___ no

2. Do you believe the "tough-it-out" hero is who really wins the day in personal change?

    ___yes   ___ no

3. Have you begun to analyze the many ways the marketplace, office politics, the media, your lack of commitment in the moment of choice, and even your friends influence the hundreds of choices you make every day?

    ___yes   ___ no

4. Have you considered that the influences mentioned in question 3 sometimes gang up on you and come at you in multiples?

___yes   ___ no

Picture an American-style football game with a quarterback (you) and a defensive line representing all the influences listed in question 3. Will you be able to make forward progress against the defense without an offensive line? Unlikely. The sad truth is we try to rely solely on a one-person offensive line—willpower. We need a team to counteract the bad-influence team working on the defensive line against us. We need real friends who are supporting our new choices, not fake friends who tempt us to return to our old ways. We need someone who encourages us when the day is long and struggles are many. We need a coach to get us back on track when we get lost on the goal's journey. We might need to learn some new skills to handle the new goal with success. We also need to make plans for those times when we are temped to lose control so we have an alternative already rehearsed. Now picture your team led by you and willpower. This time you will win the goal.

The prescription that follows will depict how to develop the offensive line that will enable your behavior change to cross the goal line. This is a process, a plan, and a set of actions with a track record of success.

PRESCRIPTION: MAKING THE PLAN TO GROW NEW LEADERSHIP SKILLS

We have studied change in organizations. Those same principles (Kotter, 1995) apply to personal change.

1. Establish a sense of urgency.

2. Form a powerful guiding coalition.

3. Create a vision.

4. Communicate the vision

5. Empower others/yourself to act on the vision.

6. Plan for and create short-term wins.

7. Consolidate improvements into your routine.

8. Institutionalize the change into your everyday life.

The method you will learn incorporates all of Kotter's eight steps. The plan-do-check-act framework describes a process for change starting with a stellar plan followed by action steps with pauses at checkpoints to allow you to modify and perfect the plan. As you read this plan, it may seem as if it is all planning and very little doing, checking, or action. The secret to success is a plan that brings many sources of influence together working for you as your offensive line. Football teams simply don't break from the huddle and run a play. They spend time with coaches developing a game plan utilizing the talent of the team to outplay the specific skills of the opponent. You have the opportunity to recruit an assortment of talent for your game plan. Who will you recruit?

1. Plan

No one can learn to adopt or change multiple behaviors at the same time. Attempting this is a recipe for failure. This book provided you with potentially 36 leadership topic areas for change. Being selective and strategic is how to develop your plan. First, you must determine what your next steps are in the immediate future of your leadership development plan (5 years or less). Is your next step one of the following?

- Spending time on the priority areas of your life, creating a better life balance
- Building a professional network
- Learning and practicing quality communication/conflict resolution skills
- Learning and practicing project- and time-management skills
- Learning and practicing better team-building skills
- Replacing unhealthy habits with healthy habits
- Doing something else

Select one of the above to work on today so that you can experience the plan-do-check-act process.

Keep in mind, a realistic goal is to identify two or three goals a year to successfully adopt or alter, and sustain the changes in your life. Therefore, determine which one from the prioritized list you will work on first.

For each of the goals you have chosen to adopt, describe in detail how you want that behavior to be once you have completed the change. For example, if you chose a goal such as creating an improved system of organization and calendaring, you could say that success might contain the following elements:

- You have identified a weekly planning day and time and you have not missed using that time in the last 8 weeks of your change effort.
- You have not missed a work or personal appointment in 8 weeks.

- You can look ahead 60 days in your calendar and see an up-to-date schedule.
- You have created a weekly, prioritized list of tasks and have successfully accomplished the top three items on the weekly list consistently for the past 4 weeks.

Notice that each of the items on the success list is a measureable result. This may not be your complete description of an improved organization goal, but it is a format that will get you on the right track of describing the results of the changed behavior. The example establishes a format of measurable results on which to base your changed behavior list.

As you do this, don't just think about the results; write them down in a formalized document. Creating a written document gives the goals legitimacy. The document must look important because it is important for you to make this change. Post it in places where you will see it daily.

Declaration of Change:

Success #1

Success #2

Success #3

Success #4

Steps of the Plan

Now that you have described the results in detail, break the goal down in to steps. Progress on goals is easily derailed if the steps are not predetermined and if they are not clearly articulated. Have you ever assembled a piece of furniture or a complex toy and spent an enormous amount of time studying the steps to put the pieces together? Now, using your knowledge and experiences, pretend you are writing instructions to make this new behavior whole. Break it into manageable pieces and identify any tools you might need for each step. Be overly specific because something you understand now might be confusing when you revisit it a week, month, or year later. Also remember, slow and steady wins the race, so be sure each step is small enough and manageable. A good way to think of your steps is by the progress you want to make on a weekly basis. Use your planner to identify target weeks to schedule when you will begin to work on each new set of behaviors.

Strategies for the Plan

Humans are social animals, and you must use this fact to your advantage. Now that you have created the formal document declaring the change you want to make, share it with important people who can be supporters and cheerleaders for you over the course of your journey. Humans fear embarrassment and will work harder if others know about their goals. Surround yourself with people who are invested in achieving goals. Likewise, distance yourself from those who have negative attitudes, or worse, are an accomplice to those behaviors you are working to change (Patterson, Grenny, Maxfield, & Switzler, 2011). You might consider a dialogue with the accomplices in your life requesting their support and encouragement regarding the behavior you want to change, turning them from an accomplice to a friend. Be open to making new friends who are positive in thought and supportive of you.

In that group of supporters and cheerleaders you have established, select someone who is faithful, kind, supportive, and reliable and who will call your bluff to be an accountability partner. Humans are more likely to change if they are held accountable. Identify rewards that will help you move forward as well as consequences that will make you say "ouch" if you slide backwards. Communicate your plan to your accountability partner. Your partner then becomes the person you do not want to disappoint until you are strong enough to not want to disappoint yourself. Breaking promises to yourself is a common affliction. Humans are also more likely to make a change if they connect with others who are attempting to make similar changes. If you are reading this book as part of a group learning experience, you can organize a leadership discussion group to meet regularly, using the time to compare success strategies and celebrate results. Groups such as Weight Watchers and Alcoholics Anonymous are designed around this strategy of group support and accountability.

Strategies to Stay With the Plan

Don't allow yourself to be distracted by a victim mentality. Being proactive is the human ability to control your thinking and choice of behaviors. No one can force you to eat the brownies at the office staff meeting when your goal is to eat more healthily. Choosing actions, which align with your goals, is no doubt a challenge. And the more often we make the choice that supports our goal, the stronger that muscle of positive choice becomes. You might call that muscle of positive choice "willpower." Willpower is the ability to say no to bad choices no matter how tempting or easy those choices might be. It is common to think that willpower is the sole force that allows people to make behavior changes. In fact, is it one of several sources of influence (Patterson et al., 2011, p. viii-ix):

- Love what you hate. If the change you wish to make is unpleasant or distasteful, you must find a way to like it. Pleasure will win every time until you can find something likable about the new behavior.
- Do what you can't. Many times the skills needed for the behavior change are not in our grasp. You may know intellectually what to do, but not have any

practice doing it. Just like an athletic skill, the skills to change a behavior require practice, practice, and more practice.

- Turn accomplices into friends. It can be surprising the negativity you might generate by announcing a positive goal for yourself. Those you thought were your friends may find sport in speaking critically or even sabotaging your effort. Only you can protect yourself by either converting accomplices into friends or creating a barrier that prevents accomplices from influencing your actions.
- Invert the economy. Make incentives both positive as well as negative by identifying rewards you enjoy and consequences that you will avidly work to avoid.
- Control your space. Listen to positive messages. Decline invitations to hang out with complainers. Distance yourself from those things that can tempt you to stray. Purge your environment of people and things that deliver a bad message.

After you develop and post your declaration of change, you must also think about how you will reframe a negative reaction to failure. What will you do or say if you feel like giving up? This is the time to write and stash a motivational letter written to yourself in advance of beginning the plan. Promise yourself you must read the letter if you decide to stop temporarily or give up. Thinking about this now increases your chances for success because it enables you to prepare for moments of weakness and self-doubt.

When you work inside your circle of influence where you have control and influence, you can grow the willpower muscle. Having a proactive perspective empowers choice and ownership of decisions that work for and against you. Ownership of decisions is necessary to accountability in the change process.

Sometimes it is helpful to have a document you can tailor to create your change initiative plan. The following document will start your journey:

A Plan for Behavior Change

Behavior Change Goal 1:
Detailed Description of Successful Change
a.
b.
c.
d.
e.
___ Motivational letter written.

(Continued)

(Continued)

Behavior Change Goal 2:

Detailed Description of Successful Change

a.

b.

c.

d.

e.

___ Motivational letter written.

Behavior Change Goal 3:

Detailed Description of Successful Change

a.

b.

c.

d.

e.

___ Motivational letter written.

Potential rewards for weekly success:

Potential consequences for not meeting weekly goal:

Accountability Partner: _____

Communication Method: _____

Frequency: _____

Cheerleaders for Your Success: _____

_____

_____

Weekly Journal

Month 1	Month 2	Month 3
Week 1	Week 1	Week 1
Goal Steps:	Goal Steps:	Goal Steps:
Results:	Additional Reinforcement of Goal #1	Additional Reinforcement of Goals #1 and #2
Challenges:		

Accountability Partner Contact: Rewards or Consequences	Results: Challenges: Accountability Partner Contact: Rewards or Consequences	Results: Challenges: Accountability Partner Contact: Rewards or Consequences
Week 2 Goal Steps: Results: Challenges: Accountability Partner Contact: Rewards or Consequences	Week 2 Goal Steps: Additional Reinforcement of Goal #1 Results: Challenges: Accountability Partner Contact: Rewards or Consequences	Week 2 Goal Steps: Additional Reinforcement of Goals #1 and #2 Results: Challenges: Accountability Partner Contact: Rewards or Consequences
Week 3 Goal Steps: Results: Challenges: Accountability Partner Contact: Rewards or Consequences	Week 3 Goal Steps: Additional Reinforcement of Goal #1 Results: Challenges: Accountability Partner Contact: Rewards or Consequences	Week 3 Goal Steps: Additional Reinforcement of Goals #1 and #2 Results: Challenges: Accountability Partner Contact: Rewards or Consequences
Week 4 Goal Steps: Results: Challenges: Accountability Partner Contact: Rewards or Consequences	Week 4 Goal Steps: Additional Reinforcement of Goal #1 Results: Challenges: Accountability Partner Contact: Rewards or Consequences	Week 4 Goal Steps: Additional Reinforcement of Goals #1 and #2 Results: Challenges: Accountability Partner Contact: Rewards or Consequences

2. Do

With your detailed plan and weekly goals, embark on your change journey. Record in a journal your successes and challenges. If a week brings no progress, adjust your plan. The goal is to implement sustainable change. Whether it takes you a week, month, or a year to make the change, the important thing is to finish, regardless of how long it takes to get there.

3. Check

This is a very important step and one that most omit. What in your plan is working? And what in it is not working? You are the scientist as well as the science project (Patterson et al., 2011). Review your journal weekly. If you have had successes, you may also find that unexpected problems appeared. How will you deal with those? Use data from the days of discouragement to provide feedback on how to make your change process more effective and successful. This data will also help you identify if you need to institute new rules, utilize your accountability partner more specifically, recruit additional supporters, adjust your calendar, or implement new rewards? The structure in your plan must correspond to your needs.

4. Act

You made a plan, implemented the plan, reviewed your results, and then altered your course to incorporate your findings. Like a moth to a flame, maintain your focus on the results you have achieved. Feel proud about what you have learned about yourself through the data and information you gathered. At the same time, keep your eye on the prize, not on the sacrifices you are making to get there. The prize is the changed behavior and the results you will enjoy. And while it is easy to get bogged down in the process, remember to enjoy the journey.

SUMMARY

Whether you are transforming a behavior or adopting it as a new ability in your repertoire of leadership skills, attitudes, and practices, you are engaged in the process of personal change. Using the plan-do-check-act process is a proven method for individuals and organizations to change. The time and thoughtfulness you invest in the plan will set the stage for the early progress of the change initiative. A great plan helps motivate the initial commitment to start. Expect to pause and reset some parts of your plan. A perfect plan is never established with the first start. Plan to investigate what is working and what is becoming a barrier to success.

Do not feel defeated by judging your current behaviors as good or bad. Instead, regard them as either effective in the situation or not. You have all completed tasks with tools that were helpful as well as struggled with tasks using tools that caused you frustration. It is time to update and add to the tools in your leadership tool bag. Every problem you face will look like a nail if the only tool you own is a hammer. If you had a job that needed a wrench, would you own only one or would you acquire a set or even an adjustable wrench. If the hardware store is not your scene, then picture your parents' kitchen. The drawer next to the stove was full of a variety of spoons, spatulas, ladles, and other cooking gear to handle all the family's favorite foods. Every task needs the right tool, and leadership tasks are no different.

All leaders are engaged in an ongoing practice of personal improvement. They recognize the importance of life-long learning and commit to the journey. This text was developed to launch you with a full leadership tool bag into the leadership positions of human services organizations. Expect to continue your learning journey with this book long after the actual course or seminar is completed. Use the method in Chapter 13. Gift yourself with a commitment to acquire the tools and to learn how to use them. You will excel as a leader and bring immeasurable positive results to your clients and communities.

REFERENCES

Kotter, J. (1995). Leading change: Why transformation efforts fail. *Harvard Business Review*, *73*(3/4), 59–67.

Patterson, K., Grenny, J., Maxfield, R. M., & Switzler, A. (2011). *Change anything: The new science of personal success*. New York, NY: Business Plus.

Index

Meetings
assessing prior experiences with, 150–151
follow-ups to, 211–212
planning, 152–155
summary, 166
time-consuming nature of, 149–150
Melan, E. H., 220
Memorandum of understanding for
alliances, 308
Memory Jogger 2 (Brassard and Ritter), 159
Mentoring, 136–137
Merchandising, 14
Merrill, Rebecca R., 90
Micro level of human services, 6–7
Mindmapping diagram, 207–208, 207 (figure),
208 (table)
Mindset, 69–73
Minority groups, 25–26, 36–37, 284
See also Multicultural leadership
Mission statements
clarifying for employees, 134
defined, 13
focusing on, 105–106
importance of, 179–180, 183
organizational, 179–183
personal, 99–100, 99 (table)
reviewing with employees, 136
Sonia's A+ example, 232, 233
updating, 188
using, 182–183
writing, 180–182
See also Goals; Values
Montgomery, C. A., 189
Morals. *See* Ethics
Morgan, N., 255
Morgenstern, J., 112, 114
Morgeson, F. P., 120–121, 121 (table)
Mort, G. S., 312
Motivation
choices affecting, 142–143
defined, 139
feedback adding to, 133
focus and, 143–146

intrinsic and extrinsic, 140–142, 144,
145–146
mattering concept, 135
mission statements and, 183
summary, 146
theories about, 139–140, 141 (table)
Motivation letter, 323
Mouton, J. S., 27–29, 28 (figure)
Multicultural leadership
assimilation and acculturation, 283–286, 284
(table), 286 (table)
diversity of society, 281–282
exclusion and inclusion, 282–283
minority groups, 25–26, 36–37, 284
social entrepreneurship, 309–313,
311 (table)
summary, 289
team challenges, 286–289
See also Collaboration; Politics
Multicultural school, 36–37
Myers Briggs Type Indicator, 61, 62

Nanus, B., 175
NASA Columbia accident, 85
Native American Talking Stick
approach, 253
Native American vision quest, 282
Negativity, 70
Nelson, R. B., 30
Net margins, 15
Networks, 291, 292
Neutrality, 273
New leadership school, 38–41
NGT (Nominal Group Technique),
162–164, 164 (figure)
Nkomo, Stella, 284
Nohria, N., 145–146
Nominal Group Technique (NGT), 162–164,
164 (figure)
Non-native speakers, 287–288
Non-sales selling, 294
North Star of organizations, 179
See also Goals

Lightning Source UK Ltd.
Milton Keynes UK
UKHW031831120822
407223UK00007B/1558